Michael Kuhn, Hebe Vessuri (eds.)

# The Global Social Sciences
## —Under and Beyond European Universalism

# BEYOND THE SOCIAL SCIENCES

Edited by Michael Kuhn, Hebe Vessuri, Shujiro Yazawa

ISSN 2364-8775

1  *Michael Kuhn, Shujiro Yazawa (eds.)*
   Theories about and Strategies against Hegemonic Social Sciences
   ISBN 978-3-8382-0586-1

2  *Michael Kuhn*
   How the Social Sciences Think about the World's Social
   Outline of a Critique
   ISBN 978-3-8382-0892-3

3  *Michael Kuhn, Hebe Vessuri (eds.)*
   The Global Social Sciences
   —Under and Beyond European Universalism
   ISBN 978-3-8382-0893-0

4  *Michael Kuhn, Hebe Vessuri (eds.)*
   Contributions to Alternative Concepts of Knowledge
   ISBN 978-3-8382-0894-7

Michael Kuhn, Hebe Vessuri (eds.)

# THE GLOBAL SOCIAL SCIENCES
## —UNDER AND BEYOND EUROPEAN UNIVERSALISM

*ibidem*-Verlag
Stuttgart

**Bibliografische Information der Deutschen Nationalbibliothek**
Die Deutsche Nationalbibliothek verzeichnet diese Publikation in der Deutschen Nationalbibliografie; detaillierte bibliografische Daten sind im Internet über http://dnb.d-nb.de abrufbar.

**Bibliographic information published by the Deutsche Nationalbibliothek**
Die Deutsche Nationalbibliothek lists this publication in the Deutsche Nationalbibliografie; detailed bibliographic data are available in the Internet at http://dnb.d-nb.de.

∞

Gedruckt auf alterungsbeständigem, säurefreien Papier
Printed on acid-free paper

ISSN 2364-8775

ISBN-13: 978-3-8382-0893-0

© *ibidem*-Verlag
Stuttgart 2016

Alle Rechte vorbehalten

Das Werk einschließlich aller seiner Teile ist urheberrechtlich geschützt. Jede Verwertung außerhalb der engen Grenzen des Urheberrechtsgesetzes ist ohne Zustimmung des Verlages unzulässig und strafbar. Dies gilt insbesondere für Vervielfältigungen, Übersetzungen, Mikroverfilmungen und elektronische Speicherformen sowie die Einspeicherung und Verarbeitung in elektronischen Systemen.

All rights reserved. No part of this publication may be reproduced, stored in or introduced into a retrieval system, or transmitted, in any form, or by any means (electronical, mechanical, photocopying, recording or otherwise) without the prior written permission of the publisher. Any person who does any unauthorized act in relation to this publication may be liable to criminal prosecution and civil claims for damages.

Printed in the EU

# Table of Contents

**Acknowledgements** ............................................................. 7

**Chapter 1:**
**Critical thought about global social sciences** ....................... 9
Michael Kuhn and Hebe Vessuri

## Section I: Critiques of critiques of the 'European' social sciences

**Chapter 2:**
**Post-colonialism and Social Theory Revisited** ................... 23
Kwang Yeong Shin

**Chapter 3:**
**21st Century Challenges to Social and
Economic Sciences: Global Sciences
of the Economy and of Individual Behavior** ....................... 41
Huri Islamoglu

**Chapter 4:**
**Towards World Social Sciences:
Why criticizing 'Western Hegemony' does not help** ........... 63
Doris Weidemann

**Chapter 5:**
**Why arriving at imperial thought is not an accident
of critical sociological thinking but the consequent
endpoint of international sociological thinking** ................... 81
Michael Kuhn

## Section II: The European universalism

**Chapter 6:**
**The European Comprehension of the World:
Early Modern Science and Eurocentrism** ......................... 101
Mauricio Nieto Olarte

**Chapter 7:**
**Institutional Re-structuring in the**
**Social Science World: Seeds of Change** ............................ 141
Hebe Vessuri and Carmen Bueno

**Chapter 8:**
**What happened to the spread of universal ideas?** ............ 169
Reiner Grundmann

## Section III: The social science world under the 'European' universalism and beyond

**Chapter 9:**
**Intervening in the Geopolitics of Travelling Theory:**
**Constraints, Limitations and Possibilities** ....................... 189
Sujata Patel

**Chapter 10:**
**The Impact of Internationalization on**
**Post-Soviet Social Sciences and Humanities** ................... 205
Igor Yegorov and Pal Tamas

**Chapter 11:**
**Poverty and Social Sciences:**
**Pauperology as Apology for Modernity** ........................... 229
Kumaran Rajagopal

**Chapter 12:**
**Academic Working Culture: Shifting from National**
**Competitions towards Transnational Collaborations** ...... 249
Kazumi Okamoto

**Biographical Notes** .......................................................... 275

# Acknowledgements

This book presents social thought about **"The Global Social Sciences—Under and Beyond European Universalism"** with contributions from social scientists across the world reflecting on the contemporary social sciences, social thought initiated by discourses on three WorldSSHNet events:

- The thinkshop *about "Multiple Epistemologies - Science and Time - Science and Space - Science and Culture - Science and Society"*, held at Universidad Iberoamericana, Mexico City, Mexico, 22–23 February 2013, funded by the Wenner Gren Foundation,

- The thinkshop about *"The global social science world—beyond the 'Western' universalism"*, held at and funded by the University for Applied Sciences, Zwickau, Germany, 27–29 September 2013,

- The WorldSSHNet panel on the *"Eighth Congress of the International Asian Philosophical Association"*, held at the Süleyman Demirel University in Isparta April 30th–May 3rd 2016.

This book publishes the papers resulting from the discourses on these events and distributes them to invite those academics who could not participate in our events but can thus join our controversial debates.

    The editors of this book want to take the opportunity to thank all participants of the WorldSSHNet activities, those who contributed papers to the events, those who contributed chapters to this book and all others who contributed in several other ways to our thinkshops and thus also supported the publication of this book.

As a funding organisation that goes beyond paying lip service to the issues of inter-disciplinary and inter-national social science activities, but really supports them, we wish to express our gratitude to the Wenner-Gren Foundation for funding our thinkshop in Mexico City.

We extend our thanks to the generous financial support from CONACYT in Mexico, who through "Space and Knowledge. Dynamics and Tensions of International Collaboration in the Social Sciences in the Context of Globalisation" contributed to the publication costs of this book.

We, the editors, consider this book not as the end, but as a new point of departure for further controversial debates and would like to take this opportunity to invite readers to contribute to the continuation of these conversations with their critical comments.

Those who are interested in the WorldSSHNet may visit our www: http://www.worldsshnet.org/

Michael Kuhn and Hebe Vessuri

# Chapter 1:
# Critical thought about global social sciences

## Michael Kuhn and Hebe Vessuri

Chasing credits, counting publications, becoming a global flagship, arguing about which national science community is a scientific centre, which a periphery, which national science community dominates theorizing around the world, is the global social science world keeping social sciences around the world busy as if global social thought was a scientific world cup. What seems a rather mundane scenario is though the very science world recent science policy "incentives" have created, serving their idea of making knowledge a global commodity and global social thought a battle between national science communities.

As with its previous publications[1], the WorldSSH Net invites to interrupt the routine work of social science academics and to think about what social sciences are doing, especially when they are theorizing beyond their nationally confined socials.

This book intends to provide some incentives for thinking about the social sciences and discusses "the global social science world— under the 'European' universalism."

The oddness in the notion of a locally confined universalism tries to point to the oddity the universalisation of the European social sciences has brought on the social science world.

This book discusses some aspects of the European social science approach to social thought spread and practiced across the world as if it was the nature of scientific thinking. If it was the case that the social science approach to social thought is the nature of theo-

---

[1] See: Michael Kuhn, Kazumi Okamoto, (eds.), (2013), *Spatial Social Thought, Local Knowledge in Global Knowledge Encounters*, ibidem Stuttgart; Michael Kuhn, Shujiro Yazawa, (eds.), (2015), *Theories about and Strategies against Hegemonic Social Sciences*, Ibidem Stuttgart; Michael Kuhn, Hebe Vessuri, (eds.), *Contributions to Alternative Concepts of Knowledge*, Ibidem Stuttgart, forthcoming; Michael Kuhn, *How Social Sciences Think about the World's Social, Outline of a Critique*, Ibidem Stuttgart, forthcoming.

rizing about the social or not, in any case the global spread of the European social science approach confronts social science thinkers with more than the oddness of the universalisation of an approach to social thought that was created in the context of the emergence of European, colonial nation states.

This book contributes some reflections about the universalized European social sciences and it does this in three sections:

*Section I: Critiques of the critiques of the 'European' sciences*

*Section II: The 'European' universalism*

*Section III: The Social sciences world under 'European' universalism*

Section I, critically reflecting on critiques of the 'European' sciences, consists of four chapters, which discuss typical critiques the European social sciences have encountered. Indeed, critiquing the European social sciences has become, thanks to and since the postcolonial discourses, an acknowledged part of social science theorizing, at least theorizing about the global social. There are hardly any contributions to the contemporary discourses about the "globalising" social sciences, which do not support their critical views about the European social sciences with arguments such as the unsuitable theories created by the "Western" social sciences, the ethnocentrism of European theories or a scientific hegemony of the "Western" social sciences, when they argue about inequalities in the distribution of scientific power between "scientific centres and peripheries". Pointing to the "Western" social sciences which do no longer want to distinguish whether this is a critique of theories created in the "West" of the "Western" social science system indicates the danger that critiquing the European social sciences may deteriorate towards a politically biased kind of scientific insult and does not do any harm to the European social sciences, which are indeed still highly appreciated among the world's academia. Not only the Western social sciences and their theories, even in their critical discussions, are considered as the world's reference theories. Not only, but especially young academics, if they have the choice to study in the discriminated "West" seemingly prefer to gain their academic degrees in those "Western" universities. One might downplay this as a mere calculation regarding their career prospects; however, if this is a calculation, then it is a calculation that counts on the global appreciation of the "western" social sciences, not just among students, but among the world's academia.

Hence, looking at the well-established and globally appreciated critique of the social sciences and questioning what and how this critique critiques the European social science, is what the four chapters in section I seek to do.

In Chapter 2 Kwang-Yeong Shin, reflecting on *"postcolonialism and social theory revisited"*, argues that *"post-colonial theories successfully undermined the validity and legitimacy of social theories in the West as the universal normal sciences but failed to provide a new paradigm of the social theories. They failed to be revolutionary sciences replacing the existing social sciences of the non-West."*

Discussing *"attempts to promote alternatives to social theories by post-colonial perspectives in the non-West"*, alternatives which *"represent historical and cultural specificity of the non-Western countries"*, Shin focuses on three issues overcoming the failure of post-colonial theories, which did not manage to replace the theories from the West while thinking about the non-West. Firstly he raises the question if and why theories from the West need to be replaced by non-Western theories, since there are *"many critical social theories, such as Marxism, Post-Marxism, critical theory, post-structuralism, feminism etc., stemmed from the West and critical intellectuals in the non-Western world which rely on those theories in their critical discourse on their own societies as well as global capitalism."*

Secondly, he argues that although the post-colonial criticism rejected the Western theories, it never managed to reveal the social reality only non-Western theories are able to reflect on, and, thirdly, that the non-Western theories need to create their theories about the non-Western "explanandum" "with *"transparent discursive approaches"*, globally communicable theories, rather than with *"obscurantism and ventriloquist discourses"*, preserved by the non-West.

In Chapter 3, unlike the prevailing trends of another critique strand of the European social sciences, critiquing them for theories that are not applicable to the social in the "non-West", as Shin phrases it, Huri Islamoglu, discusses *"trends in Western social and* *economic sciences in the post-World War II era under American hegemony during the Cold War. It does this by addressing the ways societal conceptions and solutions to social issues emerging in Europe in the 19$^{th}$ century were universalized and generalized in various social science disciplines to serve as an idiom of Western domination in non-Western world regions. Secondly, the essay addresses the challenges to societal sciences since the 1980s and the rise of global sciences responding to exigencies of the global economic order and its free-tradist understandings."*

Unlike the above critique of the unsuitable theories originating from the "West", strikingly all assuming that those European theories allow to understand the "West", this chapter discusses whether these theories and their categories are at all appropriate to understand what the societies in the very "West" are all about. Considering the extent to which on the one hand the social science theory production has accommodated its way of thinking and its categories to a new wave of marketization across the whole society, conceptualized and imposed to the world by the so called neo-liberal political rationales, while on the other hand social science theorizing is rooted and rests on the ideas of pre-industrialised capitalism *"of free-tradism in the 17$^{th}$ and 18$^{th}$ centuries"*, this chapter suggests to not only think about new theories in the "non-West".

Tracing how the social sciences since the 19$^{th}$ century developed by ever struggling to accommodate their thinking towards the historically changing concepts of nation state policies and economies within the European experiences, ever grounding the development of theorizing in the historical phases of the European history and at the same time applying these theories to the world as a whole, points to the needs to not only think about new ways of theorizing, not just in and about the "non-West", but about the whole global social.

As well as the previous two chapters, chapter 4 by Doris Weidemann, under the title *"Towards World Social Sciences: Why criticizing 'Western Hegemony' does not help"* thought, also questions the existing critique of the European social sciences. Opposing a "western hegemony" is another widespread critique of the theories created by the European approach to social sciences; Weidemann's chapter develops some arguments questioning whether this notion helps to build "world social sciences". Pointing to some typical steps, such as creating variations of opposing politically constructed entities like "North" versus "South", attach to them mostly politically constructed 'vice versa' judgments to then reject the discriminated rather than critiqued entities as being different from what is appropriate for the advocated entity. She argues that this contrasting view that subsumes in a rather odd way all kind of theories under categories, creates a critique of the social sciences entities, which opposes them in a way that "keep(s) Western hegemony intact". From elaborating on why this critique keeps the critiqued intact, the chapter develops an alternative suggestion for how to shift from those dichotomous opposing entities and from the creation of such prejudiced selection of any politically constructed theory bodies towards a mode of critique that invites critical reflections in all directions, not only towards the "West", and to thereby move towards building world social sciences and a world discourse.

Chapter 5 in this section by Michael Kuhn discusses *"Why arriving at imperial thought is not an accident of critical sociological thinking but the consequent endpoint of international sociological thinking"*. In contrast to the notions of theories, such as Islamoglu's in chapter 3, arguing that thanks to a decline of nation-states in a globalizing world traditional social sciences and their concept of the nation-state as compensating global market effects are no longer appropriate concepts for theorizing, Kuhn argues that nation-state constructs are the very categorical foundation of critical sociological thinking, not in any particular historical variation of a nation -tate rationale, but in the concepts of what any sociological thinking considers as the essential of nation-state. This sociological concept of nation-state appears as at least ideally serving its citizens by providing what sociologists consider as the genuine mission of nation-states, an ordered society. It is this idealization of the mission of the nation-state as an ordering system, a structure and alike that is responsible for theories, created by critical sociological thinkers who present their thought as a critique of the European social sciences, that these very critical theories not coincidentally end up promoting imperial thought when they think inter-nationally. Sociological thinking bound to think through categories which founded the discipline of sociology, a view of the social that looks on the social through the idea of an idealized nation-state mission, is incapable of reflecting about the global social other than as creating imperial theories.

Section II contributes thought about some aspects of social thought crafted through the European social sciences. A major concern of these debates is still the notion of a scientific universalism. And this is somehow striking, considering that, with some exceptions,[2] today's social sciences across the world are so keen on being part of the very European social sciences, opposing, however, their claim of being universal theories. No doubt, the European social sciences, as Nieto phrases in his chapter, considered their way of theorizing and their theories *"as a unique and superior kind of knowledge and its diffusion seen as a natural consequence of its universality."* Yes, it is surely the case, that the colonizers presented their knowledge *"as a unique and superior kind of knowledge."* However, concluding from the fact that the colonial powers forced the colonized world to share the views of the colonizers that the European science imposed a scientific universalism, is certainly a disputable identification of the political power of colonialists with an only imagined power no knowledge has, inviting to further debates about this notion.

In chapter 6 titled *"The European Comprehension of the World: Early Modern Science and Eurocentrism"* Mauricio Nieto Olarte argues *"that the scientific practices involved in the European exploration of new lands in the early modern period were related to the emergence of a new European self-perception that Christian Europe was legitimate sovereign of the world."* He then discusses in three sections the *"birth and diffusion of Western Science"*, the European "comprehension" of the world and finally the relation between the notion of a scientific universalism and the building of the colonial empire.

Vessuri and Bueno engage in chapter 7, entitled *Institutional Re-structuring in the Social Science World: Seeds of Change,* some of the dominant debates about globalization of the social sciences. The argument of this chapter is fivefold: First, despite the long history of several national social science communities, invisibility and marginality of knowledge production in the south continues to be accepted as a fact of life. Dominant cultural flows and institutions have deep historical roots and are closely entwined with the resulting social science production. In time, however, with

---

[2] See for example: M. Kuhn and H. Vessuri (eds.), *Contributions to Alternative Concepts of Knowledge*, ibidem, Stuttgart, forthcoming

different aims, regional and transnational associations were created and some of them represent a vivid expression of today's fashionable transnational networks.

Second, the massification of higher education has ultimately affected the identity of universities, which have been forced to compete with other institutions and social agents more aligned with corporate cultures and policy-making. What the identity of universities will be in the future is difficult to predict.

Third, new initiatives and trajectories have started to reconfigure the topography of knowledge production and diffusion. A series of technological and institutional novelties are once again altering the balance. New technologies and telecommunications, among other factors, generate global cultural flows whose stretch, intensity, diversity and rapid diffusion exceed those of earlier eras. The centrality of national cultures, national identity and their institutions is being challenged.

Fourth, original aspects in organizational infrastructure pave the way for an unprecedented transformation in the governance of knowledge production and diffusion of the social sciences. International agendas, "politics" in scientific organizations, tailored research for public policy, funding priorities and other channels of knowledge production are immersed in contradictory forces that challenge the purposes and aspiration of national academic systems and national social science traditions.

Fifth, given the dominant "inevitabilist" discourse, developing and emergent countries face new and difficult challenges to generate and use new knowledge, even social knowledge, according to social or economic goals defined with varying forms of autonomy. So far, however, the asymmetric geography of knowledge seems to persist, although some of the players have altered their strength. These five arguments move Vessuri and Bueno to explore the impact of contemporary sociocultural globalization that is transforming the contexts and the means through which the social sciences produce knowledge and are legitimated.

Chapter 8 by R. Grundmann, entitled "*What happened to the spread of universal ideas?*" analyses the role of the university knowledge production form in the relation between Western science and other forms of knowledge.

The main point of his paper is that the various critiques of the diffusionist framework have led to an abandonment of the notion of universal science, of linear transfer, and hence of the very concept of Western science. Sociologists and historians of science favour particularistic accounts with no appetite for generalizations. In contrast, researchers in the Neo-institutionalist framework invoke the existence of universalistic norms when it comes to knowledge production. The expansion of the universities on a global scale is explained through the appeal of a universal ideal, that of truth and univerwsal validity. There are reasons to be skeptical towards this interpretation and to advance a more pragmatic reading in terms of isomorphism in that societies have become convinced of the value of universities for knowledge creation that is instrumental in the search for efficacy. Governments support science in a global competitive market for talent, and individuals try to enhance their life chances by entering higher education. If we, as he does, for the sake of the argument, apply Basalla's three phases to the present case, we can probably identify phase three in the data: there is still an absolute dominance of Western authors in the field of social theory and 'grand narratives'. This could be due to the fact that Western HE institutions are still an obligatory passage point for global elites and their offspring, that the Western legacy is too esoteric for new generations across the globe, or that it has become irrelevant.

Section III of this book *The Social science world under and towards beyond the 'European' Universalism"* discusses with four chapter some phenomena of knowledge production under the regime of the European social sciences, how to oppose them, critical thought inviting to debates shifting to a science world beyond the reign of the European social science traditions.

S. Patel's chapter 9, entitled *Intervening in the Geopolitics of Travelling Theory: Constraints, Limitations and Possibilities* revises the growth of the Eurocentric episteme. Eurocentric knowledge, she argues, is based on the construction of multiple and repeated divisions or oppositions which get constructed as hierarchies, based on a racial classification of the world population. Sociology, in this view, became the study of modern (European – later extended to Western-) society while anthropology became the study of (non-European and non-Western) traditional societies. Patel aims to show that ironically and paradoxically this project found an expression in the work of indigenous intellectuals in the

Asian subcontinent, searching to find an identity against colonialism.

Patel is keen to show that Eurocentrism is not only an episteme, but also a way to organize production, distribution, consumption and reproduction of knowledge unequally across the different parts of the world. It cannot be merely replaced through cognitive supplants of concepts, theories and methods, which was what the best of nationalist social science in ex-colonial countries attempted to do. Institutionalization under the aegis of the elite nationalist orientation has reproduced practices in place across the Global North, with the consequence of 'infantilisation' of scientific practices within the Global South regions. She aims to show that merely intervening in the world of knowledge will not displace Eurocentric knowledge; intervening in the practices that structure knowledge will, and she proposes to build intellectual networks across institutions and scholarship among and between scholars of the non-Atlantic region as a practice that may help to reflect collectively on common and relevant themes that structure the experience of being part of the '*south*'.

In Chapter 10 about *The Impact of Internationalization on Post-Soviet Social Sciences and Humanities* by Igor Yegorov and Pal Tamas, the authors organize their analysis of the social sciences and humanities in the former Soviet Union into four broad categories: infrastructural, methodological (or intellectual), cultural (or rather personal), and political. They describe how the institutional infrastructure for research has crumbled. Very often individual scholars face impoverishment, a sharp decline in status, a deterioration of collegial interaction, and growing personal isolation. Russia's continuing difficulty to come to terms with the outside world wreaks havoc on a range of disciplines often identified as being inherently "Western." Professional interaction has diminished, contributing to a lack of a sense of belonging to a group. In some areas, younger scholars are left without mentors as senior scholars have left academia or are virtually unavailable as they pursue other endeavors. As the status of intellectuals declines, there is a corresponding diminished sense of mission for those engaged in intellectual pursuits.

Westernization has been largely understood as being of only one type. Descriptions of the given societies could be constructed according to the speed and character of their divergence from ideal types of the Western model. In these years, almost no work is available that compares the transitional societies with real Western societies or societal processes. Participation in large European programs of social science cooperation is predominantly determined by the interests of foreign partners. Projects in collaboration are usually not interested in the dynamics of transformation in the post- Soviet countries, but only in the 'Eastern' equivalents of problems formulated by the coordinators in their Western European social and research environments. The resulting work may be interesting or even original, but is usually only weakly related to local intellectual traditions and cultural environments; and cross-national comparative accents or efforts will normally be absent here.

Chapter 11 by Kumaran Rajagopal, entitled *Poverty and Social Sciences: Pauperology as Apology for Modernity,* unlike many other critical reflections focusing on the relation between scientific entities discusses a major theory complex the European social sciences operate with and distribute across the world as master theories for theorizing. Kumaran reflects on the concept of poverty as a key category for theorizing about the social in the "developing world" and, thus, on how it affects thinking about the majority of people across the world.

Kumaran's chapter proves how the categorical basis of theorizing about poverty consist of a concept of poverty, that provides the ideological thought thanks to which poverty is not reduced but under whose theoretical labels it not only continues to exist but its perpetuation is presented as a fight against poverty. Summarizing his arguments, it is the cardinal fault of all social science theories discussing poverty to conclude from the fact that the non-existence of paid labor is responsible for poverty, that the existence of paid labor abolishes poverty. It is the insistence of social science thinking on a social mission only social sciences know, that allows to ignore that even employment may result in poverty and to conclude by insisting on the dreamy social mission of capital, that it must be the lack of capital in the "developing" countries that is responsible for poverty with and without employment. Hence, creating the very business that causes poverty is the circle all those projects set into force, putting into practice their wishful theories about poverty—ever at the cost of the poor.

In Chapter 12 by Kazumi Okamoto entitled *Academic Working Culture: Shifting from National Competitions towards Transnational Collaborations* the author engages in thinking towards alternative discourses about internationalising social sciences. She argues that the mainstream discourse about how to internationalize social sciences accompanying a shift towards international social sciences seems to be retarded by a still national way of thinking. Mainstream discourses mainly discuss the internationalisation of social sciences as a competition among national science communities, competing about a hegemony of still widely nationally constructed theories, for which, ironically, the international comparative studies are the most obvious example. The prevailing focus in these discourses is to argue about inequalities, asymmetries and scientific hegemonies, discourses which all in different ways consider the competition among national science communities and their locally constructed theories as the main challenge of internationalising social sciences. As an alternative approach to thinking about globalising social sciences, she advocates to overcome a so far widely nationally confined theory production and to shift towards the collaborative production of knowledge across the national sciences communities and their national orientations. To do this she presents some ideas about how to investigate the social sciences to better understand their shared and particular working practices. Okamoto labels this as an investigation on "*academic working culture*", a collaborative production of knowledge beyond the contemporary modes of global knowledge production where a competition between national science communities prevails.

# Section I:
# Critiques of critiques of the 'European' social sciences

# Chapter 2:
# Post-colonialism and Social Theory Revisited

Kwang-Yeong Shin

## 1. Introduction

The recurrent issue in social theorists in the non-Western world is the meaning of the West in social theory in general. For those who are aware of the long imperial rule of the West and its lingering impact on post-colonial countries in the post war period, it has been conceived with regard to hegemony of the West in the space of academic world in the non-West. Because of the overwhelming dominance of the West in representation of non-Western societies, intellectuals in the non-West seek to find out alternative social theories to those in the West. Among others, post-colonial perspectives in literary theory and cultural studies provided important new pathways to criticize the dominance of the West in social theory and academic world. They succeeded in raising issues embedded in the power-knowledge nexus between the West and the non-West or the metropolis and the periphery or the mainstream and subalterns. In particular, debunking hegemonic dominances in social theories explicitly and criticizing the concept of sciences implicitly, they allowed us to figure out alternative understandings of the social formation of the contemporary non-Western world as well as the Western world

However, those challenges are not influential enough to redirect the academic discourses and the knowledge production in the West as well as in the non-West. The dominant social theories developed in the context of Western societies have still dominated the sphere of knowledge production in the social sciences in the non-Western region. Thus, it is hard to deny that the discourse on subalterns still remains as the marginal status in the academic sphere, particularly in the social sciences. It is one thing to pose the problematic of ideological interpellation of the dominant Western social theories over the non-West. It is completely another thing to generate alternative social theories to the dominant social theories of the West. In other words, post-colonial theories successfully undermined the validity and legitimacy of social theories in the West as the universal normal sciences but failed to provide a new paradigm of the social theories. They fail to be revolutionary sciences replacing the existing social sciences of the non-West.

In this paper I will address some issues involved in the attempts to promote alternatives to social theories by post-colonial perspectives in the non-West and try to formulate alternative concepts of social theory to represent historical and cultural specificity of the non-Western countries. I will focus on three issues which are interconnected with each other but could be dealt with separately. The first issue is that whether or not non-Westerners need the alternative social theories to the social theories developed in the West. There are many critical social theories, such as Marxism, Post-Marxism, critical theory, post-structuralism, feminism etc., stemmed from the West and critical intellectuals in the non-Western world which rely on those theories in their critical discourse on their own societies as well as global capitalism. While major post-colonial theoreticians were born in the non-West, most of them belong to major academic institutions in the metropolis. The history of dependency theory is somewhat different from post-colonial theory in that almost all social scientists posing dependency theses were Latin American scholars and stayed in institutions in Latin America.[1]

Second, how and what reality can be theoretically represented? Totalizing critiques of Western social theories is not a sufficient way to formulate an alternative understanding of social reality in the non-Western world. Without specifying explanandum and identifying explanans, any alternative theoretical attempts are doom to fail. Regarding explanadum, post-colonial theorists disclosed the collective silence of social theories, revealing hidden dimensions of the colonial power-knowledge relationship. Concerning explanans, it did not provide successful social mechanism through which reality of the non-Western world was formed and transformed, except criticizing hegemonic dominance of the West

---

[1] There were few dependency theorists who theorized unequal interdependency between the center and periphery outside Latin America. Notable exception might be Walden Bello in Philippines.

in the post-colonial countries, especially in India. In contrast, polemics of dependency theories tried to identify explanans of underdevelopment of Latin American countries, displaying exploitative economic relations between the US and Latin American countries.

Third, counter-hegemonic social theories should be communicable to social scientists of the West as well as those of the non-West and have discursive rationality among social theorists beyond nationality and spatiality. Obscurantism and ventriloquist discourses still prevail in the post-colonial discourses, producing biblical elites and followers in academics. In other words, it is still regarded as a part of literary critique or humanities rather than social sciences. In addition, counter-hegemonic social theories also should be empirically grounded as far as those are theories about society.[2] Post-colonial discourse did not provide much theoretical ramification in the social sciences except cultural studies and cultural psychology. Counter hegemonic social theories should seek to explain social reality with transparent discursive approaches.

In the following, I will discuss theoretical issues associated with the three issues and attempt to find plausible theoretical strategies to resolve the issues. Specifically, I propose a comparative mechanism based approach to social reality which de-universalizes social theories of the West and treat them as social theories based on local or national contexts of the West. It might be considered as an extension of double indigenization (Shin, 2013: 77-94), provincializing of social theories (Chakarabarty, 2008; Kuhn, 2013: 33-48), and an alternative discourse (Alatas, 2010).

## 2. Postcolonial Problematic: What is to be explained by whom?

Post-colonial discourses can be portrayed by many critiques of colonial discourses which were characterized by Euro-centrism, called Orientalism, and hegemonic episteme of the West (Seid, 1974; Spivak, 1984; Baba, 1990). While theoretical traditions of post-colonialism range from literary theory to psychoanalysis, it

---

[2] It means that social theories should be empirically grounded. Empirical ground refers to both visible and invisible social actors' experiences through social life, regardless of perception of those experiences by social actors.

has been a part of overwhelming cultural turns in the 1980s.³ They implicitly assume that a geo-political dimension embedded in knowledge and knowledge production is important in shaping the domination of the West and subordination of the non-West. That is epitomized by Spivak's argument that the West as Subject "pretends it has 'no geo-political determinations'"(1984: 66). Debunking ideology of universalism and power relations in intellectuals, she discloses geo-political dimension of desire, subjectivity and ideology.

Post-colonial discourses criticize persistent cultural domination of the West over newly liberated colonial societies. Social theories of the West played a key role in cultural and psychological formation of hierarchal relations between the metropolis and the peripheries even in the post-colonial period. European hegemony of knowledge production perpetuates the representative imbalance between the two. The metropolis' domination of psyche of the people and intellectuals of the peripheries prevents from altering the relationship between the metropolis and the peripheries. Post-colonial critiques of the dominance of knowledge production of the West over the non-West touch the meta-theoretical issues with regard to representation and understanding of their own identity and the history of the non-West.

However, post-colonial discourses suffer from simplified imaginary boundaries between the West and the non-West or between the metropolis and the periphery. They paid less attention to endogenous heterogeneity within the non-West or the periphery where some subalterns dominate other subalterns (sub-subalterns). As globalization proceeds, the global chain of exploitation and domination keeps extending its encompassing influence to individuals and families in local communities. As the web of market

---

3   Cultural turn in the 1980s took place in humanities and social sciences in the non-West as well as the West. Post-colonialism, cultural studies, cultural psychology and new labor history become a major academic discipline or sub-disciplines within mainstream academic world. The cultural turn has provided new pathways to overcome the limits of political economy and structural reductionism (determinism) overshadowed by classical Marxism. Furthermore, the rediscovery of culture has stimulated perception of heterogeneity and diversity of society rather than homogeneity and unity. See Jameson (1998), Bonnell, Hunt and Biernacki (1999), and Ray and Sayer (1999) for general and critical discussion about the cultural turn.

relations reaches villages and alleys of the Global South, simple dichotomous classification of the West and non-West conceals the web of social relations embedded in and operating at different levels of the life-world of the Global South. Though some postcolonial theorists such as Bhabha (1994:173) accentuate an analysis considering "complex cultural and political boundaries", they only focus on cultural dimensions neglecting complexity of political and economic relations between the metropolis and the periphery.

Another weakness of post-colonial discourses is that their problematic was mostly confined to an issue of identity and subjectivity. The dominance of cultural imperialism still exerts significant influence on the formation of subjectivity of the people of the Global South. Furthermore, Western dominance in mass culture of the non-West still prevails through popular songs, movies and consumer goods. However, the dominance of the West over the non-West primarily depends upon economic and military power. In addition, the formation of identity and subjectivity has been contested through the conflicting interpellation of family and local institutions. There are complex intervening and mediating factors between the Global North and identity and subjectivity of subalterns in the Global South. It is too simplistic to argue that cultural imperialism of the West directly dominates the life-world of subalterns and indentify and subjectivity of subalterns are outcomes of cultural imperialism of the West.

Thus, post-colonial discourses did not fully influence social sciences in the non-West except some relatively marginal disciplines such as cultural psychology or indigenous psychology which stresses local culture or cultural practices in the process of shaping the psyche of the people (Kim and Berry, 1993; Kim, Yang and Hwang, 2006; Sheweder and Levine, 1984). Cultural traditions stemmed from local historical experiences affect the mind-set of the people and thus resists universal application of psychological theories developed in the West. Culture specific psychology challenges Western psychology which assumes universal validity of psychological theories based on universal psychological beings. However, as Weidemann (2013) argues, indigenous psychology proclaimed by some psychologists in Asia still remains within the perimeter of

Western psychology in the sense that their research still follows the Western model of science.[4]

Alternative models of science do not exist yet, competing with all the other (bourgeoisie, Eurocentric or Western) models of sciences. Rather alternative social theories might be feasible to explain social reality which includes social and historical events, social institutions, and culture and ideology of societies at a given time and space. It implies that alternative social theories also tend to explain social phenomena or social reality, identifying generative causal dynamics in a narrative way or in a more formal way. In spite of difference in ontological and epistemological foundation of social theories, all social theories have a common aim to understand the formation and transformation of society or societies.[5] Alternative social theories also seek to provide understandings of social reality different from those originated from the West, assuming cultural and historical specificity exert strong causal influences on the psyche of the people, institutional arrangement, social relations and social actions.

## 3. New Strategies for Theory Construction

Those who seek to promote alternative social sciences against the hegemonic and universalizing social sciences developed in the West face harsh reality of social sciences outside the mainstream academic world. Above all, the social sciences have been completely dominated by the West. As some alternative social theories such

---

[4] An alternative concept of science seems to be only possible outside the space of institutionalized academic world. Recruitment of researchers and research funding for them are based on research agenda proposed in their grant proposals. Those proposals are evaluated by researchers who have the dominant concept of science. See Benton and Craib (2001), Keat and Urry (1975), Manicas(2006), Rosenberg(2012), Bhaskar(1987).

[5] The meaning of understanding includes two dimensions. One is a hermeneutic dimension in which an understanding of subjective status, such as intention, purposes, subjectivity, and emotion, as Max Weber (1904) or Peter Winch (1958) argued. Another is a naturalist understanding of objective causal processes visible or invisible to actors and observers as Durkheim (1985) and Marx (1873) argued. The meaning of understanding, I argue, should include the third dimension in the social sciences. In addition, a complete understanding should include an understanding of the relationship between actors' subjective status and objective causal processes.

as dependency theory emerged, it did not succeed in becoming alternative social theory of economic development in Latin America.

Since academic institutions associated with education, research and publication are totally controlled by established institutions in the West, it is hard to find alternative space for new challenging and critical social sciences in the non-West. Paradigms developed in the West still dominate academics in the non-West simply because academic norms with regard to perspectives, research methods and writing styles are set by the 'Western standard'. Violating those norms is sanctioned by various institutional norms.

With regard to further developing problematic articulated by post-colonialism in social sciences, I propose five elements in order to develop non-hegemonic alternative theories. The five elements are prerequisite for representing local and national contexts, at the same time for recognizing multiple layers of causality, partially accepting the possibility of universal foundation of social theories, and formulating social scientific explanatory models based on lived experiences of 'subalterns.'

**Social Totality**

The first step is a totalizing perception of the relationship between the West and the non-West. The social formation of the non-western societies has been affected by the social formation of the West. Since Portugal had expanded its influence beyond the European continent since 15$^{th}$ century, the vast area of the world had been under the direct control of western countries. The formation of the modern world system has affected not merely the world economy but also the global transaction of knowledge and information, exerting hegemonic power of the West over the non-West.

However, the recognition of hegemonic power of the West is only a beginning step for developing non-hegemonic social theories. It becomes the fact of life that the global power relations shape the lives of the people through the web of commodity chains in the economy and political/cultural domination in the domain of sciences and ideology. That is 'the first order conditions of determination' within which local and national institutions are operating and individual and family lives are managed. Capitalist globalization has reinforced the economic impact of the West on the lives of the people in the non-West. This overwhelming and encompassing reality have been easily neglected by social researchers focusing on individuals at the micro-level, ignoring the global power relations as the macro-structural factors. Thus, social theories and researches in the non-Western world have been kept in the "territorial trap" in which global power and domination are assumed to be outside of the framework of local and national territory (Agnew, 1994).

Of course, world system analysis (Wallerstein, 1974, 1983 and 2000) attempts to build radically different theory of social changes based on geopolitical dimension. It radically discloses the limits of the analysis of local and national social changes under the framework of capitalist development of a single country, or a single nation state. He suggested a macro-economic system which went beyond the geographic territory of the individual nation state. Industrial development and trade expansion took place simultaneously in some regions with multiple cultural systems. Though cultural dynamics might be confined to smaller regions due to ethnic divisions and different cultural heritages from the past, the global division of labor made locals and nationals integrated into the world economy, generating an unequal transaction of surplus from some regions called the periphery to other regions called the core.

Both indigenous social science researches and mainstream social science researches tend to overlook dominant global forces which reveal itself very differently at the individual level as well as the local/national level. The global forces have operated analogous to magnetic fields in the nature, though invisible or intangible, influencing every aspects of the physical world we are living. Compartmentalized social science disciplines do not allow researchers to perceive and theorize the overarching global forces that operate beyond the local and national boundaries properly. While an analytical rigor has been appraised as a core of the mainstream social sciences, the failure to recognize the importance of the global forces has resulted in fragmented and incomplete understandings of individuals, societies and the world.

**Social Mechanism Centered Approach**

The second step for an alternative theory construction is to theorize the linkage between globalization and social changes at national or local levels. Recognition of the global power relations exerting influences over the national and local social changes is not enough to fully comprehend social changes taking place at the local or national level, since local and national societies consist of local institutions and actors with their own culture and local histories. Thus, we need to understand the interplay of the global forces and the local and national factors to fully comprehend social change. Because there have been various modes of interaction between the global and the local, the mechanism of interaction should be theorized. Dependency theories in the 1970s or post-colonial theories in the 1990s might be regarded as alternative theoretical attempts to identify relations of domination between North America and South America and between the mainstream and the subalterns at different levels. But they did not fully specify the operating processes of unequal exchange between the core and the periphery or temporal or spatial sequences of dominations by the West over the non-West.

In order to reveal how domination of the West over the non-West is taking place through the nation state and the global market, the mechanism specific approach, which seeks to identify the processes of domination of the West over the non-West through various institutions and local and global agencies, is needed.

Hitherto, there have been two major approaches considered as models of social sciences. One is a deductive model to which mainstream economists, among others, stick, assuming that theoretically constructed hypothetical conditions are identified by empirical observation and commonly mathematical tools are used to prove theoretical deduction from those conditions. Another is to find correlations between events or among variables to explain events or the state of affairs. Rather than identifying causal dynamics between events or variables, correlation or sometimes called association has been considered as a proof of theoretical argument or hypothesis. This approach has been common in the contemporary sociology and the political science as well. Even though some causal relations are assumed in the theoretical discussions, causal processes are not investigated directly. The analysis of correlation and association has been wrongly assumed to be a verifying method of the existence of the causal relations.

Social mechanism centered approach focuses on sequential processes in which social actors and institution are interacting at different spaces and times. Both social actors and institution are temporal products of interactions and also constraining factors for both social actors and institutional changes. Thus, social mechanisms have limited generality and that defies universal or general social theories (Elster, 1991: 7-8). While society consists of individuals, individuals are not atomized and do not act in the vacuum. They are differently inculcated by different national cultures and influenced by class experiences at the workplace and local community. For example, a Japanese worker employed in Toyota Motor Co. who is at the same time a member of Toyota Motor Co. union has quite different subjectivity and ideology from that of a South African coal miner, a member of the COSATU in South Africa. They have experienced different power relations between labor and capital as well as the national politics. Identity and ideology of workers are outcomes of social and cultural processes deeply grounded in the national and local context. The structure of authority within work organization, the relationship between union and management, historical legacy of labor struggle etc. have affected the formation of workers' perception of themselves, their union organizations, capitalists and the state. The configuration of institutions and social relations has generated different social and political actors between the Japanese Toyota Motor Co. and a South African coal miner.

Social mechanism centered approaches are different from variable centered approaches which decompose individuals or groups into the sum of properties described by variables. For example, based on individual information, social actors, respondents, are dissected into variables, eventually numbers, such as gender, education, age, etc. The major concern of variable centered approach is to find out significant correlations among variables and the relationship between dependent variable and independent variables. The variable centered approach is a correlation based social analysis, assuming variables are major causal factors and correlations represent real causal relations or possible indicators of causal relations. Ontologically actors are not causal factors in social events or social phenomena. Instead, variables are causal factors (for more details, see Hedstrom and Swedberg, 1996: 291-293). C. W. Mills (1959) called it "abstract empiricism" by which statistical models are assumed to represent research interests.

A search for social mechanisms between an explanandum and its explanans might prevent researchers from over-generalization of the experiences of the West to the non-West. Because there are diverse possibilities of social mechanisms in social formation, the same explanandum can be generated by different explanans across nations. For example, major causes of the economic growth in South Korea in the late 20th century were different from those of England in the 19 century. Economic growth as the same explanandum can be explained by different causal factors and different social mechanisms of economic growth can be identified between South Korea and England. Thus, the division between the West and the non-West is also an oversimplified dichotomy, assuming homogeneity within the West and within the non-West. Social mechanism approach rejects oversimplification of social formation.

Furthermore, the social mechanism centered approach is an attempt to interrogate causal processes which are culture specific or context specific, differentiating real causal processes from pseudo-causal processes frequently observed among over-generalized social theories and empirical research based on survey data.[6] Identifying "nuts and bolts of social mechanism" would help researchers reveal specificity of causal factors or causal processes which represent cultural differences and institutional idiosyncrasy (Elster, 2007: 31-52). Thus, the social mechanism centered approach is inter-disciplinary or trans-disciplinary approach because constituents of social mechanisms consist of various factors which cannot be confined to traditional boundaries of social sciences disciplines. The classification of social sciences and humanities are artificial demarcations with institutional power in universities.

**Trans-disciplinary Approach**

However, the social mechanism centered approach is not welcomed by each discipline in the social sciences because it demands new approaches to the society with different understanding and an explanation of different layers and aspects of the society, trans-

---

[6]  Context free social theories tend to ignore specific assumptions which those theories rely upon. Collective ideology and institutional trajectory strongly reflect path dependency. Individuals and collective actors are influenced by collective memory and group experiences heavily embedded in collective ideology or culture and institutional configuration. Comparative studies emphasize not only macro context or background but also dynamics between macro-micro processes. See Mahoney and Rueschemeyer eds. (2003).

gressing traditional boundaries within social sciences which were established in the late 19th century and the early 20th century. Each discipline has its own explanandum by which each discipline establishes its institutional identity and maintains organizational autonomy within higher academic institutions. The formation and transformation of each discipline within universities have accompanied academic politics, claiming and maintaining the genuine area of research and sometimes monopolizing professional jobs. Economics try to understand economic activities and economic outcome such as economic growth, business cycle, price change, wage determination, and so on. Psychology attempts to explain cognitive structure, psychic change including emotional depression and metal disorder of individuals. Political sciences pursue an understanding of the relationship between political parties and voters, policy making processes, and political power and legal order. Sociology tries to understand social behavior, social structure and social transformation.

Variation in explanadum results in differential emphases on explanans in social sciences. While emphases on interdisciplinary approach bring about convergence of explanans in social sciences in recent years, it is still limited in some areas. In particular, specialized journals developed in the 20th century prevent social scientists from searching for theoretical understandings beyond particular disciplines in the existing academic boundaries in the social sciences. The institutional boundary exercises strong constraints on research activities from choosing research subjects to finding plausible explanations and the ways of publication of research findings.

The diffusion of Western education system into the world has brought about the almost same institutional boundaries in the non-Western world. The university system in the Third World followed the university system in the West, including disciplinary boundaries made in the West, the contents of curriculum, and evaluation of students and teachers. The model of sciences including both natural sciences and social sciences developed in the West was also transplanted into the newly liberated countries in Asia and Africa, where Western higher education system was established during the colonial rule. Even though there has been an indigenous development of education and research in each country in the non-West, the model of sciences developed in the West, mostly in the United

States of America, dominates the idea of sciences and its institutional configuration in the non-West, that is, as hegemony of scientific education and research among universities in the non-West.

## Hermeneutic Reflection or Mental Experiment

As Spivak (1984) argues, the subalterns cannot speak out by themselves. They are not fully represented by academic representatives either. Furthermore, they cannot present their own history and collective experiences in an academic discourse. While they are living in the life world, they do not exercise their existential power at the sphere of knowledge production. Therefore, the agency centered approach to knowledge might end up with an emphasis on practice because agency cannot produce a scientific theory based on lived experience by itself.

Then the remaining issue will be 'what is real in the real experience of the subalterns' and 'how it can be presented and represented by whom? More fundamentally, how can reality be identified? One way to go beyond the essentialist approach to reality is to go further to empirical reality rather than transcendental reality. The Kantian conception of reality can be comprehended only by "noumena" which cannot be perceived by experience due to limitations and even distortion of sensibility of human beings. The reality in this case can be captured by a priori knowledge that is independent of experience. How is a priori knowledge possible? If reality is independent of our experience and only a priori knowledge provides some possibility of understanding of reality, what is the basis of a priori knowledge? The Kantian concept of reality cannot be a proper way to promote social scientific discourse because it moves the issue to the speculative metaphysics.

Instead, an empirical reality can be perceived by sensory experiences. However, we should recognize the fact that sensory experiences are imperfect and limited in its reliability and validity. Thus, knowledge about reality in the social sciences cannot be a final and definite one. Rather it is a tentative explanatory scheme made via thought experiment or mental experiment. To use Lakatos' term, it should be a "scientific research program" that defies simple and degenerative methodological falsificationism.[7] Mental experiment

---

[7]  Imre Lakatos distinguishes sophisticated falsificationism from naïve falsifica-

identifies causal mechanism that generates what we observe as events or phenomena. The causal mechanism perceived by researchers' mental experiment includes unobservable causal processes. However, if we assume the operation of the unobservable causal processes, we can explain social events or phenomena much better.

To use the term invented by C. W. Mills, sociological imagination captures the mental experiment or mental reconstruction of social reality to interrogate and indentify power relations embedded in social relations in a society and across societies. The issue raised by post-colonial discourses concerns power relations that underwrite

**Toward Complex Theory**

To formulate counter-hegemonic social sciences, we need to avoid overarching parsimonious universal social theory. Instead, we should seek complex theories. That is one way to localize social understanding and indigenize social theory. The hegemony of universal theory developed in the West has not been challenged by social scientists in the non-West recently. While the issue of hegemony of mainstream social sciences has been raised by critical social scientists, universalism has been accepted as core criterion of a good theory. Thus, theoretical discussions of social theories have been done without contextualizing those social theories. Decontextualized social theories have been imported from the West to the non-West in the 20th century, generating speculative understandings of Western social theories. For example, there has not been a clear demarcation between social theories and philosophical theories in theoretical discourse in sociology. That is the reason why philosophical discussion could be easily transplanted into sociological discussion, exemplified by structuralism Marxism and post-modernism, invoking Louis Althusser and Jacque Derrida (Rusch, 1992 and Seidman, 1994).

However, the level of complexity in social theory depends on the concrete relationship between an explanandum and its explanans.

---

tionism, arguing that a scientific theory can be falsified if and only if another theory has been proposed with the excess empirical content. Otherwise, naïve falisification leads to degenerative scientific research (Lakatos, 1970: 182-191).

The core principle of theory construction of non-hegemonic social sciences is that social scientific understanding should be fully contextualized spatially and temporally. One way of contextualization is double indigenization of social theories developed in the West by which social scientists in the non-West scrutinize its validity by contextualizing Western social theories for Western societies with specific historicity and temporality. Of course, social scientists should bear in mind that the West is not monolithic and homogeneous. The unit of contextualization also depends on explanandum. For example, as world system theories argue, the unit of analysis of social development should be a broad region rather than a country because several countries in the same region have experienced common social changes (Amin, 1976; Arrigi, 2003; Frank, 1998; Wallerstein, 1974) On the contrary, an analysis of the political psychology of social groups should pay attention to local cultures or races, subalterns, in the local area within a country (Bhabha, 1990; Hall, 1996).

The formation of the modern world has been dominated by the supreme power of the West. Social theories that attempted to explain social changes in the West have been imported to the newly liberated non-West after the postwar era. To use Foucault's term (1980), the episteme of dominant social sciences of the West has been firmly articulated in the social sciences in the non-West. That the common feature of mainstream social theories in the West has been a pursuit for parsimonious and abstract explanatory models. Thus, hegemonic social sciences in the non-West, heavily influenced by the West, have produced knowledge that failed to represent the wretched of the life world.

## Concluding Remark

Post-colonial perspectives in literary theory and cultural studies raise an important problematic, revealing hidden dimension of social theory in the West, considered as seemingly neutral and scientific. It argues that social theories of the West have excluded voices of the oppressed which cannot represent their own history and historical experiences of the non-West. They include both the ordinary people and the academicians. In short, hegemony of social theory of the former imperial societies in the West still persists over the liberated societies in the non-West, shaping the captive mind of the people of the former colonial societies.

Post-colonial critique of social theories of the West has been done by transcendental reflections on ontological and epistemological foundations of social theories, historical research, genealogical exploration of theories and knowledge taught at various educational institutions in the non-West. However, as many critics also agree, the post-colonial perspective has not paved a new way to the development of social theories in the non-West. It is mainly because post-colonial perspective is fundamentally oriented toward the literary theory. Although critique of knowledge derived from the West included debunking epistemological foundation and distortion of the historical and social reality made by imperial perspectives, it did not succeed in providing alternative non-hegemonic social theory to those of the West.

Hegemonic social sciences in the West have been entrenched in academic institutions in which culture and norms have evolved in tandem with higher education and knowledge production in the West. Institutional bases of hegemony comprises of sets of scientific customs including research practices, methods used in the research, writing journal papers and review system, excluding non-mainstream research and issues. Compliance of individual social scientist in the non-West to the "hegemonic social sciences of the West" cannot be easily deplored, particularly for young social scientists in the non-West, simply because defiance of hegemonic social sciences may hinder his or her academic career by violating institutional rules and norms of the academics in the non-West.

As an attempt to construct non-hegemonic social theories, I suggest that at least five elements should be considered in formulating social theories based on spatiality and historicity; social totality, social mechanism centered approach, trans-disciplinary approach, hermeneutic mental experiment, and toward complex theory. In principle, the five elements are suggested to enhance validity of social theory fully representing historical specificity and complex social dynamics at various levels. Recognizing the problematic raised by post-colonial discourses and its limitations to social sciences, I discuss that consideration of five elements in theory construction contributes to non-hegemonic social theories in the non-West as well as in the West.

# References

Agnew, J. (1994). The territorial trap: the geographical assumptions of international theory. *Review of International Political Economy, 1(1),* 53–80.

Alatas, S. F. (2010). The Definition and Types of Alternative Discourse. In M. Burawoy, M. Chang & M. F. Hsieh (eds.) *Facing An Unequal World, Challenging For a Global Society* Vol. II. Taipei: Institute of Sociology, Academia Sinica. (pp. 139–157).

Amin, S. (1976). *Unequal Development: An Essay on the Social Formations of Peripheral Capitalism.* New York: Monthly Review Press

Arrigi, G. (2003). *The Resurgence of East Asia: 500, 100, 50 Year Perspectives.* London: Routledge.

Benton, T. & Craib. I. (2001). *Philosophy of Social Science: Philosophical Issues in Social Thought.* London: Palgrave Macmillan.

Bhabha, H. (1990). *Nation and Narration.* London: Routledge.

Bhabha, H. K. (1994). *The Location of Culture.* London: Routledge.

Bhaskar, R. A. (1987). *Scientific Realism and Human Emancipation.* London: Verso.

Bonnel, V. E. & Hunt, L. A. (eds.) (1999). *Beyond The Cultural Turn: New Directions in the Study of Society and Culture.* Berkeley: University of California Press.

Elster, J. (1991). Patterns of Causal Analysis in Tocqueville's *Democracy in America. Rationality and Society,* 3, 277–297.

Frank, A. G. (1998). *ReOrient: Global Economy in the Asian Age.* Berkeley: University of California.

Hall, S. (1996). The West and the rest: discourse and power. In Hall *et al.* (orgs.) *Modernity: introduction to the modern societies.* Oxford: Blackwell. (pp. 185–227).

Hedstrom, P. & Swedberg, R. (1996). Social Mechanisms. *Acta Sociologica, 39,* 281–308.

Jameson, F. (1998). *The Cultural Turn: Selected Writings on the Postmodern, 1983–1998.* London: Verso.

Kaidesoja, T. (2013). Overcoming the Biases of Microfoundationalism: Social Mechanisms and Collective Agents. *Philosophy of Social Sciences, 43(3),* 301–322.

Keat, R. & Urry, J. (1975). *Social Theory as Science.* London: Routledge.

Kim, U. & Berry, J. W. (eds.) (1993). *Indigenous Psychology: Research and Experience in Cultural Context.* New York: Springer.

Kim, U., Yang, K. & Hwang, K. (2006). *Indigenous Psychology and Cultural Psychology: Understanding People in Context.* New York: Springer.

Kuhn, M. (2013). "Hegemonic Science": Critique Strands, Counterstrategies, and Their Paradigmatic Premises. In M. Kuhn & S. Yazawa (eds.) *Theories about and Strategies against Hegemonic Social Sciences*. Tokyo: Center for Global Studies Seijo University. (pp. 31–54).

Lakatos, I. (1970). Falisification and the Methodology of Scientific Research Programmes. In I. Lakatos & A. Musgrave (eds.) *Criticism and the Growth of Knowledge*. Cambridge: Cambridge University Press.

Mahoney, J. & Rueschemeyer, D. (eds.) (2003). *Comparative Historical Analysis in the Social Sciences*. Cambridge: Cambridge University Press.

Manicas, P. T. (2006). *A Realist Philosophy of Social Sciences*. Cambridge: Cambridge University Press.

Marx, K. (1990) [1873]. *The Capital*. New York: Penguin Books.

Mills, C. W. (1959). *Sociological Imagination*. London: Oxford University Press.

Ray, L. & Sayer, A. (1999). *Culture and Economy After the Cultural Turn*. London: Sage.

Resch, R. P. (1992). *Althusser and the Renewal of Social Theory*. Berkeley: University of California Press.

Seidman, S. (1994). *The Postmodern Turn: New Perspectives on Social Theory*. Cambridge: Cambridge University Press.

Shweder, R. (1991). *Thinking Through Cultures*. Cambridge. MA: Harvard University Press

Shweder, R. & Levine, R. A. (1984). *Culture theory: Essays on mind, self, and emotion*. New York: Cambridge University Press.

Shin, K-Y. (2013). The Emergence of Hegemonic Social Sciences and Strategies of Non(counter) Hegemonic Social Sciences. In M. Kuhn & S. Yazawa (eds.) *Theories about and Strategies against Hegemonic Social Sciences*. Tokyo: Center for Global Studies Seijo University. (pp. 77–93).

Spival, C. C. (1984). Can the Subaltern Speak? In C. Nelson & L. Grossberg (eds.) *Marxism and the interpretation of Culture*. Chicago: University of Illinois Press, (pp.271–313).

Said, E. (1974). *Orientalism*. New York: Penguin Books.

Rosenbeger, A. (2012). *Philosophy of Social Science*. (4th ed.) Boulder: Westview Press.

Wallerstein, I. (1974). *The Modern World-System I: Capitalist Agriculture and the Origins of the European World-Economy in the Sixteenth Century*. New York: Academic Press.

Wallerstein, I. (2000). *The Essential Wallerstein*. New York: New Press.

Weber, M. (1904). Objectivity in Social Science and Social Policy. In E. A. Shils & H. A. Finch (eds. and trans.) *The Methodology of the Social Sciences*. New York: Free Press.

Winch, P. (1958). *The Idea of Social Sciences and its Relations to Philosophy*. (2nd ed.) London: Routledge.

# Chapter 3:
# 21st Century Challenges to Social and Economic Sciences: Global Sciences of the Economy and of Individual Behavior

Huri Islamoglu

## 1. Introduction

Since the closing decades of the 20th century global market interests have posed a challenge to the supremacy of national states, as well as to economies and societies which these states helped to shape. Coinciding with this challenge was a questioning of social and economic sciences, of their relevance in a globalized world interconnected through trade and financial flows and through migration of peoples. Social and economic sciences had emerged initially in the 19th century in contexts of state and nation-making in Europe; they played a central role in similar processes in the post-World War II era in Europe's former colonies in Asia and Africa. This essay primarily discusses trends in Western social and economic sciences in the post-World War II era under American hegemony during the Cold War. It does this by addressing the ways societal conceptions and solutions to social issues emerging in Europe in the 19th century were universalized and generalized in various social science disciplines to serve as an idiom of Western domination in non-Western world regions.

Secondly, the essay addresses the challenges to societal sciences since the 1980s and the rise of global sciences responding to exigencies of the global economic order and its free-tradist understandings. Margaret Thatcher's statement 'There is no society' summarized the vision of the new era. Thatcher was pointing to the priority of the economy, of the economic activity of 'rational' individuals acting to maximize their gains interacting in markets as producers, investors, and consumers continuously making decisions to exchange their labour power, capital, and goods. Economic growth depended on the fact that this activity was unimpeded by political concerns of the state responsive to demands of social actors (including interventions in the labour market by setting a minimum wage) and that prices of labour (wages), goods, and capital (interest rates) are determined according to market rules (or supply and demand in different markets). Accumulation of capital in the hands of maximizing individuals (often identified with major economic actors or corporations) was, in turn, expected to have trickle down effects on other individuals in the form of jobs, or charity. In a word, new global sciences that are taking the place of social and economic sciences do not claim to be social; instead, they address economic individuals, their activities and institutions and behavior patterns to facilitate those activities.

Hence, resting on a faith in universal market principles, global sciences focus on institutions (e.g. property rights) facilitating the workings of markets in accordance with those natural and universal principles. In that relation, governance studies addressed expert knowledge about formulation of technical rules or institutions. At the same time, global sciences draw attention to those factors that influence decisions or choices of rational individuals as had been the case with cognitive sciences and behavioral economics as well as cultural studies. At issue is a raising of the level generality and universality of assumptions about movements in economic activity and individual behavior to an higher level, that of natural laws while the very substance of these assumptions remain rooted in yet another European experience, that of free-tradism in the 17th and 18th centuries.

## 2. Social and Economic Sciences and the Social Democratic Disciplining of Industrial Capitalism in the 19th century

Historically, social sciences and initially sociology as well as administrative sciences (including administrative law) developed in the midst of societal dislocations occasioned by industrialization and Napoleonic wars throughout Europe. It was part of an attempt to introduce some form of a cognitive order at a time of immense societal changes and uncertainty. At the same time social administrative sciences and later economic science, addressing the 1870s crisis of European industrial capitalist economies, were integral to the process of the articulation of a social democratic challenge to free-tradist capitalism that preceded industrialization. That challenge in the 19th and the 20th century involved a conceptual incorporation of policy or political decisions, most notably, those of states, in the steering of industrial capitalism to address its excesses in the form of peasant dispossessions, unhindered exploitation of factory workers and mounting poverty both in towns and the countryside. Such excesses had led to disruptions of societal order thus rendering the 'Social Question' a primary threat to industrial capitalism.

Hence, in the 19th century securing of societal order became a central concern of the emerging industrial middle classes. Societal and economic sciences addressed this concern functionalizing knowledge about human behavior to place in the service of disciplining individual behavior in the different institutional settings of industrial society including schools, factories, barracks or the army, and prisons (Foucault 1973). In keeping with the legacy of the Enlightenment, just as nature was understood to be the object of scrutiny by the physical sciences, human society was understood the object of scrutiny by the human or social sciences. Physical sciences had put knowledge about nature in the service of mankind in the form of technology to enable exploitation or domination of nature. Similarly, societal sciences were expected to place knowledge about human behavior in the service of 'reforming' that behavior to create an orderly society. In this relation, the science of society, addressed by Comte-ian sociology, or Bentham's utilitarian legal science, were conceived as 'techniques' essentially to attain societal cohesion, stability and some amount of equity.[1]

In the 19th century social and economic sciences were pivotal to the normalization of tremendous changes unleashed both by the industrial revolution and the French Revolution, and the Napoleonic wars throughout Europe. (Wallerstein 1991) In fact, in this world turned upside down, ideas of equality, fraternity, solidarity,

---

[1] Similarly, Marx's more revolutionary work was very much imbued by this positive or instrumentalist perception of society- whereby his analysis of class struggle in capitalist society, led him to a prediction of inevitability of a universal triumph of the working classes and societal liberation signaling the end of the capitalist order.

and liberty unleashed by the French revolution and spread by Napoleonic wars were turned into demands against the new order of industrial capitalism, of property and colonial expansion. Normalization entailed formulations of norms of human behavior in the emerging contexts of nation-states, as citizens as conscripted soldiers, as prisoners, as students; of industrial societies as workers, as entrepreneurs. Put differently, normalization implied the formulation of universalistic assumptions about human behavior and human expectations, so as to render outcomes of such behavior that would be predictable, therefore controllable.

In this period, normalizing idioms of societal sciences and economic sciences competed with different strands of social revolutionary thinking, most notably, Marxism in addressing the 'Social Question'. The latter addressed the injustices and inequalities which the social and economic order of capitalism had given rise to, putting knowledge about society, its conflicts or struggles in the service of revolutionary change by societal agents e.g. working classes or their representatives. To counter social revolutionary claims, a functionalist social science (most notably sociology) cast as *positive science* comparable to or on par with physical sciences, emerged as part of the governmental environment, placing knowledge about society in the service of controlling and reforming it for the public good. It meant countering the revolutionary assault with a new vision of society, with a new 'normal' of conformity to a societal order increasingly identified with the government of centralized, national states. Such conformity was the end-point for all disciplinary action.

Economics, as a scientific discipline, emerged in the latter part of the 19th century. In this context, economics as a mathematical general equilibrium model (initially formulated by the French economist Leon Walras), represented the prices for the point at which supply and demand for all goods would be equated and individual markets (labor, capital, goods) would clear simultaneously (Walras 1874; Morishima 1977).[2] As such, equilibrium, mathematically calculable, was the point at which maximum gains accrued to all parties engaged in exchange activity. That equilibrium, in turn,

---

[2] Supply and demand trends represented decisions on the part of self-interested individuals set out to maximize their gains with respect to choices regarding supply and demand, inputs and outputs.

represented a norm in relation to which the economists could make predictions about future trends (in prices) on the basis of the past and present equilibrium points. Walras was adamant about the independence of his formulations from any consideration of value and utility; for him, the general equilibrium model was simply a tool to assist in individual decisions regarding investment, production, trade etc.

In the 19$^{th}$ century such predictability and measurability was increasingly important when decisions on the part of capitalists regarding levels of investments and profits; availability of jobs, production conditions and food prices in increasingly individual European national societies and their colonial possessions were all increasingly among the concerns of European governments. Walras' equilibrium model introduced a measure of discipline to economic decisions, proposing an 'objective,' 'positive' way of measuring (as well as predicting) outcomes of individual decisions in economic activity. In doing so, notwithstanding his reticence about addressing issues of utility, he was responding to exigencies of the economic uncertainties in his time and his mathematical formulations sought to introduce a measure of certainty in market activity.

Alfred Marshall, on the other hand, addressed head-on the issue of utility in relation to economics. For Marshall, economics was to serve human welfare. He placed his theory of price at the center of economic science establishing relationships between price shifts and the shifts in supply and demand. Confronted with conditions arising from the first global crisis of capitalism involving falling prices for agricultural goods world-wide, shrinking demand for industrial goods and falling rates of profits, Marshall looked for possibilities of reversing these economic trends. It meant policy interventions to alter demand for and supply of goods, thus affecting price and profit levels as, for instance, that which could be achieved through taxation measures. Marshallian economics represented a de-mystification of the economic domain, of the free-tradist faith in self-regulation of markets or in unhindered decisions of individuals as sole movers of markets (Marshall 2009; Cook 2005). Marshallian economics was a predecessor of Keynesian challenge to that faith in the 20$^{th}$ century and, most notably, during the 1930s Great Economic Depression in the European economies with world-wide repercussions. At a time when markets collapsed and millions were left jobless, goods were not produced, and capital was not available, J.M.Keynes upheld the priorities of national economies and the role of state policies to intervene in the economy, in markets, to ensure that jobs were created, and consumption and production stimulated. Keynes, like Marshall questioned the faith of free-market advocates that all would be set right in the long term once the markets were allowed to take their natural course and achieved equilibrium states.'In the long term, we are all dead,' Keynes famously quipped.

As I will later discuss, Keynesian economics was the main source of inspiration for developmental economics in the post-World War II era.

Notwithstanding their subsequent claims to scientific universality (more specifically in the post-WW II era under American hegemony), social and economic sciences initially belonged to Europe, to the struggles and debates in the 19th century in the context of societal upheavals addressing the ills of industrial societies and critical of free tradist understandings grounded in universalistic and naturalistic explanations with their priorities of economic growth and gains for individual entrepreneurs. The 19th century was also a period of European expansion and establishment of European domination in non-European areas. Orientalism developed in Europe as a separate body of knowledge about the Orient or of non-European areas, their societies, cultures, politics, as well as their law (Hodgson 1974; Said 1979; Islamoglu-Inan 1987; Lockman 2009). Trade provided Europe's main link and interest in the non-European areas. Hence, Orientalism primarily rested on freetradist assumptions with a spattering of European Enlightenment thinking. Orientalists posed a binary vision of the world with Europe representing a domain of commercial prosperity and economic growth enabled by the law's autonomy or the rule of law upholding individual rights and freedoms; most importantly, property rights, and by governments representative of commercial interests. By contrast, economic deprivation, lawlessness or lack of individual rights and freedom, and tribalism or despotic, arbitrary rule, at best benevolent absolutism, prevailed in non-European regions.

Orientalism also embodied a culturalist, historicist vision, very much imbued with civilizational perspectives of the nineteenth and early twentieth century, whereby each civilizational entity represented an unfolding of a cultural essence. While the golden age of a civilization was understood to have coincided with a time of utmost potency of that essence, of institutional effervescence, its decline pointed to its exhaustion, and hence, its institutional depravation and degeneration ( Islamoglu-Inan 1987).

A civilizational/ culturalist perspective enjoyed a revival at yet another era of free-tradism, when America led Western expansion in the 1990s and the 2000s in the oil-rich regions of Middle Eurasia (Afghanistan as converging point of pipelines from Central Asia, Iraq) I was cast following September 11th, 2001 events in terms of a crusade of Western Christian civilization against the civilization of violent, backward Islam. Samuel Huntington summed up the Western mood of that times in the phrase 'clash of civilizations.'

Orientalism, its binary vision of history contrasting Eastern absences with presences in Europe, underlining Europe's incontestable superiority to non-European areas, provided justification for Europe's presence in and domination of these regions. That superiority was posed in free-tradist terms both in the 19th century and presently. In the 19th century, while Europeans advocated free-trade in non-European regions, a vibrant social democratic critique of free- tradism was underway in Europe with an eye to containing free-tradist excesses. [3] The latter discourse was not to 'travel' to non-European regions which were designated as domains of free-tradism whereby Europeans (together with their local allies) held non-European economies, law, and government to idealized universals (including expectations of unobstructed individual rights or freedom rooted in natural law, market activity clear of all government intervention). In the 19th century as it has been in the 21st century, European 'reformers' did not hesitate to introduce draconian measures to implement free-tradist policies with little regard for the social dislocations these measures caused. Moreover, coupled with the European rejection of non-European histories (or European representations of these histories[4]) which denied any dynamics to those histories, free-tradism, inseparable from European domination, was posed as the only policy option or as the

---

[3] In this relation one could point to the emergence of Marshallian economics rejecting natural, self-regulating markets and of historical economics as well as to Benthamite questionings of natural law, to historical law debates and, finally, to the practice of administrative law and courts throughout Europe.

[4] Reinstatement of a history of castes in India by the British is a case in point. For an excellent fictional account, see Gosh 2015.

only solution for non-European regions, if not the only one for these region to join 'world history'.

Yet, notwithstanding its haughty claims embodied in Orientalist formulations, free-tradism introduced by European domination did not offer any prospect for economic development to non-European regions neither in the 19th century nor in its present revival in the era of global market development. Instead, often undermining the existing social and economic dynamics,[5] free tradist domination tended to condemn the non-European regions to a cycle of perpetual dependence on Europe which remained the center for capitalist development (Wallerstein 1974), if not to total devastation and societal disintegration, as has been the case in following the American invasion of Iraq to the trumpet of free-tradist Orientalism (Mattei &Nader 2008).

## 3. Post-World War II Developmentalism or a Modernization Perspective in Social Sciences and Economics

Not unlike the 19th century free-tradist Orientalism, Western social and economic sciences in the post-war era rested their universality claims on Western superiority this time represented by American world hegemony. That hegemony was grounded in what seemed like the infinite possibilities of the American economy to generate wealth to enable a reconstruction effort of vast proportions extending from war-torn economies in Europe and Japan to former European colonies in Asia and Africa, suffering from adverse effects of colonization. As significantly, American hegemony was grounded in a universal promise of 'freedom;' it represented the 'free world' as opposed to the totalitarian Communism of the Soviet Union. Social sciences and economics became instrumental to the delivery

---

[5] Here dynamics includes not simply the local trade and production structures but also historical institutions and discourses which had developed in the course of long histories of non-European regions prior to European advent. More often than not these regions have been ruled by trading empires (Qing, Mughal, Safavid, Ottoman) as had been in most of Middle and Eastern Eurasia with extensive experiences in balancing the growth of exigencies in a commercial environment with those of equity- not dissimilar European quests for social democratic solutions in the 19th century.

of the promise of freedom resting their universality claims on it. In the post-war era, increased use of sophisticated quantification techniques, further reinforced the universality claims of social sciences, and especially of economics, imparting these sciences as having scientific legitimacy or at least the appearance of one.

The 'promise of freedom' which social sciences took upon themselves to realize assumed a model of modern development borrowing heavily from Max Weber's model for the development of Western industrial capitalism in the 19th century. First and foremost Weber's formulations had sought to reconcile the often contradictory strands in the development of Western industrial capitalism by means of a Kantian understanding of a rationality driving human society; for Kant that rationality was rooted in the idea of universal human interest in survival. For Weber, such rationality was represented in the West by Protestant ethics enabling individuals to behave in ways which were conducive to capitalist development. In the 19th century, given the primacy of nation states, Weber assigned the bureaucratic states the task of (institutionally) realizing that rationality. Western domination worldwide, in turn, made possible the diffusion of Weber's model of rational development.

The universal validity of a Western model of rational capitalist development was questioned in the first half of the 20tth century witnessing waves of senseless destruction by western capitalist powers in the two world wars of the early 20th century. In the post-war era the rise of American hegemony sparked a renewed faith in that rational development inspiring a new model for modern capitalist development in social and economic sciences (Corkin 2000).

This model of modern development, first, highlighted the virtues of free-market capitalism and development of entrepreneurial middle classes while looking to rational bureaucratic states to facilitate the rise of middle classes (Rostow 1956). At the same time, the model called for the dissemination of rational thinking and rational law which encouraged behavior conducive to capitalist development. For instance, Weber regarded Islamic religion and law as having been adverse to capitalist development. This perspective on Islam made secularization a priority in Islamic societies. Finally, while states, and state-steered economic development was viewed to be essential for capitalist development, state actions were to be subjected to scrutiny by democratically elected parliaments and subjected to the 'rule of law' or to rational law. These properties of modern capitalist society corresponded to and were articulated by the different social science disciplines including development economics, sociology, and political science.

From the perspective of economic science *per se*, in the post-war period a near-consensus developed around the necessity of state intervention or state action to deliver means of livelihood to populations devastated by war and colonization, what the markets could not or would not. (Marglin & Schor 1991; Crouch 1979; Crafts 1995). Keynesian intervention in the 1930s with its emphasis on state policy to affect recoveries of European and American national economies from the Great Depression, loomed large in the minds of policy-makers faced with the post-war reconstruction effort. Also of concern for builders of the 'free world' was a revival of socialist movements in war torn Europe and Japan; and socialism had an appeal to poverty ridden Third world societies. Socialist models of development accorded important presence to the state and achieved important returns at least in pulling the Soviet Union out of dire poverty and devastation in the 1930 albeit at great human costs. The latter were either not known to or did not interest Western observers in the immediate post WWII era when Stalin was glorified for his victories against the Nazis.

Since Marshall's favoring of policy decisions to intervene to set 'things' right in the national economy in the 19th century, it became increasingly difficult for economic theory to claim its lofty distance from the state and society, finding itself entangled in state policies addressing multiple societal interests. Macroeconomics, the dominant trend in economic theory in the post-war era, adopted Walras' general equilibrium model on a scale of national markets. On the one hand, this assumed that equilibrium prices for goods, labor, capital were to be formed in national markets where individuals made decisions affecting the supply of and demand for goods. On the other hand, national markets were also sites for state policy, for state interventions in price-making responding to various demands of /pressures from different societal groups. Such interventions took the form of agricultural subsidies, public provision for health, education, and transport services, subsidies for industries and for entrepreneurial activities; it also meant high taxes, most notably on the wealthy or the entrepreneurial classes to sustain these services or subsidies. Of course, the liberty of national governments to set prices was limited by trends in and pressures from the international economy further complicating the equilibrium picture pointing to continuities between national and international economies which assumed priority under conditions of development of global economies after 1980s.

## Social and Economic Sciences and the Actual Makings of the American Hegemony

These idealized properties of Western development pre-supposed their opposites in the 'eastern' power of the Soviet Union, the rival of the West in the Cold War and in the 'underdeveloped' Third World in Asia and Africa. Hence, reminiscent of 19$^{th}$ century Orientalism, the Weberian modernization perspective posed an idealized 'modern' against its opposite in a similarly idealized 'traditional other' with the modern/ traditional divide overlapping with the West/East divide. For instance, both Communist China and Russia were amply endowed with descriptions of eastern barbarity and despotism (Wittfogel 1957). At the same time, modern/ traditional also addressed a divide within Europe's own history, that between traditional agrarian societies before industrialization and modern industrial societies. Just as free-tradist openings were seen as the only solution to Eastern stagnation and backwardness in the 19$^{th}$ century, modernizing reforms were viewed as the only hope of the Third World, as well as of the socialist areas, for catching up with the West and becoming modern. Yet, unlike the free-tradist/Orientalist vision states, state-building was central to the post-war modernization project. In the Third World as well as the developed world modernizing reforms were expected to be carried out by the 'new states'.

Primacy of state-building in societal modernization also coincided with the security and policing interests of American hegemony, or in the language of that hegemony, with the concerns for the defense of the free world. To this end, 'militarization' became a center-piece for modernizing reforms. In the Third World creation of 'new nations' more often than not amounted to no more than creation of 'armies', trained and equipped, against a supposed Soviet threat. This, in turn, placed the militaries in the forefront of the capitalist modernization project, giving the lie to a host of 'liberal' reforms introducing parliamentary democratic regimes, the rule of law etc. Third World militaries proved to be most effective in suppressing their own populations often to protect investments by American corporations. Resistance of agricultural and industrial workers to exploitative practices of foreign corporations often met with brutal action of 'modern ' armies. In fact, 'militarization' often rendered the Third World countries as well as European countries as members of an US led military alliance (NATO) lucrative markets for arms-trade by American corporations. For the most part, that trade was underwritten by the US government itself whereby the military aid constituted a major part of the US aid received by these regions. Similarly, the fact that the bureaucratic states, their armies were direct recipients of US aid which, more often than not, did not find itself to other groups in society.

Most importantly, to the extent a middle lass developed it consisted of bureaucrats, the army and a weak entrepreneurial class dependent on state subsidies enjoying monopolistic control over protected national markets. Furthermore, especially after the cutting of US aid in 1970s most notably to the Third World region following the downturn in the American economy, these government turned to borrowing in international banks paving the way to severe that crises which contributed to their discrediting in the 1980s. The heavy borrowing by Third world government also contributed to the further expansion of international financial institutions, the leading actors in the era of global capitalism that followed.

Social and economic sciences in the post-war era were intimately involved in ventures of societal reconstruction in Europe, Asia and the Third World. American social scientists, sociologists, political scientists and development economists working for the US government advised European and Third world governments in economic policy, state-building, and in matters of social reconstruction including education reforms. Furthermore, children of Third world elites educated in the US, returned home to participate in the enforcement of modernizing reforms. When the post-war world order came to end in the 1980s and 1990s, its social democratic bend favoring state presence in the economy, its focus on national economic, social development, and state building came under scrutiny; social and economic sciences, their universal validity claims, which had been a mainstay of that order, were also questioned. ultimately giving way to new ways of understanding capitalist reality.

## 4. Economics of Growth, Human, Behavioral and Market Sciences

The discrediting of Keynesian economics, its developmentalists' statist thrust in the Third world and subsequently in the developed world, however, cannot be understood independently of the increased significance of global capitalist interests in financial institutions and corporations in the developed world, most significantly in the US and subsequently in western Europe. Neither can the undermining of state led socialist economies be understood independently of this development. Major American corporations and financial institutions greatly benefited from investment opportunities both at home and abroad, in Europe and the Third World. Financial institutions (or banks) were empowered as a result of increased capital flows from oil-producing areas occasioned by high oil prices in the 1970s and also from Third World debt at high levels of interest. At the same time, American multi-national corporations weary of high levels of taxes and high wages due to power of trade unions in the States, sought investment opportunities abroad seeking markets where cheap labor was available. This drive on the part of multinational capital led in the 1990s to the opening of new markets in the former Communist regions.

Beginning in the1980s, global markets reforms imbued with free-tradist ideology and introduced by the IMF, World Bank and the EU, addressed the aspirations of multinational corporations and financial institutions to expand globally. To this end, market reforms first and foremost sought to eliminate state presence in economies including privatization of health, education services, and public transport services; removal of agricultural subsidies, elimination of minimum wages, tariffs and exchange rate controls. Simply, these reforms aimed to open the national economies to the activities of global capital interests (financial institutions, corporations) and to their investments. An economics of growth, led by maximizing individuals (synonymous with corporations), in pursuit of profits in self-regulating markets that were not interfered with by states, gained priority over developmentalist economics and its statist thrust.

The shift from a development to growth perspective, involving a demonizing of the state and its involvement in the economy and society signaled the demise of social sciences deeply implicated in state policies of the post-war era. Free- tradist growth models redefined 'modernization' in terms of the makings of global market environments and the dismantling of the post-war societal order in the making of which economics and social sciences played an important part. In the brave new world of global markets both the nature of policy and modalities of knowledge production were radically transformed.

First, economic policy-making regarding economic activity was no longer the domain of national states with priorities in national societies. Instead policy-decisions regarding local economies were increasingly made by expert bodies at international or global organizations, most notably, those at the IMF, the World and the European Union. These expert bodies engaged drafted the rules of global markets; in doing so, they addressed a world of products - goods, capital- and their global movements rather than societal actors or activities, for instance, of production. At the same time, expert bodies called governance bodies claimed objectivity and universality for what were described as technical rulings. Such rulings, the experts claimed, represented signals from self- regulating markets; as a result they were free of entanglements in societal claims, in a word, from societal politics. At issue was the transparency of rulings meaning their freedom from politics; this feature, in turn, distinguished the new governance rulings from the former state or government rules which were understood to have been grounded in the political interests in national societies.

The reality of global market environments, however, have given the lie to their claims of 'objectivity' of global market rulings; in practice, the new global market order rejecting the broad based politics of underlying governmental policy (which included the workers and the peasants), often and unabashedly spoke to the singular interest of global capital actors, transnational corporations and financial institutions.[6] Governance rulings claimed a univer-

---

[6] For instance, the Common Agricultural policy of the European Union (exemplary of governance rules in agriculture) required that agricultural exports were given certification and subjected to quality standards . Notwithstanding its universalistic claims, this requirement served to favor from large farmers who had the means to fulfill such requirements and engage in production for export markets at the expense of those who did not. Similarly, market rules of Common Agricultural Policy which made access to bank credits by farmers incumbent on submission of title deeds, discriminated against smaller farm-

sality for the interests of global capital actors with the media (another global corporate interest) continually reminding us that if these actors prospered we will all do so through enjoyment of 'trickle down effects' or crumps of corporate gains. It appeared that what was emerging was a 'privatized Keynesianism' with private capital continually interfering to ensure the interests of the global capitalist order (Crouch 2009). Equally pertinent has been the fact that promotion of global capital interests at the expense of other societal actors was concealed through abstract and universal legal definitions of the sovereign individual, his/her rights and freedoms with respect to economic activity- embodied in universal human rights (focusing on property rights) packages that were introduced alongside governance packages.

Furthermore, their claims to objectivity that were grounded in the natural workings of self-regulating markets, served to shield expert governance bodies from political or societal accountability, from taking responsibility for their decisions (Scharpf 1999; Islamoglu 2009). In practice, experts primarily answered to global capital interests; they did not take take any responsibility for any consequences their decisions might have had on other groups or interests including workers, farmers and the poor who, for the most part, are left with no option but to accept their lot, and wait for the time when markets might favor them!

Amidst the conservative upsurge of the 1980s and celebrations of the collapse of socialist regimes in the Soviet Union and eastern Europe, the free-tradist perspective with its assumption of self-regulating markets disseminated through the reform packages introduced by the the IMF, WB and the EU, prevailed in the shaping global market environments and served in the dismantling of national and socialist states. In the 1990s new institutional economics, somewhat distanced itself from the initial ideological fervor of free-tradist revival and its naturalistic assumption of self-regulating markets, and emphasized the centrality of rational, profit maximizing decisions/choices of individuals in achieving economic growth. New institutional economists pointed to the importance of institutions or rules to facilitate the making of those decisions/ choices

---

ers in favor of those with large holdings, leaving the former no alternative but to take recourse to usurers, ultimately a cause for the destruction of small farmers.

regarding consumption, investment, and exchange (North 1990). Yet while critical of free-tradist assumption of natural, self-regulating markets, new institutionalism remained ambivalent about the relationship of economic activity, of individual decisions to societal concerns and to political power relations. [7]

Consistent with that position, new institutionalist thinking provided conceptual openings for studies which addressed constituents of human behavior occasioning the rise of behavioral economics and the interest of economists in cognitive science. At the same time, new institutionalist thinking infiltrated social sciences; for instance, political science, addressing institutions in terms of their capacity to enhance rational behavior of human beings in markets . In this relation, the political science discipline adopting an institutionalist perspective and, relying on a rational choice model, assigned a central role to a 'technical' state shorn of all social and political entanglements, acting as a reservoir of institutions to facilitate the rational economic decisions of private individuals in pursuit of profits (Evans 1995; Rueschemeyer *et al*.1985).

As such, the new state was assigned the task of shaping the institutional mapping of global market environments, most importantly, property rights. How the states did so without reference to politics or different social/ political interests in a given region, however, remained theoretically problematic.[8] Put differently, at issue has been the question whose state are we talking about or whose politics prevailed in state decisions. The reality of global markets environments point to the politics of major corporations and financial institutions as a prevailing force.

In this relation, it is important to point to the centrality of law in the present context of global capitalism. From an institutionalist perspective, law as legal studies has been pivotal to the makings of global market environments; above all, it implied a recasting of legal institutions to partake in the ordering of market environ-

---

[7] Initially for Douglass C. North, leading theoretician of new institutionalisms, politics and political power relations represented transaction costs to be removed , or at best accommodated, for individuals to be able to make rational decisions in order to further economic growth ( North 1990). However, in his later work, North considerably distanced from this position.

[8] North pointed to the importance of a political consensus among different landed interests in defining property rights on land in England in the 18th century.

ments as witnessed in the case of practices of European Courts of Justice. As such, there has been an attempt to replace bureaucracies with the courts cast as governance institutions entrusting them with implementation / formulation of market rulings. At the same time, human rights inclusive of individual rights and freedoms, most importantly, property rights, has been central to the making of global market environments.

While the free-tradist perspective adopted a naturalist vision of rights rooted in natural law; the institutionalist perspective emphasized their character as rules or institutions subject to individual decisions. This proposition—as is the case with other institutionalists propositions, however, remains overladen with all the ambiguities about who these 'individuals' shorn of political power or societal concerns are. In practice, individuals are generally identified with major corporations, the legal personhood of which is repeatedly confirmed through court decisions e.g. US supreme court's recent decision on Citizens United. In countering the influence of corporations, of major bank over economic decisions that directly affects the everyday lives of people; all the critiques among them some individual social scientists ' with a conscience' (including Douglas C. North) can do is to offer feeble homage to social democracy or dapple in various theories about how to alter human behavior in doing so perhaps to shift central motivation of individuals away from greed to more altruistic ends (Sunstein 2014).

On the other hand, institutionalist emphasis on the individual and his behavior (distanced and at the expense of societal concerns) as a center-piece of growth-oriented capitalism, coupled with trends towards disintegration of national environments, opened the way for a focus on the constituents of individual identity-ethnicity, gender, religion- leading to a prominence of cultural studies. The obverse side of the concern for individuals, their behavior and identity has been the concern for security of individuals, their property and their identity; hence, a phenomenal expansion of security industries and the rise of security studies.

## 5. By way of Conclusion

This essay questions the universalistic claims of Western understandings about economic development, the society as well as about the state and the law embodied in social and economic sciences in the post-war era and in global market sciences since the 1980s by grounding them in Europe's historical experiences since the 18th century. Most centrally these universality claims were grounded in conditions of European / Western world domination since the 19th century while these claims served to legitimate or justify that domination. This venture in questioning the universality claims of Western understandings coincides with the dramatic changes in conditions of European world domination since the 1970s gaining momentum since late 2000s. It also points to possibilities for new thinking about social realities in the global economic environment—both historically and presently.

One unintended consequence of global economic development since the 1970s has been an emergence of competing regional economies steered by sovereign governments. China has been the most notable of these regional formations. On the one hand, regional economies are integrated into the global economy through investment and trade networks; non- Western multi-national corporate bodies, Chinese as well as Russian, Indian, and Brazilian are increasingly a common phenomenon in global markets, pointing to a true globalization of capital interests no longer confined to Western interests. On the other hand, non-Western regions, their governments ( most notably in China) increasingly seek to distance themselves from governance reforms which accompanied market reform packages introduced by international organizations (IMF,WB and the EU).

*Governance studies* had told us that new governance relied on technical rules drafted by disinterested experts; they simply transmitted signals from universal markets which, if allowed to operate without interference from special interests, we were told by *market economics,* would deliver prosperity to all. Instead, global governance had for the most part eliminated all special interests but those of global corporations. In the developed world it meant abandoning large segments of society to declining trends in their standards of living if not impoverishment while privileging a small corporate elites as a well as islands of skilled work. Outside of the developed world free-tradist governance allowed free rein to transnational corporations to plunder resources in different part of the global economy; fragmented states, fractured societies; it resulting in plunging of entire regions into chaos with religious, ethnic groups engaged in incessant warfare. The present Middle East is witness to the disaster of this failure of free-tradist market development.

One overriding issue, at the heart of human suffering in the global market order and the Western hegemony it represented, has been the exclusive character of its politics, admitting to no other societal interest but that of big capital to the exclusion of all other actors. Questioning of free-tradist governance or ways of ordering global economic reality points to new ways of conceptualizing that reality, most importantly, of its politics. That politics has to address concerns or interests outside of the enchanted sphere of global mega corporations. It would also mean 'bringing back broad -based societal politics and the state as the institutional domain of politics. This would be speaking to Sinicization not in the sense of introduction of autocratic government of central states all too reminiscent of Orientalist reflexes which are fashionable among Western journalists and intellectuals (Szijek 2015).

At issue is politicization of governance in the global economy whereby those who are responsible for drafting and implementing governance rules are politically accountable and these rules address the concerns of multiple societal actors including workers, peasants, service sector people (and, in the Chinese case, the different state actors belonging to local and central states). As such, rules are not exclusively concerned with improving the lot of major corporations in the hope that they might invest their gains to contribute to the well-being of others if the latter are patient enough to wait for their turn. Politicization of governance would also mean setting into motion processes whereby societal actors actively engaged in the making of global market environments, its rules or institutions negotiating their interests, voicing their claims, expressing their dissent. Characterization of this process as Sinicization would be accurate in that, for instance, in China rules ordering landed property and labor relations drafted by central government, were fiercely contested and deliberated in light of the concerns of the different parties involved over a number of years (Hsing 2013). As a result, the property law of 2007 and the labor contract law of 2008 represented texts of negotiated settlements rather than edicts issued by an autocratic government.

Viewed in this perspective, the study of global environment would no longer be considered to be one of governance or technical management of natural markets but to address those markets or economic activity as these are embedded in societal and political concerns, in the actual lives of people, in the relations between workers and their employers, between consumers and producers, in terms of who gets what and how much of what is produced, from exchange activity. Does this suggest a return to post-war understandings of social and economic sciences separated by rigid disciplinary boundaries with such compartmentalization remaining faithful to an essential liberal separation between the economic or market activity and politics, and the state. In the post-war period admittance of politics and states into study of market society economics) was part of the social democratic compromise grounded in historical conditions of strong labor movements in this period as well as to the prominence of socialist politics in the world as represented by the Soviet Union. When those conditions came to an end into 1980s and 1990s, in a new of age of global corporations states and politics were demonized and banished from the purview of societal analysis. Presently, however, while the conditions for a social democratic compromise are not there, developments worldwide have pointed to an urgency for creating political domains to enable participation of different groups in the making of the global economy, to ensure the survival of that economy. Yet, this does not suggest a return to nation-state environments with politics confined to boundaries of the state or the nation. Politics of global environments, regions which form those environments include national, transnational, state, societal, trans-state actors; furthermore that politics is inextricably linked to market activity, to how much does it get from that activity—or to how to distribute gains, of to expand employment and enable growth, for whom. Hence, inter-disciplinarity will be an in-built feature of societal analysis in the post- free-tradist global market contexts.

Finally, the intense experience of globalization of interaction among people in different world regions through trade, immigration, travel is bound to render absolete binary visions of the world into the west and its 'Other', notwithstanding the continuing grievances incurred earlier as well as certain archaic reflexes on the part of the West harking to former patterns of dominance. The binary vision had been central to Western world supremacy; with that supremacy in doubt, its model of global market model questioned, we may begin thinking of a world of, shared histories, shared concerns, while solutions remained specific and political.

# References

Cook, S. J. (2005). Late Victorian Visual Reasoning and Alfred Marshall's Economic Science. *British Journal for the History of Science, 38(2)*, 179–195.

Corkin, S. (2000). Cowboys and free markets: Post-world war II Westerns and US hegemony. *Cinema Journal, 39(3)*, 66–91.

Crafts, N. F. (1995). The golden age of economic growth in Western Europe, 1950-19731. *The Economic History Review, 48 (3)*, 429–447.

Crouch, C. (ed.) (1979). *State and economy in contemporary capitalism.* Croom Helm, Limited.

Crouch, C. (2009). Privatised Keynesianism: An unacknowledged policy regime. *The British Journal of Politics & International Relations, 11 (3)*, 382–399.

Evans, P. B. (1995). *Embedded autonomy: states and industrial transformation.* Vol. 25. Princeton, NJ: Princeton University Press.

Foucault, M. (1973). *The Order of Things.* New York: Vintage.

Gosh, A. (2015). *Flood of Fire.* New York: Farrar, Straus and Giroux.

Hodgson, M. (1974). *The Venture of Islam.* Chicago: University of Chicago Press.

Hsing, Y. T. (2013). *The Great Urban Transformation: Politics of Land and Property in China.* Oxford: Oxford University Press.

Islamoglu-Inan, H. (1987). Oriental Despotism in World system Perspective. In H.Islamoglu-Inan, *The Ottoman Empire and the World Economy.* New York: CUP.

Islamoglu, H. (2009). Words That Rule: Bureaucratic Commissions /*Komisyon* to Expert Boards / *Kurul.* In C. Gluck and A. Tsing (eds.) *Words in Motion.* Chapel Hill: Duke University Press.

Lockman, Z. (2009). *Contending Visions of the Middle East: The History and Politics of Orientalism.* New York: CUP.

North, D. C. (1990). *Institutions, Institutional Change and Economic Performance.* New York: CUP.

North, D. C. & Weingast, B. R. (1989). Constitutions and Commitment: The Evolution of Institutions Governing Public Choice in Seventeenth-Century England. *The Journal of Economic History, 49(04)*, 803–832.

Marglin, S. A. & Schor, J. B. (1991). *The golden age of capitalism: reinterpreting the postwar experience.* Oxford University Press.

Marshall, A. (2009). *Principles of Economics.* (Unabridged 8th Ed.) New York : Cosimo Classics.

Mattei, H. & Nader, L. (2008). *Plunder: When The Rule of Law is illegal.* New York: Wiley-Blackwell.

Morishima, M. (1977). *Walras' economics : a pure theory of capital and money.* Cambridge University Press.

Rostow, W. (1956). The Take-Off into Self-Sustained Growth. *The Economic Journal*

Rueschemeyer, D., Evans, P. & Skocpol, T. (eds.) (1985). *Bringing the state back*. Cambridge: Cambridge University Press.

Said, E. (1979). *Orientalism*. New York: Vintage.

Scharpt, F. (1999). *Governing in Europe: Effective and Democratic?* Oxford: Oxford University Press.

Sunstein, C. R. (2014). *Why Nudge?: The Politics of Libertarian Paternalism* (The Storrs Lectures Series). Yale University Press.

Walras, L. (1926). *Elements d'économie pure, ou théorie de la richesse sociale*. Paris: R.Pchon & R.Durand-Auzias.

Wallerstein, I. (1974). *The Modern World System I: capitalist agriculture and the origins of the European world-economy in the sixteenth century*. New York: Academic press.

Wallerstein, I. (1991). *Unthinking Nineteenth Century Social Sciences: The Limits of Paradigms*. Oxford: Polity.

Zikek, S. (2015). Sinicisation. *London Review of Books, 37(14)*. (16 July)

# Chapter 4:
# Towards World Social Sciences: Why criticizing 'Western Hegemony' does not help

Doris Weidemann

## Introduction

Criticism of the global social science system has been voiced for some decades now. Social theories have been found to represent the perspective of the rich, the male, the capitalist, the countries of Europe and North America. English has become the global language of science, leaving those at a disadvantage who do not speak, read and write it well. Grant policies and publication standards favor research that follows what Raewyn Connell (2010) calls interests of the "metropoles". Social science disciplines have been shown to be Eurocentric in design and in topics, while upholding the assumption that their theories possess universal validity. Regarding the discipline of sociology, Connell summarizes: "mainstream sociology turns out to be an ethno-sociology of metropolitan society" (2010: 226), and Allwood and Berry call global academic psychology an "indigenous psychology of Western societies" (2006: 244). Even representatives of the academic centers, the "metropoles," agree that we need to "open the social sciences" as the well-known Wallerstein report put it (Wallerstein et al. 1996).

It would appear from these quotes that critiques of the global social science system are widely shared across disciplines and world regions. But this is not entirely the case. It might be true that in Europe and North America "questioning the global hegemony of Eurocentric social science has acquired the status of a new fashion" (Dirlik 2012: 23), yet a large majority of researchers—in the "metropoles" as well as in the "periphery"—uphold the idea that current theories are universal and fear that localizing research fosters cultural relativism that would ultimately jeopardize international dialogue or open up roads to 'unscientific' studies. However, as will become evident, my remarks concerning critiques of "Western science" do not mirror their concerns. Despite my critical comments I am not saying we should abandon critiques of Eurocentric science and Western hegemony. Instead, I believe that we should have more of them, better argued, and supported by a larger number of evidence that alternatives are possible.

In this paper I aim to present a critical view of arguments that are usually used in cases against hegemonic Western science. I will forward the idea that by way of connotations and subtext, these critiques actually support Western academic power, instead of abolishing it. The last section contains some thoughts on how to avoid argumentative pitfalls and sketches trajectories towards more balanced world social sciences.

## Criticizing Western hegemony: Typical steps of argumentation

Critics of Western hegemony take different positions and draw on different arguments. First, there are those who critically take stock of the international social sciences from what may be called a "position of center", such as the 'Wallerstein report' (1996), or the World Social Science Report (UNESCO 2010). Authors typically point to existing inequalities, modes of exclusion, dominance of English as the language of science, or Eurocentrism and a North-Atlantic Hegemony in research agendas and funding. They often rely on statistics and bibliometric analyses. They usually take the foundations of what others call "Western science" for granted and are mainly concerned with mechanisms of exclusion, though they also address consequences for the epistemology of the social sciences. Other researchers extend their criticism and point to Western imperialism and misrepresentation of cultural others in theory and methods, i.e. in the foundations of the scientific endeavor itself. They draw our attention to power mechanisms that allow some actors to define scientific discourses while ignoring the voices of the underprivileged and suppressed. Postcolonial theory, Academic Dependency Theory (Alatas 2003), subaltern studies and related approaches identify with the position of the weak and the colonized and focus on "writing back", "researching back" and "provincializing Europe" (e.g. Chakrabarty 2008). Thirdly, there are researchers (mainly from countries of the scientific 'periphery') who are struggling to develop additional and alternative approaches within the existing science system. Endeavors to develop an Asian indigenous psychology are a case in point and could be called an attempt to reform the system from within. Finally, there are scholars, who strive to develop truly "indigenous", "endogenous", or "autochthonous" social science that would offer genuine 'alternatives' to current Western science. Contributions are still few, scattered and disintegrated, often published in local languages.

These different approaches, arguments and positions are interlinked and draw on each other: The aim of developing alternatives is unthinkable without prior critical assessment of the status quo. And those who criticize the world social science system are usually also concerned with suggesting alternatives. Instead of going into details of these different approaches (and more can probably be added), I will take a meta-perspective and look at the premises and typical steps of argumentation that can more or less be observed across all of these discourse strands. Argumentations typically unfold in three steps:

In a first step two contrasting entities are being created: "West" (Global North) and its other ("East", "South", "indigenous populations", "the colonized", "periphery" etc.). In her introduction to the problem of "decolonizing methodologies" Linda Tuhiwai Smith states, for example:

> "In a very real sense research has been an encounter between the West and the Other. ... This book reports to some extent on views that are held and articulated by 'the other sides'." (Smith 2012: 8)

In 1988 Ho used a fictitious dialogue of Dr. West and Dr. East in an article that was devoted to the prospects of developing an "Asian psychology", and Connell (2010) rests her argumentation on the distinction of "Northern theory" and "Southern theory". Notions of the "West" are usually roughly identical with a definition by Syed Alatas as "the contemporary social science powers, which are the United States, Great Britain and France" (Alatas 2003: 602). In other cases, West is spelled out as "Europe, the United States and the Anglophone Commonwealth nations" (Newcombe 2012: 202). Alternatively, "OECD countries" are contrasted against the "non OECD world" (Vessuri 2013), or simply against the "majority world."

In a second step, it is observed that West is imperialist in politics and science: West and other differ in terms of power (money, research participation, scientific impact). West imposes theories, methodology, values, and world views. It is pointed out that social sciences are Western science. For example:

> "Research is one of the ways in which the underlying code of imperialism and colonialism is both regulated and realized. It is regulated through the formal rules of individual scholarly disciplines and scientific paradigms, and the institutions that support them (including the state). It is realized in the myriad of representations and ideological constructions of the Other in scholarly and 'popular' works, and in the principles which help to select and recontextualize those constructions in such things as the media, official histories and school curricula." (Smith 2012: 8)

The third step consists in the observation that Western science does not fit non-Western contexts, and thus misrepresents the other. This is because local cultures are different from Western culture (which is implicit in Western science). It is argued that local, indigenous science needs to take local cultural context into account. For example:

> "Indigenous methodologies tend to approach cultural protocols, values and behaviours as an integral part of methodology. They are 'factors' to be built into research explicitly, to be thought about reflexively, to be declared openly as part of the research design, to be discussed as part of the final results of a study and to be disseminated back to the people in culturally appropriate ways and in a language that can be understood." (Smith 2012: 15/16)

These steps of argumentation can be found in other contributions, as well. Another example is derived from the field of psychology: In a special issue of the International Journal of Psychology on indigenous psychologies, Allwood and Berry (2006) write on the "origins and development of indigenous psychologies". In a first step they contrast "Western psychology" and non-Western "indigenous psychologies". In a second step they explain that Western science is the dominant model (also called "master psychology" by Teo 2013: 13):

> "We can view the discipline of psychology as a complex set of behaviours (including concepts, methods, and interpretations) that emerged in one cultural region of the world (European-American). These behaviours had their roots mainly in one religio-philosophical tradition (the Judeo-Christian), and had been passed on to the West mainly by one thought-tradition (the Greco-Roman). The outcome is the widespread presence of one indigenous psychology (that of Western societies) which has been exported to, and largely accepted by, other societies." (Allwood/Berry 2006: 244)

Because this psychology is rooted in a specific cultural context, its applicability to non-Western contexts is limited. As a result (this is step 3), indigenous approaches that provide a better cultural fit are called for:

> The IP [indigenous psychology] approach can be characterized as attempts by researchers in mostly non-Western societies and cultures to develop a psychological science that more closely reflects their own social and cultural premises. (Allwood/Berry 2006: 244)

The same argumentative build-up is also observed by Chang (2012: 241). Regarding indigenous social sciences in Taiwan, he points out:

> Finally, we need to comment on the general meaning of indigenization. First, it is concerned with the construction of an "us-them" dichotomy. Second, it is concerned with the existing hierarchical relation between "us" and "them," with "them" perceived to be dominant. Indigenization has often arisen from calls to overcome that perception of inequality. (Chang 2012: 241)

As may be noted, two central concepts keep recurring across these various statements: the concept of power (imperialism, dominance) and the concept of culture. They are both important cornerstones of critiques of the current science system, and they both play a role in constructing world social sciences. They will therefore be dealt with in more detail below. Yet, other aspects of the argumentative pattern also deserve attention.

## How critiques keep Western hegemony intact

Because these argumentative steps are so widely used and also present valid arguments, they look convincing at first glance. Yet, I believe that, despite intending to be (and indeed being) critical of the current global science system they help to reproduce it, not explicitly, but by way of subtext and connotations.

1. They perpetuate the simple contrast of West and East that European colonizers used to create fundamental distinctions between "us" and "them" and to justify colonial rule. Using this dichotomy contributes to an essentialist view of collectives that (wrongly) implies homogeneity on both sides. While essentialist notions of cultures have largely been abandoned in the cultural sciences, they curiously survive in critiques of Western academic dominance. They probably have because these critiques serve polemic aims, rather than analytical distinction.

2. Describing the social sciences as Western obscures the many international sources of science and social theory. Instead, it supports the meta-narrative of an innovative, creative "West" and a passive, receptive "East". In the 1950s Joseph Needham startled western audiences by providing detailed proof of the early scientific achievements made by Chinese scholars in the fields of engineering, botany, astronomy, medicine, etc. This was at a time when Europeans held stagnation and intellectual incapacity to be Chinese national traits. Needham showed that central criteria that define science today were also applied by early Chinese scholars: predictive accuracy and consistency of theories, among them (Needham 1979). There are many other proofs that science is no Western invention. The Greco-Roman tradition that is often pointed to as the source of Western social science (as in the above quotation by Allwood and Berry 2006) is a Eurocentric construction in itself and ignores Arab, Persian, Indian, and even Chinese influences on 'Western' thought.

3. Stressing the contrast between East and West leads to a problematic focus on the Western academic centers while inter-regional cooperation is being largely ignored. Whereas mutual exchange of researchers of marginalized scientific communities would be essential for constructing a more global social science, their

attention remains directed at Euro-American theories. A Eurocentric outlook is thus confirmed (Dirlik 2012: 28).

4. Reducing the debate about scientific power to Western imperialists and non-Western victims ignores the manifold relations between science and power at all levels that postcolonial and gender theory remind us of. It prevents us from carrying out inter-regional analyses of power structures within "the North" or "the South". As Burawoy (2010) warns us: "The model of academic dependency shouldn't lead us to overlook pattern of inequality and domination within countries" (p. 8). Age, gender, and ethnicity define discourse power in many places, in the academic centers as well as in the peripheries.

5. The simplistic talk of imperialist science also prevents us from understanding if and how scientific hegemony is being "co-constructed". Krige (2008) reminds us of the European postwar situation when American science was not only exported to, but also eagerly embraced by European nations. China and Japan are other examples of countries that actively imported Western science as part of their 19$^{th}$ and 20$^{th}$ century modernization efforts (Mitter 2010, Huang 2010, Okamoto 2010). When talking about "academic colonialism" (Atal 1981: 189), the dynamics of "self-colonization" (Gu 2013: 60) should also be taken into account.

6. The description of West as imperialist and non-West as (misrepresented) recipients of Western science creates a semantic field of perpetrators and victims. This rhetoric of "strong West" and "weak East" attributes moral faults to Westerners, but otherwise leaves their superior position unchallenged. It does not tackle the question of scientific quality and validity of Western research, at least not strongly enough. In some cases the stereotypical diagnosis of "being colonized" is even being upheld in countries that have turned from

formerly dependent Third World countries into global players in their own right.

7. The argumentation is prone to mixing up issues of power and culture: The critical response to "imperialist science" probably should be to understand and eliminate its motivation, driving forces and mechanisms. Responding to it by attempts to establish research that is meaningful in local cultural context misses the point. It introduces a new (and relevant) category, but it does not logically relate to arguments of power. In short: Culture is no good argument in the fight against Western imperialism. It does have its merits, however, as an analytical category in philosophy of science.

8. The call for adapting research to local cultural needs is only made with respect to non-Western societies. This assumes that Western research is meaningful in Western cultural contexts (is it?). More importantly, it insinuates that analyzing the relationship between culture and science is only of relevance in non-Western context. It clearly is not. This is one of the factors that silently push the idea that Western theories are universal: if only non-Western research needs to pay heed to culture, Western science is being treated as mainstream, universal science. As Wang Hui put it from a Chinese point of view:

   > "In taking our own perspective to be particular, we are already presuming that the pre-existing framework of knowledge is the universal one. We already recognize the universalization and naturalization of the Western framework of knowledge—we say that it is "natural" or that it is a "natural phenomenon." In light of this, our application of our own particularities to argue against that universality actually affirms it. (Wang 2009, p. 115)

9. Indigenous approaches stress the importance of local perspectives, yet they also risk getting lost in them. This includes the possibility that studies remain focused on local trivia. More importantly, indigenous research runs

the risk of becoming entangled with local political agendas and nationalist rhetoric (cf e.g. Hong/Yang/Chiu 2010 on the interrelated discourse on Chinese identity in research and politics)

While these points raise a host of complex issues that cannot be dealt with here in detail, I would like to point to a shared assumption that is recognizable across the field: the subtext of the listed arguments can be summarized as follows: West has power, East has culture. Which implies (even if texts explicitly argue against these statements): West is strong, East is weak; West is universal, East features particulars. This might help to explain the curious phenomenon that despite five decades of vehement criticism of Western hegemony, nothing much has changed in the fundamental distribution of global power. While it is true that international participation of non-Western scholars has increased, Western researchers are still enjoying a position of center, claiming universal validity of their theories, while others are allotted a playground that deals with cultural particulars. My suspicion is that this strategy of peaceful coexistence has benefits for both sides: Western academics feel tolerant and open-minded when enlarging participation, while non-Western academics feel gratified to be allowed a seat at the table, i.e. to take part in international conferences, editorial boards, scientific associations, etc. This is all the more the case because international engagement, especially the recognition by the Western academic centers, is an important career factor in peripheral science communities. Non-western scholars can thus build rewarding academic careers, while on the international scene they mostly remain experts for cultural particulars. This pattern does not change the often-criticized division of academic labor that leaves theory construction to Western scholars and local data gathering and replications for everybody else.

## Conclusion

There are several questions that result from the above debates that we need to find answers to. They all address the same overarching theme: How can we argue our case that social sciences are systematically biased in favor of the rich, Western countries better? Which steps should be taken towards truly global social sciences that provide space for hitherto excluded perspectives? I will take up some questions that are central to these debates and venture some preliminary thoughts.

## How to leave dichotomies behind?

While relying on the binary notion of "us" and "them" has been identified as one of the factors that lead us astray, dichotomies do have their value, provided they make valid distinctions and highlight dimensions that serve analytical or heuristic purposes. Most of the time, they are more correctly understood as representing endpoints of a continuum. They may be useful as long as we remember that they are constructs, rather than existing entities. Still, East/West, and North/South are unlucky concepts. It is not helpful to rely on categories that were created for different purposes. Instead we should employ analytical categories with descriptive power and focus on what we need to distinguish. Geographical concepts are useless (and don't even serve as meaningful metaphors) when we wish to point to different degrees of academic influence or economic power. This purpose is served better by distinguishing between "metropoles" (academic centers) and "periphery", or by employing other notions that conceptually link the construct to the phenomenon at hand. Thus, distinguishing between OECD-countries and the non-OECD world is helpful when we want to stress the effects of economic development and commitment to a certain (democratic) society model on the organization of academic work. Dichotomies may then be valuable to analyze the status quo and also to describe where we want to arrive. At the same time, we should resist assuming homogeneity of either category and actively search for counterevidence. We may then discover that some universities outside of Western countries would more correctly be described as part of scientific metropoles, while many research institutions in the geographical West would more adequately be classified as peripheral.

## Do we need to open the social sciences?

Yes, absolutely. But what does that imply? As Wallerstein et al. (1996: 54–55) remind us of, in opening the social sciences we are faced by two different, yet interrelated challenges: the political challenge and the epistemological challenge.

> The political challenge had to do with the recruitment of personnel (students, professors) within the university structures (going in tandem with a similar challenge in the larger political world). [...] The solution that was advocated followed quite clearly: if we expanded the scope of recruitment for the scholarly community, we would probably expand the scope of its objects of study. (Wallerstein et al. 1996: 54–55)

Increasing participation does not, however, reduce the epistemological challenge that results from the Eurocentric thought pattern engrained in the social sciences:

> The challenge to parochialism has, however, been deeper than the question of the social origins of researchers. The new voices among social scientists raised theoretical questions that went beyond the questions of the topics or subjects of legitimate study, and even beyond the argument that evaluations are made differently from different perspectives. The argument of these new voices was also that there have been presuppositions built into the theoretical reasoning of the social sciences [...] (ibid.)

Linking these observations to concepts of power, and culture that were identified as important earlier, we may conclude that the *political challenge* is where *power* is concerned: It addresses questions of enlarged participation and increased diversity of researchers' background. It relates to the ways academic institutions are shaped and run, to research policies, definitions of curricula, etc. In order to open the social sciences researchers should be aware of power mechanisms that lead to the exclusion of others and institutions should be shaped in a way that reduces them. The *epistemological challenge* is where *culture* comes into play: We need to reflect the silent assumptions of our scientific thinking, including its cultural foundations, apply theories of *Verstehen* in order to recognize different standpoints in scientific dialogue. Philosophy of science helps us to understand that dealing with different world views is not a matter of politeness or moral obligation, but an epistemological necessity. My point is: we should be aware of power and of also of culture. We just should not mix both things up and argue for culture when we should fight power mechanisms that work against us. We should also avoid treating culture as a "soft" category. Culture does have an important impact on scientific thinking and research everywhere, not just outside of the metropolitan centers (Weidemann 2013)

**Do we want one science or many sciences?**

Where does all that lead us? One of the horrors of social scientists is the idea that we end up in a large number of ethnocentric sciences that exist alongside one another. Apparently, this is nothing anyone aspires to. I would argue that it is not likely to happen, either, because central ideas of what characterizes science are not "Western" at all, but are in fact shared across many societies around the world. It should be possible to reach an understanding of what world social science would consider as science, and as non-science. In order to arrive at a shared understanding we do not even have to agree on a single definition. Instead, we could follow a suggestion by Kochinka (2006) who reflects on ways of reconciling different ways of doing science without resorting to a hierarchy of "hard" and "soft", "exact" and "inexact" science. This would entail giving up on the idea that physics constitutes the ideal, prototypic science, whereas all other endeavors are regarded as more or less deficient varieties. As has been argued before, this understanding of science—that places the discovery of causal relationships and the functions of explanation and prognosis center stage—does not do justice to much of social research and the humanities that are rather concerned with appropriate description and reconstruction of meaning. Kochinka proposes to employ Wittgenstein's concept of family resemblances (Familienähnlichkeiten) as a way to assemble different approaches under the same theoretical roof of "science". Just as "games" (to use Wittgenstein's example) have some characteristics in common that mark them as members of the same family, sciences do too. Games share common features (they entertain, invite us to compete, challenge our dexterity, etc.), yet we will not be able to discover a specific characteristic that is shared by *all* varieties of games. Still, we have no difficulty recognizing a game when we see one. In analogy to this example science could be treated as a "family" in the above mentioned sense. We could then ask for resemblances of different members of this family and would arrive at a "list of attributes or criteria, of resemblances between groups of sciences, but not at indispensable preconditions of what ultimately constitutes science" (ibid., 101). As Kochinka points out, many of these criteria have been previously addressed by theory of science, such as: "science provides descriptions", "science offers explanations", "science is systematic", "science makes unambiguous statements", "science is objective", among others (ibid.).

Looking for family resemblances may offer a theoretical framework for overcoming a narrow Eurocentric (mostly positivistic) understanding of science. It would offer space for integrating different varieties without succumbing to arbitrariness.

Another reason why I consider it unlikely for social sciences to fall apart into completely alienated indigenous varieties is the fact that we live in a world that is interlinked and where people relate to ideas of other people. I agree with Raewyn Connell who states:

> Every significant development in the social sciences in the periphery makes *some* use of concepts or techniques from the metropole. It is therefore not realistic to imagine the future of world social science as a mosaic of distinct knowledge systems—as a set of indigenous sociologies, indigenous economics, and so on, all functioning independently. (Connell 2010: 223)

Some of the mechanisms by which concepts of the metropoles transpire to the periphery may be undesirable. We should be mindful when it comes to implicit knowledge structures that mirror Western worldviews and imbue scientific thinking with Eurocentric content. Orientalism (Said 1979) is a case in point, "sinologism" (the "implicit system of ideas, notions, theories, approaches, and paradigms, first conceived and employed by the West in the encounter with China to deal with all things Chinese") another example (Gu 2013: 7). These mental patterns are not, as Gu stresses, restricted to Western scholarship, but have become part of the cognitive landscape of people around the globe. In a similar vein, the disciplinary structure of modern social sciences has been shown to preconfigure social thought in Eurocentric ways (Wallerstein et al. 1996, Staeuble 2009).

Still, during the last one hundred years, Western social sciences have become part of the intellectual reality in many locations. Western ideas and methodologies have undergone local adaption and can now with some right be regarded a new cultural tradition.

> The Western culture we have accepted for more than a century—from notions of equality or evolution introduced by missionaries, to the advocacy of science and democracy by the May Fourth Movement, or the widespread adoption—and later national implementation—of Marxism, has accumulated so many meanings in our daily life that it has itself become a new cultural tradition. (Chen 2005: 119)

The current situation leaves "many questions unresolved" (ibid.). Resorting to unrelated, indigenous social sciences does not seem a feasible outcome. But we should also not be complacent and seek unity in science without addressing the many pressing epistemological questions involved in internationalization.

## Integration or unification?

Social science should abandon the claim to speak for all, when in fact it only speaks for the privileged metropole. It should overcome the ethnocentric practice of judging others against one's own norms and expectations. It should take into account the periphery, and also recognize the change of and diversity within peripheries. This means it would have to extend its research topics to include experiences of subalterns, the colonized, which would establish new topics on the research agenda: Connell (2010) lists "loss" (of land, social structure, traditions, religions, etc.), and "destruction" as significant, yet under-researched, topics. Meaningful science requires the metropole to also learn from the periphery. Integration of different science approaches neither needs nor means homogeneity. Instead, we should aim for "a pluricultural universe where each culture can hope to live in dignity with its own distinctiveness" (Nandy 1998: 147).

## From metropolitan social science to world social science

World social science would thus have to allow for plurality of viewpoints that are not always capable of being integrated in a harmonious universally valid model. Yet, because it rests on dialogue and on identifying interrelations among experiences and interpretations it would also not be likely to succumb to relativism. In a globally linked world, it would "multiply the directions of knowledge flow" (Chen 1998: 4) and be able to produce social theories of higher validity. It would include lateral globalization, such as networks of researchers in the periphery, as have indeed been developing in recent years. It also requires institutions that support world social science and intercultural competences of researchers (Weidemann 2010). Its prospects strongly rest on a shared willingness to overcome Eurocentric knowledge structures, and on innovative theories of science and internationalization.

## References

Alatas, S. F. (2003). Academic dependency and the global division of labour in the social sciences. *Current Sociology, 51 (6)*, 599–613.

Allwood, C. M. & Berry, J. W. (2006). Origins and development of indigenous psychologies. An international analysis. In C. M. Allwood & J. W. Berry (eds.) *Special Issue on the Indigenous Psychologies. International Journal of Psychology, 41 (4)*, 243–268.

Burawoy, M. (2010). Facing an Unequal World: Challenges for a Global Sociology. In M. Burawoy, M. Chang & M. F. Hsieh (eds.) *Facing an Unequal World: Challenges for a Global Sociology. Volume One: Introduction, Latin America and Africa.* Taipei: Institute of Sociology, Academia Sinica, (pp.3–27).

Chakrabarty, D. (2008). *Provincializing Europe. postcolonial thought and historical difference.* Reissue, with a new preface by the author. Princeton: Princeton University Press.

Chang, M. (2012). The Movement to Indigenize the Social Sciences in Taiwan. Origin and Predicaments. In A. Dirlik (ed.) *Sociology and Anthropology in Twentieth-Century China. Between Universalim and Indigenism.* Unter Mitarbeit von Guannan Li und Hsiao-pei Yen. Hong Kong: The Chinese University Press, (pp.209–253).

Connell, R. (2010). *Southern Theory. The global dynamics of knowledge in social science.* Cambridge: Polity.

Dirlik, A. (2012). *Zhongguohua*: Worlding China. The Case of Sociology and Anthropology in 20th-Century China. In A. Dirlik (ed.) *Sociology and Anthropology in Twentieth-Century China. Between Universalim and Indigenism.* Unter Mitarbeit von Guannan Li und Hsiao-pei Yen. Hong Kong: The Chinese University Press, (pp. 1–39).

Ho, D. Y. (1988). Asian psychology: A dialogue on indigenization and beyond. In A. C. Paranjpe, D. Y. Ho & R. W. Rieber (eds.) *Asian contributions to psychology.* New York: Praeger, (pp. 53–77).

Hong, Y., Yang, Y. & Chiu, C. (2010). What is Chinese about Chinese psychology? Who are the Chinese in Chinese psychology? In M. H. Bond (ed.) *The Oxford Handbook of Chinese Psychology.* New York: Oxford University Press, (pp. 19–29).

Huang, H. (2010). China's Historical Encounter with Western Sciences and Humanities. In M. Kuhn & D. Weidemann (eds.) *Internationalization of the social sciences. Asia - Latin America - Middle East - Africa - Eurasia*. Bielefeld: transcript, (pp. 21–43).

Kochinka, A. (2006). Über Wissenschaft und Wissenschaften. *Handlung Kultur Interpretation, 15, (1)*, 96–108.

Krige, J. (2008). *American Hegemony and the Postwar Reconstruction of Science in Europe*. Cambridge & London: MIT Press.

Mitter, R. (2010). *A Bitter Revolution. China's Struggle with the Modern World*. (2nd ed.) New York: Oxford University Press.

Nandy, A. (1998). A New Cosmopolitanism: Toward a Dialogue of Asian Civilizations. In K. Chen (ed.) *Trajectories. Inter-Asia Cultural Studies*. London & New York: Routledge. (pp. 142–149).

Needham, J. (1979). *Wissenschaftlicher Universalismus. Über Bedeutung und Besonderheit der chinesischen Wissenschaft*. (Ed. & trans. By T. Spengler). Frankfurt a.M.: Suhrkamp.

Okamoto, K. (2010). Internationalization of Japanese Social Sciences: Importing and Exporting Social Science Knowledge. In M. Kuhn & D. Weidemann (eds.) *Internationalization of the social sciences. Asia - Latin America - Middle East - Africa - Eurasia*. Bielefeld: transcript. (pp. 45–65).

Smith, L. T. (2012). *Decolonizing Methodologies: Research and indigenous peoples*. (2nd revised ed.) London & New York: Zed Books.

Newcombe, S. (2012). Global Hybrids? 'Eastern Traditions' of Health and Wellness in the West. In S. Nair-Venugopal (ed.) *The gaze of the West and framings of the East*. New York: Palgrave Macmillan. (pp. 202–217).

Teo, T. (2013). Backlash against American psychology: an indigenous reconstruction of the history of German critical psychology. *History of psychology, 16 (1), 1–18*. DOI: 10.1037/a0030286.

UNESCO & ISSC (eds.) (2010). World Social Science Report 2010. Knowledge Divides. Online available under : http://www.unesco.org/shs/wssr. Paris: UNESCO.

Vessuri, H. (2013). The transformation processes in global social knowledge. In M. Kuhn & K. Okamoto (eds.) *Spatial social thought in international knowledge encounters*. Stuttgart: ibidem. (pp. 263–283).

Wallerstein, I., Juma, C., Keller, E. F., Kocka, J., Lecourt, D., Mudimbe, V. Y. et al. (1996). *Open the Social Sciences. Report of the Gulbenkian Commission on the restructuring of the social sciences*. Stanford: Stanford University Press.

Wang, H. (2009). *The End of the Revolution. China and the Limits of Modernity*. London & New York: Verso.

Weidemann, D. (2010). Challenges of International Collaboration in the Social Sciences. In M. Kuhn & D. Weidemann (eds.) *Internationalization of the social sciences. Asia - Latin America - Middle East - Africa - Eurasia*. Bielefeld: transcript. (pp. 353–378).

Weidemann, D. (2013). Culture as a dimension of international social science encounters. In M. Kuhn & K. Okamoto (eds.) *Spatial social thought in international knowledge encounters*. Stuttgart: ibidem. (pp. 201–215).

# Chapter 5:
# Why arriving at imperial thought is not an accident of critical sociological thinking but the consequent endpoint of international sociological thinking

## Michael Kuhn

## What imperial thought means

What does the term "imperial thought" mean? Unlike all those categories used in a discourse about such issues like "in-equalities", "academic dependence" or a scientific battle between a "global South and "North", which all discuss and—critically—share the view of national science policies forcing academics in to a science world that instrumentalizes science as a means for the global battle among nation states about global political power, the notion of "imperial thought" means a theoretical view theorizing about the social world. Imperial thinking is about the contents of thinking, not as the above mentioned discourses about the conditions under which social sciences, presented as the sociological constructed subjects of competing "national science communities" compete about "scientific power and the like. Imperial thought is about what theories say, not about the many wheres and hows of theorizing. This view of imperial thought constructs its theories through the perspective nation states have on the world of the nation states. It is a view, a way to see the world that essentially shares the view political power has on the world's social, a view that considers the world's people and the nature as a potential means for the growth of political power and the other nation states as an obstacle to use their people and nature, because it is under the control of the sovereignty.

Secondly, calling such imperial thought idealized imperial thought means that such thought are created through a view nation states have on the world of nation states thinking about the power relation towards other political powers, however, they are thought created through a imperial rationales, which are not the real rationales imperial views of nation states reflect on, but rationales such theories attach to them as rationales only these theories wish to be the imperial rationales of nation states, idealized imperial rationales establishing them with objectives transforming them into agendas these theories only wish there were what imperial agendas are aiming at.

Having said this, it is the intention of this paper to say two things: Firstly, it will show with a few examples of imperially thinking theories, created by leftish sociological theorists, what such imperial thoughts are and why they are idealized imperial thought. It does this along theories created by sociological thinkers who are considered to be critical, politically leftish sociologists. Theories from politically leftish sociologist were chosen, to show secondly, that such imperial thoughts are not the result of the political position these theorists have, but the consequence of sociological theorizing.

Critiquing theorists for creating imperial thought does not oppose any political position they might have or not, critiquing imperial thought points on the thought which even presents such thought as a critique of nation state policies and its imperial agenda, as it is the case with Wallerstein, and reasons this critique as a failure, a failure measured against the idealized objectives of the political subject that is the only subject that sui generis is able to practice imperial actions, the nation state. Thus sharing the imperial objectives of nation states and critiquing them for failing a nations state mission only sociologists attach to them, is imperial thought and it is false thought. Just as if a nation state was not the political power of the private property owners as a whole, that considers its political borders as contradicting with the borderless growth of wealth of the private properties and thus arrives at imperial actions against other nation states with the same concerns, just as if a nation state was nothing but a political tool that can be instrumentalised for any political purposes, imperial theorizing advocates theorizing through nation states rationales as a means for the ideal missions they attach to them—in Wallerstein's case he discusses such idealized imperial thought as an argument against the fake justification of imperial actions of the US—the justification, not the wars. Just as if nation states are the only political subjects sociology can imagine they engage the nation state as the subject for any ideas or missions sociological thinking ever imagines and ever imagines that they must be aims of nation states, just as if nation states were subjects awaiting any orders from sociologists. It is therefore the second intention of this paper to show why such imperial thinking is not an accident of some sociological theories, but a consequence of the categorical essentials founding sociological thinking.

## Wallerstein: A "universal universalism"— a concept of science welcoming wars by the attacked[1]

Contributing to debates about the internationalisation of social sciences, notions such as *"cosmopolitan", "local", "global" or* "glocal" theorizing, in short, all sorts of variations of spatiological thinking[2], created mainly by sociological thinkers, contributing discourses reflecting on social thought going beyond thinking about confined national societies, a leading sociologist, E. Wallerstein, who is considered most critical and certainly not an imperial thinker, contributed to this debate the notion of a "universal universalism" and demonstrates how easily sociological thinking arrives from epistemological reflections at imperial social thought.

While discussing the epistemological issue of a "European Universalism",[3] *Wallerstein* arrives at a question, a question this sociological thinker feels that it *"goes to the heart of the political and moral structure of the modern world of the modern world-system"*. [4]

This question, concluded from his discussions about the epistemological issue of a "European universalism" is nothing less but the question how to legitimate global wars. Arriving at a discussing the question how to legitimate wars as the result of discussing epistemological issues, such as critiquing " the concept of science that

---

[1] Wallerstein I., (2006) European Universalism, The Rhetoric of Power, New York,
[2] See: M. Kuhn, Notes on a Critique about how social sciences think, Ibidem, Stuttgart, forthcoming
[3] Wallerstein I., (2006) Ibid
[4] Ibid, p 27.

was outside of 'culture'" as the "the most subtle mode ideological justification of the powerful" [5], for the critical sociologists such as Wallerstein, works like this:

> "The question—Whose right to intervene?—goes to the heart of the political and moral structure of the modern world of the modern world-system. Intervention is in practice a right appropriated by the strong. But it is right difficult to legitimate and therefore always subject to political and moral challenge. ....It is not that there may not be global values. It is rather that we are far away from yet knowing what these values are. Global universal values are not given to us; they are created by us. The human enterprise of creating such values is the great moral enterprise of humanity. This issue before us today is how we may move beyond European universalism—the last perverse justification of the existing world order- to something much more difficult to achieve: a universal universalism, which refuses essentialist characterizations of social reality, historicizes both the universal and the particular, reunifies the so-called scientific and the humanistic into a single epistemology, and permits us to look with highly clinical and quite sceptical eye at all justifications for 'intervention! By the powerful against the weak." [6]

Finding justifications for "interventions"—he talks about the imperial wars, just to clarify this -, finding *"a universal universalism"*, shared by the whole world...., wrongly phrased. Wallerstein is an idealist sociological thinker, so we have to re-phrase the same question in his own words this way: Having a *"quite sceptical eye at all justifications for 'intervention,"* is *the* mission of global social thought which refuses to seek a "single epistemology", and, instead must search for a *"universal universalism"*, must search for *"global universal values"*, as he phrases the dream of any global empire, making their imperial wars against others a desire of those, *"the weak"* they attack. Doing this, finding *"global universal values"* which justify imperial wars as a request of the attacked, is not only nothing less than fulfilling the *"great moral enterprise of mankind"*, but the final development of a debate that started with Merton's notion of a scientific universalism, now further developed by Wallerstein towards the scientific "universal universalism", that is *"global universal values"*, which provide, unlike the naive believe in a "single epistemology", a world wide shared justification for imperial wars, making imperial wars missions on behalf of this "universal universalism".

---

5 Ibid, p 77
6 Ibid, p 79

# Chapter 5: Why arriving at imperial thought is not a accident

This is how a most critical social science scholar bothers the world of science with *the* moral headaches of a very sociological and imperial mind, with what he tells us is *"the great moral enterprise of humanity"*, longing for a world that is concerned with the headache of imperialism where their victims never welcome imperial actions, presented by this sociological thinker as if solving this question of imperial nation states was precisely the same as a solution of the epistemological troubles of global social thought, the final true substance of all the debates about universal sciences. Searching for *"global universal values"*, now really justifying, unlike the "powerful" and their values ever only pretend, imperial interventions, are for this profound thinker, what all the debates about overcoming the idea of a *"single epistemology"* are after all essentially about. This identification of epistemological reflections with reflections on how to make wars fulfilling the moral mission of global values is what makes a critical sociologist publish his reflections on how to justify imperial actions as reflections under the title of a book about the *"European Universalism"*.

Reflecting on theorizing about the world's social and on social thought about the world's social as thinking about the same as serving to solve the moral problems of the imperial nation state rationales, only a view has, that appropriates the essential of an idealized rationale of imperial thinking, interpreting the concerns of nation states and their imperial agendas, the only subjects in the world who are able to carry out wars, as their mission to care about the values of mankind, only this view, idealizing wars as a moral missions on behalf of the moral values of mankind, can critically raise its concerns and warn the world *"that we are far away from yet knowing what these values are."* Only thinkers, who quite naturally identify their scientific mission to create theories as the mission to provide mankind with moral values, and cannot think about mankind other than through a global "we", thinkers who ever embrace social thought as nothing less but as representing social thought as thinking on behalf of the global "we" of the world, only such thinkers cannot only not be irritated by the fact that the members of this global "we" are those who carry out wars against each other, and who are the only subjects in the world who can be subjects of wars, but critiques wars among nation states, wars which are not shared by the world's mankind moral values, as failing the world's mankind moral missions. To clarify this, Wallerstein is not at all arguing against wars, he is no pacifist thinker, he is arguing against wars which are not carried out on behalf of the world's shared values. He is arguing against wars which are wars against—an enemy, against wars which are not welcomed by the attacked! War's against enemies are therefore interpreted by this sociological thinker as a proof that mankind lacking globally shared moral values, the "universal" not only the "European" universalism and it is the mission of social thought, namely critical sociology to provide mankind with such globally shared moral values, social thought he therefore accuses for failing their global mission: *"The human enterprise of creating such values is the great moral enterprise of humanity. It is not that there may not be global values. It is rather that we are far away from yet knowing what these values are"*.

Wallerstein is not at all nationalist; advocating the nation state agenda of a single, particular nation state, but, as a sociological thinker, he identifies what he believes is the rationale of any nation state as the rationale of the world's "we" he constructs from a world of nation states, which for Wallerstein are the same as what the world's "we" is, a "we", constructed as *"the great moral enterprise of humanity"*, a *"we"*—sociologist would call it a "community"- to which sociological thinking attributes the mission to carry out wars only against those who accept wars because they violated *"the great moral enterprise of humanity"*. It is the way of imagining the world of imperialism and wars as a failure, caused by lacking shared "global values", a lack social sciences are responsible for due to their idea of a "European universalism", not having reached a "universal universalism, which is not at all an exotic exception in sociological thinking, but a most typically way of thinking that demonstrates how sociological encompasses what Beck critiques as the *"national outlook"*.

## Beck: "Cosmopolitan" thinking", overcoming the "barrier to the effective pursuit of states".

U. Beck is another politically left and most critical sociologist, who discusses the same epistemological issue of what these thinkers call "truly global science" and coined what Wallerstein named "universal universalism" with the notion of a "cosmopolitanism"—and

## Chapter 5: Why arriving at imperial thought is not a accident

arrives with his reflections about "cosmopolitanism" just as Wallerstein at promoting imperial thinking and imperial theories.

> "The idea of '(enforced) cosmopolitanization' is to describe the transition from the first to the second age of modernity: cosmopolitanization is a non-linear, dialectic process in which the universal and particular, the similar and the dissimilar, the global and the local are to be conceived, not as cultural polarities but as interconnected and reciprocally interpenetrating principles'.[7]

Beck rightly observes that social sciences are indeed not only used to think about isolated nation states socials as if an outside world does not exist, though the outside world "determine(s) *the relations within and between nation-state repositories of power'."*

> "My second point involves the critique of methodological nationalism in the social sciences. My thesis is: 'the zombie science' of the national that thinks and researches in the categories of international trade, international dialogue, national sovereignty, national communities, the 'nation-state' and so forth, is a 'science of the unreal'. This 'national sociology' is beset by a failure to recognize—let alone research—the extent to which existing transnational modes of living, trans-migrants, global elites, supranational organisations and dynamics of the world risk society determine the relations within and between nation-state repositories of power'."[8]

Caught by the categorical impossibilities of sociological thinking about the social in thinking in another way but through sociological categories which see the nation state as a—critically to be observed representation—of the "structures", the "system" and alike, all ordering the otherwise dis-ordered life of citizens , detecting the *'epochal disillusion'* (ibid) of social science theorizing, the sociological critique that *"the national outlook is consistently identified as a barrier to the effective pursuit of states"(ibid),* is a critique that can only phrase the opposition against the national outlook—as "a barrier to the effective pursuit of states". It opposes the national outlook from the very national outlook and ends up discussing the effects of the outside world on the nation state societies as a concern about *"the repositories of power"*, an outlook that not only itself practices the methodological nationalism as the critiqued "zombie science", but therefore consequently also arrives at theo-

---

[7] Beck, U. http://www.ulrichbeck.net-build.net/index.php?page=cosmopolitan
[8] Ibid

rizing about the world through the *imperial* rationales of nation state, he sociologically calls "the repositories of power", a view through which nation states look on the world of nation states.

Beck rightly argues that social science theorizing that only looks inside nation states is a barrier, but, a barrier to what? Thanks to sociological thinking the critique of thinking about the "national outlook" detects this national outlook—as a "barrier *to the effective pursuit of states"*. Not looking at the nation states beyond is a "zombie science", since it ignores to reflect on the world beyond the nation social, not as a barrier to understanding how the international affairs beyond an individual nation state affects people's lives within the nation states and how their lives are used for the international affairs of the nation states' battles for world power, but as a barrier *"to the effective pursuit of states"*—how could one better apply the critiqued national view of looking at the global social and to arrive at promoting the imperial view that national state rationales have on it.

Thinking about the social, sociological thinking always combines a national realism with a national idealism: For imperial thinkers concerned about the pursuit of nation state power in the *"meta game' of power in the area of globalization"* among all the global nation states, *while* concerned about the pursuit of nation state, imperial thinkers know that *with* the increasing power of nation states *"the greater our individual power in this global age will be."*[9]

It must be the art of sociological thinking, to present the battles among nation states about their economic and political power other but as a loss of sovereignty of nation states and to discuss the loss of national sovereignty as a loss for the individual human. A loss of what—of power! Sociological thinking would also not be sociological thinking, if it would discuss the battles among nation states about power as a problem of power, not as the power problems of any particular nation state, but as the problem of the sociological idea of what the nation state as such is, of the concept of nation state, sociological thinking believes nation states are all about. Looking at the world facing the power battles among nation states, sociological thinking is not only concerned about the image they have of nation state, but, so much convinced that what they

---

[9] Ibid

believe a nation state is supposed to be, imagine that the global battle among the powerful nation states about global power not only- mysteriously—increases the global power of all nation states, they all increase their sovereignty and believe that this increase of the sovereign power of all nation states against the other nation state results in the greater individual power of the world's citizens, of those very citizens that all nation states use as their means and material to fight these global power battles. Remarkably, sociological thinking about the world, shifting from the "zombie" sciences towards "cosmopolitan" thinking, detects the imperialism of nation states as serving its citizens, as serving—serving their "individual power". In the imperial version of sociological thinking, cosmopolitan sociology thinks beyond *"a barrier to the effective pursuit of states"*, accommodates the objectives of citizens to the imperial objectives of nation states and presents the objectives of citizens as being interested in nothing else but in what only imperial nation state rationales aim at—power.

## Calhoun: The nation state—allowing distinguishing between nationals and foreigners

A third example from Calhoun, if political left or not, in any case another critical sociologist, critiquing the idea of cosmopolitanism may serve as another example for how naturally sociological thinking arrives at imperial thought.

One might wonder about the logic of what causes what in the headline and ask the question, if it is not only the nation state that creates the distinction among nationals and foreigners. No, for this sociological thinker it is the service of nation states to allow distinguishing between somethings which without nation states would not exist and is thus one of those sociological theories, interpreting thinking through nation states as a way to create any order among the otherwise indistinguishable human creatures. And: It is precisely the risk losing this service for sociological thinking allowing to make this distinction, for which Calhoun critiques the idea of cosmopolitan sociological thinking and it is therefore that he insists that "nation states matter".

Theorizing about and through the perspective of nation state constructs, must have a narcotizing effect, when it advocates imperial thought. While people like Beck present thinking through the imperial power of nation states as an invitation to increase the global power of individuals across the world, calling this imagination "cosmopolitanism" and encourages the social science " to kiss the frog", just as if imperial thinking was deliberating a princess from its disguise, other more realistic social science thinkers feel that the sociological idea of "cosmopolitanism" is about to dissolve the nation state world order, social scientists like Calhoun simple admire, thanks to his scientific expertise he has in thinking about nation states:

> "I have been writing on nationalism since the early 1990s and reading about it much longer:"[10]

Summarizing his knowledge about nationalism he articulates his concern about theorizing about the imperial concerns of nation states under the notion of "cosmopolitanism":

> "Nationalism matters not least because it has offered such a deeply influential and compelling account of large scale identities and structures in the world— helping people to imagine the world as composed of sovereign nation states. The world has never matched this imagination, but that does not deprive the nationalist imaginary of influence." [11]

> "Nationalism, then, is the use of the category "nation" to organize perceptions of basic humans identities, grouping people together with fellow nationals and distinguishing them from other members of nations. It is influential as a way of helping to produce solidarity within national categories, as a way of determining how specific groups should be treated (for example, in terms of voting rights or visas and passports) and as a way of seeing the world as a whole. We see this representation in the different coloured territories on globes and maps, and in the organisation of the United Nations" [12](ibid, 39)

> "We need to respect the importance of belonging to nations and other groupings of human beings smaller than humanity as a whole. We need to understand that such belonging does different sorts of work for different people— inspires some, protects some, consoles some, as well as makes political opportunities for some." [13]

---

[10] *Calhoun (2009) Nations Matter, Culture, History, and the Cosmopolitan Dream. Routledge, , p.vii*
[11] *Calhoun (2009) Nations Matter, ....p.8*
[12] *Calhoun (2009) Nations Matter, ....p.3*
[13] *Calhoun (2009) Nations Matter, ....p.9*

# Chapter 5: Why arriving at imperial thought is not a accident 91

One wonders, what is more striking about this social science thinker, his style of phrasing things as a giving advice like a science priest if not to "humanity as a whole", but at least to the whole "we" of the social sciences on behalf of which he seems to give his warnings or his paranoid, very sociological idea that "humanity as a whole" seeks nothing more but what sociologists find the most essential desire of humans, belongingness, and the nation state as an offer for those who seek to satisfy their nationalism, however, for non-sociological people something smaller than "humanity as a whole", something smaller than "cosmopolitanism", yes, precisely something like nationalism and precisely of the size of nation states is the appropriate scale of thinking for nationalist thinkers to understand—a world of nation states. Which, one, the Unites States of America?

Anyway, a great sociological constructs, nation states, already thanks to their size, less than "humanity as a whole", easily to identify by people, he considers intelligent enough to know about their "belongingness" thanks to *"colored territories"*. If these are not enough reasons *"to respect the importance of belonging to nations"*, if one imagines nationalists, seeking their belongingness to their home nation state and the world was without—the small—nation states, only the huge "humanity as a whole"! What a great idea having passports *"as a way of seeing the world as a whole"*. Otherwise, who are "we" in a world of many national we's?

> "The constitution of nations—...—is one of the pivotal features of the modern era. It is part of the organisation of political participation and loyalty, of culture and identity, of the way history is thought and the way wars are fought."[14]

Imagine a world of a "humanity as a whole", a world without nation states, how could humans know to which political entity they must prove their loyalty? And, how could "humanity as a whole" know whom to shoot on?

---

[14] *Calhoun (2009) Nations Matter, ....p.49*

> "The most basic meaning of nationalism is the use of this way of categorizing human populations, both as a way of looking at the world as a whole and as a way of establishing group identity from within....The two sides come together in ideas about who properly belongs together in a society, and in arguments that members have moral obligations to the nation as a whole—perhaps even to kill on its behalf or die for it in a war"[15]

This imperial thinkers, advocating imperial social science thinking via nationalism as opposed to cosmopolitanism, knows what the whole talk about nation states as a means for people "that organizes people's sense of belongingness in the world" is all about. It is the service for the sense of belongingness that knows how to distinguish the world into friends and enemies and to know whom to kill and for which nation state to die. Fighting wars without nation states, fighting wars without knowing who is the enemy? No, impossible, nation states are a "pivotal"—to not forget, sociological thinking is critical thinking, therefore nation states also for this fanatic nation state advocate are only "pivotal"—organisation allowing us to know precisely, whom to shoot and whom not.

Sociological thinking about nationalism seemingly has a narcotic effect blurring the senses making this sociological thinker a case of particular sociological paranoia, the paranoia of non-structured life, that makes sociological thinkers discuss killing and dying in wars for the nation state as a nation state service for the "sense of belongingness". Sociological thinkers are so deeply concerned about imagining the subalterns of nation states without their ruling power, thinking the creatures of nation states without its creator, that they admit that rationale of nation states might be also be responsible for all kind of violence, such as poverty, racism, "the way wars are fought", and claim to sacrifice the lives of its inhabitants for the nation states imperial wars as a service for them and that essentially even wars are about organizing orders, structures and identities. Imagine passport holders of another nation state, just mentioning the name, but without any nationality, impossible to imagine how "*how specific groups should be treated*", which are not "determined" as nationals and are even without nation states. How could one see the world without nationalism "*as a way of seeing the world as a whole*" if the globe was not a globe of nation

---

[15]  Calhoun (2009) Nations Matter, ....p.39

# Chapter 5: Why arriving at imperial thought is not a accident 93

states ". A globe *"we see ...in the different colored territories on globes and maps."*, thanks to the existence of nation states.

## Dos Santos: Anti-hegemonic thinking with alternative imperial thought

There seem to be nothing in the world of social sciences, may this be not only advocating, like Beck, or practicing imperial thinking, like Wallerstein, that does not receive a critical response—with an alternative of the same. While Wallerstein constructs the world of science as a mission of a global we, alternative sociological thinkers advocate and practice a counter model of an alternative imperial view, consisting of a battle between two global entities, a "Northern" and a "Southern" body of theories.

Thinking through an idealized state view on the social, founding the reflections of sociological thinking to reflect on the world's nation state social, is, thanks to the universalisation of the social science approach to social thought, no longer the privilege of social science thinkers among social sciences in the imperial world.

Once the formers colonies found nothing more desirable but imitating the very society system that oppressed them as colonies and imitated the rather discriminated but critiqued "North", the former colonised countries not only imitated the society system of the former oppressors but also their science system and are unhappy that the theories from the "North"—not coincidentally—not correspond to the society system the former colonies imitated despite of their divers social and economic reality and complain that the "North" "dominates" theorizing.

Sociological thinking in a science world calling themselves "peripheries"- thus revealing that their opposition to the sciences in the imperial world is a gradual difference regarding their lacking possibilities to develop their sciences towards the same impact of knowledge—has learned its lessons from the colonizers in thinking from the view of an idealizied nation state perspective on the word's social as on the social sciences, the following sociological thinkers from the "developing" part of the world reflects on.

Theorizing about the social sciences in the "Third World" countries, he articulates the following concerns:

"If we consider the parallels between economic dependence and academic dependence we may define the latter as a condition in which the social sciences of certain countries are conditioned by the development and growth of the social sciences of other countries to which the former is subjugated. The relations of interdependence between two or more social science communities, and between these and the global transactions in the social sciences, assumes the form of dependency when some social science communities (those located in the social science powers) can expand according to certain criteria of development and progress, while other social science communities (those in the Third World, for example) can only do this as a reflection of that expansion, which can have mixed effects (positive and negative) on their development according to the same criteria." [16]

With the odd construction of "parallels" between economic relations between the imperial world and the developing countries and the relations between social sciences in the "peripheries" and the "center",—a comparison in which they present the conflicting economic relations as the rather harmless relation of "dependence" extinguishing the essential conflictual relations -, this sociological thinker in this "peripheral" world demonstrates his mastership in thinking in idealized nation state rationales and proves that his way of thinking is very much in the centres of social science thinking, discussing the contributions to knowledge from thinkers in the third world as a concern for what? The concerns—of the "Third World's" nation states.[17]

While Wallerstein's grumbled about a monstrous "universal universalism", thinking about how to find nothing less but a global moral "we", not only sociological thinkers from the "Third World" ever also construct the "Third World" as another global counter-"we", in which they do not want to know anything about the many conflicting interests between all the subjects, constituting this regional "we" in the former colonised world, now also nation states, conflicting interests, may this be between the nation states, may this be among the citizens within these new nation states and not to mention those among the also competing social sciences within this regional "we". They master the sociological manor gathering

---

[16] Dos Santos (1970) The Structure of Dependence, American Economic Review, p 603
[17] See also just as numerous other examples the paper from I. Marques titled "What can Science and Technology Studies do with and for Latin America?..." I. Marques, in: M. Kuhn & H. Vessuri, Contributions to Alternative Concepts of Knowledge", ibidem, Stuttgart, forthcoming

## Chapter 5: Why arriving at imperial thought is not a accident 95

subjects under a shared "dependency" only they suppose share distinguished from another global/regional "we", generously ignoring all kind of dependencies these subject have among themselves within all these nation states, as among the nation state within the "developing" world. Sociological thinking in the "developing" countries also appreciates to create the ideal of a "we" of the "dependent". They unify not only imperial and imperialised nation states with a region and gather them under the same notion of "dependency", easily ignoring not only their wars all these dependent nation states and subjects fight against each other. They also practice sociological thinking in and across these countries seeing them as a unit only they see, a unit, they construct negatively as sharing a victimization of the—what they therefore call—the "Western sciences", not of a science approach or theories, but of a science characterized as an opposed group of nationally constructed entities, the "scientific centers", they also present as the revers false unity as their "developing" science from the "peripheries", constituting the very meaning of the very category of "scientific dependence", under which they are gathered as victimized nationals.

It requires a very non peripheral determined sociological view on the sphere of science, to accommodate thinking about the competitive academia in the developing countries to call this competing academia the "social science community" of the "peripheries", those in the "third world", and to present their contribution to knowledge as a problem, not for the world's knowledge, but for these multi-nationally constructed imagined entity, the "South", the imagined social science "community" of the "Third world", opposed to the accordingly imagined "Western sciences".

From there on—not only—academics from the "Third World", as the social science generally do, they also count the nationalities of thinkers, whose thought do not only not matter. The view on science as a nationally identified activity, not just a few scientific thinkers in the developing countries share, thinking about social sciences even radicalizes the view on science as a matter of the position nation states have on science, just as if the view of national policies and the view of thinkers on the world of sciences was the same, and engage themselves in discussing the inter-national status of their "Third world" nation states in what they construct in their sociological sciences minds as a global battle about an "expansion" of science. For sociological thinking in the developing world, creating knowledge about the world's social and to strengthening the Third World's nation states position in global social thought consisting of a multiplicity of politically biased knowledges, is in their imagined battle between an imagined "center" and a "periphery", seemingly the same.

Sociological thinking from the developing countries thus compliments the view on social sciences from an imperial view and constructs an alternative global imperial counter "we", gathering social thought under an alternatively constructed politically "southern" science entities, entities only sociological theorizing can construct that identifies global social thought as matter of the competition among a multiplicity of nationally constructed knowledge bodies, unified in a global battle among imperial knowledge bodies and thus contribute its own imperial view on the social as on the social sciences.

To conclude: Considering the sociological ways of thinking, arguing about nationalism imagined as providing nothing but "order", "structure", "identity",[18] concluded from off-thinking the very ordered subjects without their ordering power, one tends to overlook the concept of organisation, thinkers must have in their mind, brashly presenting nation states as "pivotal" organisations structuring human live. Presenting the live of nation state citizens that is setting into force to practice live as the vice versa dependency of achieving ones interests by preventing the others to achieve his one, the other interests, which at the same are needed to strive for ones owns, presenting this nation state social life of an everybody against everybody as—though not an ideal, sociological thinking is critical thinking—but a possible not yet perfect though "pivotal" model to organise a society, is a bizarre view on the reality that cannot originate from looking at the reality.

Not even mentioning the organisation of economic life in a market economy with its economic battles among all economic subjects, presenting this nation state social life that articulates in any law how to find arrangements between all the interests that essentially conflict with each other to avoid their societal blast, presenting this battle among nation state creatures set into force with the power of nation states as a "pivotal" way of organising

---

[18] How sociological thinking creates sociological theories, see: M. Kuhn, Notes on a critique of how social sciences think, ibidem, Stuttgart, forthcoming

human live, is only thinkable for a mind, that, indeed, imagines these nation state humans and their live arrangements as competitors without the ruling power of nation states, nation states which for good reason need above all nothing more but a monopole on power in front of the society the very nation state forces into this everybody against everybody.

Considering as Calhoun, who certainly is no typical critical sociologists, but who shares the essential logic of sociological theorizing, considering the nation state as a not a perfectly, though at least as a possible "structured" society, that needs to be ever critically observed by sociologists, imagining the scenario of a world of nation states creatures without nation states and arguing from there that nation states are undeniable the only guaranty to identify the world of nation states as a world of nation states, is no insane logic, but most distinguished sociological thinking, which interprets the nation state society as an ever imperfect "system" to get any order over the otherwise dis-ordered individuals.

Therefore, most seriously presenting a book, arguing about the question if thinking through the imperial view of nation states is not eroded by a notion, such as cosmopolitanism, that in the eyes of such a nation state freak like Calhoun insinuates for his paranoid worries about a world with no "structures" the dooming end not only of nation states and their ordering services but, to make it worse, the doming end of sociological thinking, is not accident of a fanatic sociologist, but corresponds with the essentials of how sociological thinking thinks:

> "Nationalism is easily underestimated.....Analysts focus on eruptions of violence, waves of racial or ethnic discrimination, and mass social movements. They fail to see the everyday nationalism that organizes people's sense of belonging that leads historians to organize history as stories in or of nations and social scientists to approach comparative research with data sets in which the units are almost always nations."[19]

Worse than imagining all the nation state creatures without its ruling creator, nationalism without nations, patriotism without home lands, in short a world without "*nationalism that organizes people's sense of belonging*" and to conclude from these frightening scenarios that nation states are the best organizers of the socie-

---

[19] *Calhoun (2009) Nations Matter,....p 27*

ty only they create, to then imagine how nationalism without nation states would be confused to which nation which nationalism belongs, worse than all these imagined cases of any dis-order in *"people's sense of belonging"*, any un-structured society for sociological thinkers is at the end to imagine sociological thinking without the nation state as their unit of analysis and their national data sets for comparing nation states—unthinkable.

At least it is a very correct observation that nation states "lead historians" and, one should add, not only historians, but obviously also sociological thinking which therefore arrives quasi naturally at imperial thought, once sociological thinking goes beyond its *"methodological nationalism"*. It is, though, a less worrying scenario to imagine a world without both.

# References

Beck, U. (n.d.). Available online under : http://www.ulrichbeck.net/build.net/index.php?page=cosmopolitan

Calhoun, C. (2009). *Nations Matter, Culture, History, and the Cosmopolitan Dream*. Routledge.

Dos Santos, T. (1970). The Structure of Dependence. *American Economic Review*

Kuhn, M. (forthcoming). *How Social Sciences Think about the World's Social – Outlines of a Critique*. Stuttgart: Ibidem.

Marques, I. (forthcoming). What can Science and Technology Studies do with and for Latin America? In M. Kuhn & H. Vessuri (eds.) *Contributions to Alternative Concepts of Knowledge*. Stuttgart: Ibidem.

Wallerstein, I. (2006). *European Universalism : The Rhetoric of Power*. New York.

# Section II:
# The European
# Universalism

# Chapter 6:
# The European Comprehension of the World: Early Modern Science and Eurocentrism

## Mauricio Nieto Olarte

## Introduction

The aim of this chapter is to illustrate the strong bond that existed between European expansion and the claim of the West that it possessed a universal science; the intention is to expose the relationship between Eurocentrism and Western science. This is, in other words, a contribution to a political history of modern science.

The European claim of possessing a superior kind of knowledge, and the emergence of a new self-perception that Christian Europe stood at the center of the world, must be explained historically, and the actual practices that enabled such a claim should be described. How, and when, did it become possible for the West to claim ownership of a unique rational and universal form of knowledge? This chapter argues that the scientific practices involved in the European exploration of new lands in the early modern period were related to the emergence of a new European self-perception that Christian Europe was legitimate sovereign of the world. The notion of *comprehension, as* we shall explain, is a useful concept to clarify that process; it implies an act of *appropriation* and a process of domestication. Comprehend can also mean to take in, to embrace, or to include, a process of translation of the unknown into something familiar.

The chapter makes no attempt to resolve the historical problem of the birth of modern science. Too much ink has been spilt already and too many trees sacrificed nourishing the story of the emergence of this unique kind of knowledge in Western Europe. However, a critical examination of early modern science and technology, and a clarification of the political nature of scientific practice, allows a different way of thinking about the very nature of

Western science and about its role in the political history of the modern world. Science and technology constitute an active exercise of power and their dissemination can be seen as commitment to gain control; as Roy Macleod suggests, the point is to study science not within imperial history but as imperial history[1].

The first section of the chapter is devoted to presenting the old problem of the birth and diffusion of Western Science, while the second introduces the idea of "comprehension" as a notion that is useful in explaining the scientific practices that allowed the Europeans to claim dominion of the world. The third and main section of the chapter is an attempt to illustrate the close relationship between European expansion and the idea of universal knowledge. This section deals with two major scientific and political projects of the 16th Century European Christian Empires: the commitment to mapping the world and the need to catalog and name the animals and plants of the New World. Geography and natural history are presented as forms of distance control that required the systematization of information and data, that is to say, the construction of a new and widely accepted knowledge. The fourth section illustrates the relation between comprehension, systematization, distance control and science. Finally, the last section of the chapter discusses ways in which the new European self-perception as the center of the world was related of the 16th Century's exploration and conquest of unknown seas and lands.

# 1. The tried, tested and ever-problematic question of the origins and diffusion of Western Science

## 1.1 The European birth

Despite the endless debates and the vast literature associated with the birth of modern science, until recently—few decades ago—most authors identified it with the "Copernican Revolution": with the overthrow of Aristotelian physics and geocentric cosmology, and with the subsequent foundation of modern physics. All of this seemed to have been possible because of the triumph of European reason and of experience over dogma and faith.

---

[1] Macleod, 1982: 1-16.

A quick look at some of the most important narratives of the birth of modern science makes it clear that the most influential works published in English in the 20th century focused on explaining a radical epistemological turn that occurred in Western Europe.[2] Historical and philosophical debates concerning the birth of modern science have been focused on a particular period: the 16th and 17th centuries; and on a single place: Western Europe. Not only were the Asian, Arabic and American worlds inexplicably absent from this narrative, so were Catholic Spain and Portugal. The oft-repeated story of the Scientific Revolution was not just confined to the European Renaissance, it focused on particular fields of science such as astronomy and physics. Areas of natural knowledge of the utmost importance to understanding modern culture, such as cosmography, cartography, navigation, or natural history have been treated only superficially.[3]

One of the most important assumptions of the traditional notion of scientific knowledge is that its success rests on its internal characteristics, its epistemological foundations, its method, and its rational and empirical nature. This implies that there is but one science, which can be clearly distinguished from other ways of explaining or interacting with nature or society.[4] As a consequence of these historiographical and philosophical traditions, "Modern

---

[2] Burtt, 1932; Hall, 1962; Butterfield, 1957; Koestler,1959; Dijterhuis, 1950; Kuhn, 1957; Koyré, 1961; Wightman, 1962; Debus, 1972; Westfall, 1977; Webster, 1982; Cohen, 1985; Shapin, 1996.

[3] See for instance: Olby, Cantor, Christie and Hodge (eds), 1990. That same year, David Lindberg and Robert Westman published *Reappraisals of the Scientific Revolution*, a volume that included a dozen articles by experts on the topic, none of which referred to any country other than Italy or England. Neither Spain nor Portugal is mentioned. In the vast literature on the history of modern science it is difficult to understand why so little attention has been paid to the role of major changes in the history of cosmography, geography, natural history and astronomy—both in terms of content and their theoretical frameworks—that occurred in the early modern Iberian Atlantic. In 1992, Roy Porter and Mikulás Teich published yet another book on the subject, *The Scientific Revolution in National Context*; in this case—finally!—British historian David Goodman contributed with a chapter titled "The Scientific Revolution in Spain and Portugal." In this piece, despite demonstrating the importance of 16th Century Iberian science, Goodman concludes that the scientific boom of the 16th Century contrasts with later stagnation and states that it is impossible to find any Iberian contributions to the European scientific revolution of the 17th Century.

[4] De Greiff, Nieto, 2005.

Science" has been understood as a unique and superior kind of knowledge and its diffusion seen as a natural consequence of its universality.

However, the belief that a more rational mankind or an infallible scientific method suddenly emerged, somewhere in Western Europe, at some time in the 17$^{th}$ century and that this scientific revolution gave birth to a modern science created uniquely in the West and subsequently diffused elsewhere without major modifications, is no longer sustainable. [5] Contemporary historians of science seem to recognize that it is not possible to identify either a single moment, or a particular place that marked the birth of a specific form of knowledge that might be called "Modern Science". Steve Shapin's widely read book on the The Scientific Revolution opens with the statement: "There was no such a thing as the scientific revolution..."; and the third volume of the Cambridge History of Science dedicated to "Early Modern Science"—edited by Katherine Park and Lorraine Daston and containing more than 30 contributions by recognized scholars on the subject—explicitly avoided the notion of a "Scientific Revolution".[6]

The history of modern science, it is now apparent, cannot be limited to the Copernican Revolution nor to the achievements of a few genial minds in North-Western Europe. The view that the origins of scientific modernity are to be found in crucial experiments or in the ideas of a few extraordinary modern philosophers is ever more complicated and less convincing. On the contrary, there is good reason to question the very idea of a Scientific Revolution as well as to reformulate the notion of the West as the birthplace of a unique and universal science.[7]

Studies of more mundane cultural processes such as the development of the modern printing press[8] or the configuration of large empires and the great commercial enterprises of the early modern period—as well as new perspectives on the relations

---

[5] Raj, 2007.
[6] Park and Daston (Eds), 2003.
[7] Raj, 2007; Dackerman (Ed.), 2011.
[8] Eisenstein, 1983; Latour, 1990, pp. 19–68; Johns, *The Nature of the Book: Print (AÑO)*

between religion, magic, art and science[9]—seem to offer richer historical explanations of the emergence of a European Subject that claimed for itself the possession of a universal kind of knowledge.[10]

## 1.2 The diffusion and triumph of Western Science

The assumption that Europe was the birthplace of modern science confronted historians with another historiographical problem: how to explain the diffusion and success of the new science in the rest of the world.

In 1967 George Basalla published "The Spread of Western Science"[11], which advanced the argument that western science spread beyond Europe in three consecutive stages: a period in which places with non-scientific societies provided sources for European science (phase 1), a period of "colonial science" (phase 2) and finally a process of "transplantation" involving a struggle to achieve an independent, national, scientific tradition (phase 3). Such a linear approach to the study of the history of science has been the target of repeated criticism.[12]

For the most part, the criticisms refer to a problematic assumption in the diffusion model: the idea that modern science left the confines of Western Europe as a finished product that was then disseminated naturally from its place of origin to the rest of the planet without undergoing major alteration.

An enormous amount of research in the history and sociology of science has made evident the contingent nature of scientific knowledge and has questioned the traditional conception of a single, unique, neutral, a-historical way of understanding nature or society. One of the major contributions of the sociology of scientific knowledge is to have removed the traditional distinction between the context of discovery and the context of justification, showing that the production and the diffusion of knowledge are

---

[9] See for instance, Conpenhjaver, "Magic"; Feldhay; "Religion"; Swan and Niakrasz, "Art", In: Park and Daston (Eds.) 2006.
[10] Cook, 2007.
[11] Basalla, 1967, p. 156.
[12] Macleod, "On Visiting the Moving Metropolis: Reflections on the Architecture of Imperial Science," in Reingold and Rothemberg, 1987; Lafuente and Ortega, eds., 1993.

simultaneous processes. Once the obvious conclusion that knowledge is communication was accepted—that there is no science without circulation, a public, and consensus—the diffusion model presented above became worthless.

Knowledge becomes legitimate only once a particular way of explaining the world has been shared and accepted by a large community. That is to say, universal truth is only possible once it is recognized as such by many. Therefore "discovery" and justification, or the production of knowledge and its communication are not separable. The triumph of Western science, then, is not a consequence of its nature and its privileged epistemological status, and the scientific hegemony of the West cannot be explained simply by the rigor of a specific method. Very much to the contrary: its status and its success as a universal form of knowledge should be explained in terms of the actual practices that made the European claim of universality possible. It is no coincidence that the emergence of what is understood today as modern science occurred during the same period as the rise of the global European empires and simultaneously with the emergence of a global economy.[13]

This belief in the natural spread of Western science is not only an obvious expression of eurocentrism, but also presupposes that non-Western cultures and traditions are obstacles to the development of knowledge, whose only effect on European science is to interrupt the natural progress of a truly rational system of thought.

Such a process of diffusion implies that the unity of Western science and its superior and a-historical character entail a process involving the elimination of other ways of representing and interacting with nature and the homogenization of culture, which have played such an important role in strengthening a world order centered on Europe.

The idea of European expansion as a natural consequence of its cultural superiority has been subject to revision and criticism. First of all, it is evident that the expansion of Western scientific practices did not always have a positive impact on colonized cultures and places. Furthermore, several historians have demonstrated the close relationship between imperialism and science and have

---

[13] Cook, 2007.

shown how practices such as medicine, natural history, geography or ethnography have been powerful instruments of control and domination.[14] Historians of science such as Kapil Raj, and others, have also shown the impact of Eastern cultures on the history of Western science and the idea that the origins of science are purely Western has become problematic. [15]

Before we try to explain the bond between modern science and eurocentrism, it is necessary to make clear that by eurocentrism we mean the assumption that Western culture is capable of explaining any other culture in its own terms. As Arif Dirlik puts it: "The distinguishing feature of eurocentrism is not its exclusiveness, which is common to all ethnocentrisms, but rather the reverse: its inclusiveness. Eurocentrism is not the result of ignoring others but rather the consequence of organizing the knowledge of the world, including other ways of knowing, into one single systematic whole"[16].

The area we call Europe is home to a remarkable cultural diversity as well as to geographical, cultural and economic centers and peripheries. However, the aim here is, precisely, to understand the process by which the "West" was consolidated as a geographic and cultural entity—a process that was only possible to the degree that Europeans were faced with something different and was able to create a referent of an 'other' that was common to the entire Christian world.[17]

The very idea of a "Western Science" creates a dichotomy and opposition between "Science" and other, purportedly inferior, forms of knowledge or belief, often referred to as "local knowledge". This opposition of *"western"* and *"local"* implies that European science is not bound to any place or to any culture in particular but belongs to every place and culture on earth. Thus, the dichotomy between *science* on the one hand and *local knowledges* on the other is inadequate since it assumes the universal character of Western civilization, in opposition to the particular, local (and hence partial) nature of all non-European knowledge.

---

[14] For instance: Nieto, 2001.
[15] Raj, 2007. Hobson, 2004.
[16] Dirlik, 2002.
[17] Dussel, 2000, 41–53.

The attempt to escape a Eurocentric account of history, and the need to make other voices heard, cannot be reduced to denying the importance of Europe in modern history, or neglecting the central role of Western science. Instead, its success, and the consequences of this success for the geo-political transformation of the world must be explained historically, socially, culturally and politically.

How did it become possible for a particular social group to claim possession of a unique and universal way of understanding nature or society and the right to speak for all? That is the really interesting question for the history of Western science.

The Cambridge History of Science, mentioned above, seems to cover all the relevant topics: the classical protagonists of the Copernican revolution are all present, and the variety of topics and approaches offer a larger picture and a more complicated history beyond the scope of this essay. The last chapter of this extraordinary compilation of historical research, "European Expansion and Self-Definition", by Klaus A. Vogel is noteworthy because it makes evident a relation between European imperial expansion and modern science. Vogel's claims might serve as an appropriate starting point for this attempt to understand the relationship between eurocentrism and the idea of a unique and superior kind of knowledge.

The growth of knowledge and technological innovation in the fields of navigation, cartography, natural history, engineering, mining, and medicine that developed in $15^{th}$ and $16^{th}$ century Europe are all expressions of vigorous empires. It is also true that empires themselves result from thriving scientific and technical activity. The question of whether the science and technology of the early modern European empires were or were not the basis of the "Scientific Revolution" is a less interesting one than the task of demonstrating the enduring relationship between science and empire, between world exploration and the consolidation of a global order in which the expansive European culture became a dominant frame of reference. This process, involving the appropriation and consolidation of European global control, we shall argue, was simultaneously a political, technological and scientific achievement.

European expansion from the $15^{th}$ Century onwards was possible because the Portuguese and Spanish developed new technologies in marine navigation, orientation and cartography;

but at the same time the exploration of new seas and lands was for Europeans a permanent source of new knowledge in natural history, astronomy, and geography. "Encounters with previously unknown lands, peoples, animals, plants, and minerals expanded the frontiers of the ancient and medieval knowledge of the world and changed theoretical understanding of nature."[18] That is to say, the growth of science and the technological innovations of the 16th century were both a precondition for European imperial expansion and a consequence of it.

## 2. The European comprehension (appropriation) of the world

One of the most frequent and deeply rooted ideas used to explain European history in the 16th century is the notion of "discovery". This identification of European expansion with the "Age of Discovery" forms a part of a historical vision that is centered on Europe and which has profound implications for our understanding of modern history.

A "discovery" presupposes a heroic deed or an individual achievement in which someone, in a specific moment, sees or finds something that no one else has witnessed before; furthermore, it assumes that the object discovered existed as such, in itself, before it was found and independently of its discoverer. This notion of discovery has been central to the construction of an idea of modern science which, in its turn, has been fundamental to the consolidation of Western Europe as the center and driving force of the history of the modern world. It has become commonplace to assume that the history of modern science, and subsequently, the successful expansion of the European world and the conquest of nature, can be reduced to a series of crucial discoveries and individual feats. Assertions such as "Christopher Columbus discovered America in 1942" or "Vasco Núñez de Balboa discovered the Pacific Ocean", or that Johannes Kepler discovered the laws of planetary motion, William Harvey the circulation of the blood and Isaac Newton the law of gravitation, are common and generally accepted statements.

---

[18] Vogel, 2006, p. 818.

Furthermore, discoveries are presented as mechanisms of appropriation in which discoverers claim rights of possession and dominion over the places and peoples they have discovered; the notion of *discovery* assumes a one-way and asymmetrical process in which non-European places and their aboriginal populations are reduced to the status of objects, whose reality is dependent upon a European feat. In this way, the narratives of discovery constitute celebrations of the power of man over nature, contributing to the idealization of the scientific practices through which Western culture claims control and dominion over the world.

In response to this panorama of an extended process of appropriation, in which the New World was gradually incorporated into European culture—a process through which Europe was both transformed and simultaneously constructed its own identity—this chapter argues for the centrality of the idea of *comprehension*. This concept has considerable advantages and might contribute to our understanding of the conquest of the New World as an epistemological problem in which scientific practices played a crucial role.

The notion of *comprehension* derives from the Latin verb *comprehendere,* (*cum*, with, and *prehendere*, to take) and may suggest a process of *appropriation* whereby the meaning of something is internalized. Comprehend can also mean to take in, to embrace, or to include. As well as an act of appropriation, then, comprehension can also imply a process of translation of the unknown into something familiar, of incorporation and domestication, as well as of recognition of the strange.

This first connotation of the term aids the understanding that practices associated with the discovery and conquest of the New World, such as cartography, natural history or ethnography, were, in themselves, powerful ways of asserting ownership and the right of dominion over peoples and over nature—acts of *appropriation* in other words. However, this initial definition is insufficient and maintains the perception of one-way traffic, according to which Europe is the subject and the rest of the planet the object of such comprehension, and it seems to leave us once more with the limited perception of a passive New World that is appropriated by Europe.

So, the *comprehension of the New World* suggests an implicit reflective action that cannot be reduced to the process of apprehension or understanding of something external; on the contrary, the idea is that a process occurs in which both the *subject* that comprehends and the *object* of comprehension actively participate and are transformed. It is a process during which the agents and objects of appropriation are constructed simultaneously.[19]

1492 should be remembered as much as the year of the "discovery of Europe" as of the discovery of America. As José Rabasa has suggested, this means that the expression "New World" should not be limited to a geographic space different from Europe that was the object of European exploration and exploitation from the 16th century onwards.[20] It also signifies the constitution of the modern conception of a new world—the entire world—that resulted from the conquest by Europe of the greater part of the planet.

The construction or invention of the New World is thus inseparable from the invention of Europe. Sixteenth century Iberian sailors, explorers and naturalists, committed to an ambitious commercial, political and religious project to conquer the world, and confronted with geographies, natural worlds, cultures and races unknown to Europe, were forced to put aside or to critically examine the paradigms of classical antiquity, and to construct a new way of understanding nature.

The Spanish and Portuguese ships that crossed the Atlantic in the 15th and 16th centuries may have failed in their goal to reach India, but in the attempt they found a new world with an exuberant and unknown natural world. The encounter between Europeans and the unknown American natural world implied new challenges for European science; 16th century explorers, cartographers and naturalists had to name and describe the unknown, to put into familiar language the strange natural world. These new experiences, however, should be understood in the context of a rich cultural tradition in the Portuguese and Spanish courts and universities of which the legacies of Arab science and the practices of Renaissance humanism were a part. The gradual incorporation of a new part of the globe into the scheme of classical cartography, the detailed descriptions of animals, plants and cultures using domestic referents, the use of Christian and familiar names, and in

---

[19] Gadamer, 1992, p. 121.
[20] Rabasa, 2003.

general the production of texts and images, were major strategies in the task of taming the wild.

In this way, the voyages of exploration and the need to create catalogues and inventories of nature, the production of maps and the studies of population, the climate or of medicine, were all fundamental practices in the consolidation of modern Europe.

As Klaus A. Vogel has argued, the voyages of exploration and expansion changed European self-perception. "Europeans used not only Christianity but also the undisputed primacy of European natural knowledge—and technology—to legitimate their global regency in Africa, Asia and America."[21]

## 3. European Empires, Christian expansion and Western Science: the cases of geography and natural history

European imperialism and expansion have a long and complex history, which it is far beyond the purposes of this chapter to explore. European attempts to control the world might be said to have originated with the Greeks or the Roman Empire and to extend through to 19th century imperialist designs in Asia, Africa and the Americas, or beyond. The close relation between science, technology and control is evident in all these different periods and places, as has been shown by historians of technology such as Daniel Headrick.[22] This section concentrates on a particular moment that marked a significant change in the world order, namely the Christian conquest of the sea in the 16th century.

It is not easy to pinpoint the precise moment in which the process known as globalization began. Nor is there a known birthdate for phenomena like world trade or universal science. There is no doubt, however, that the 16th century witnessed changes that were unprecedented on the world stage. The Iberian exploration of the Atlantic during the first half of the 16th century consolidated two enormously important trade routes and monopolies: the route between Portugal and India (more specifically, between Lisbon and Goa), and that between Seville

---

[21] Vogel, 2006, p. 820.
[22] Headrick, 2012.

and the different ports of the Caribbean and the Gulf of Mexico.[23] These were the two principal European trade networks outside the Mediterranean and also the foundations upon which a new world order was built, in which Christian Europe proclaimed its dominion over a large part of the planet.

In Spain, the *Real Consejo de Indias* and the *Casa de Contratación* were institutions created with the explicit purpose of implementing efficient instruments of conquest, the latter acting as the center for the collection, systematization and diffusion of an inexhaustible source of new information: the New World. The Spanish enterprise of cataloging, naming and describing the nature and geography of the New World was a colossal venture and its results were noteworthy: complex legal and moral debates, detailed ethnographic descriptions, linguistic studies, encyclopedias of natural history, treatises on medical botany, countless maps, manuals and navigational instruments, ships, cannons and sails. All of these scientific and technological products not only served Spain in its purpose of controlling the New World but also circulated outside the country and opened up new horizons to the Christian world.

Let us, in the following sections, have a look at two major scientific enterprises of the early modern Christian Empires, two clear examples of the European commitment to comprehend the New World: geography and natural history.

## 3.1. Mapping the World

In order to appreciate the true scientific and political dimensions of the *Casa de Contratación* it is necessary to look, if only superficially, at the most ambitious scientific venture, certainly of the Casa or of Spain, and perhaps of the entire 16th century: the manufacture of a map of the whole world, the *Padrón Real*.

The ideas of historians of cartography such as J.B. Harley[24]— who understand maps not as simple representations of existing things but as ways of constructing order—allow for a better understanding of the political meaning of a cartography at the service of empire.

---

[23] Braudel, 1997, p. 399.
[24] Harley, García Cortés and Rodríguez (trad.), 2005.

There is no better way to organize such vast extensions of land and sea and so much information than with a map. Maps are the most efficient way of gathering together time and space in a plane and mobile two-dimensional representation. Thus, the great legacy of this geometrical conceptualization of the globe is the possibility of reducing it to a single sheet of paper. This possibility of representing and visualizing great extensions of land and sea—or even the entire globe—on a flat surface made the idea of global control plausible.

Though we know that most of the maps still in existence are in fact copies of earlier ones, we are confident that the information that permitted the New World to be set down on paper came from voyages of exploration. This is why so much emphasis was placed on providing adequate training for navigators so that they could take useful information back to Seville. The great technical challenge consisted in mobilizing the information and representing and controlling it at a distance. Communication between sailors and cosmographers, between navigators and cartographers, posed an extremely interesting epistemological problem. The solution lay in constructing a way of observing and gathering information according to a single unified framework. It was, therefore, necessary to standardize instruments and units of measurement, to train a disciplined group of navigators equipped for exploration and, of course, to ensure their return.

The project to create the *Padrón Real* required the construction of an enormous technical and scientific enterprise, involving a very large number of people. Far from being an individual achievement, the production of a map of the world was a labor carried out by powerful institutions capable of systematically bringing together the experience of many, according to a shared frame of reference. As it has been suggested above, Eurocentrism can be defined in similar terms: as the capability to integrate or translate the unknown into a familiar framework. This, precisely, is one of the essential attributes associated with modern science and it should, therefore, be included in any narrative that has pretensions to describe its birth.

It could be argued, as has in fact been suggested by Klaus A. Vogel, that the emergence of a new geography combining theory, empirical method and the handiwork of artisans constituted a

## Chapter 6: The European Comprehension of the World 115

model for the creation of natural knowledge in the early modern era.[25]

Today, no map bearing the name "El Padrón Real" is known to us. However, world maps such as the ones produced by the Portuguese cartographer Diego Ribero working for the Spanish Crown, could be an example of maps constructed on the basis of data collected together in the *Casa de Contratación* in Seville.

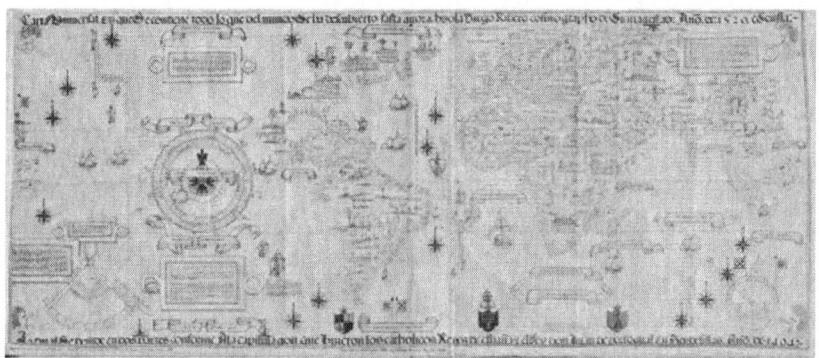

**Image 1**. Carta Universal en que se contiene todo lo que del mundo se ha descubierto hasta ahora. Hizola Diego Ribero cosmografo de su majestad: Año de 1520, Sevilla. La cual se divide en dos partes conforme a la capitulación que hicieron los católicos Reyes de España y el Rey Don Juan de Portugal en Tordesillas: Año de 1494, Seville, 1529. The Vatican Library, Rome, copy in the Madrid Naval Museum.

The purpose of this map is clear from its title, which expresses the pretension to represent the entire world and its division between the Spanish and Portuguese crowns: *Universal Map containing the entirety of the world discovered to date. It was made by His Majesty's cartographer Diego Ribero: in the Year 1529, Seville. It is divided into two parts in conformity with the treaty entered into by the Catholic Monarchs of Spain and King Don Juan of Portugal in Tordesillas: Year 1494, Seville, 1529.*

Although by 1529 the world was very different from that of the 15th century, these maps preserve the conventions of medieval Mediterranean cartography. Routes converge on the wind roses so that the networks appear to cover the entire globe. The central aim of the map continues to be the definition of the line of demarcation

---

[25] Vogel, 2006, p. 472.

between the domains of Spain and Portugal. Equally apparent is the presence of the classical astronomical coordinates: North at the top of the map, the Equator and the Tropics of Capricorn and Cancer. One element that is worthy of mention, and which distinguishes this map from that of Juan de la Cosa published 30 years earlier, is its toponymical richness, introduced not only to describe the Old World but also the Americas, and in particular its Eastern seaboard. The map's sumptuous decoration is also worthy of note. Numerous European ships, duly identified by their imperial insignia, are dotted across the seas, indicating the Christian presence across almost the entire world.

**Image 1.1.** *Carta Universal de Diego Ribero,* 1529, detail. Finely detailed images of ships appear throughout the map, giving an idea of a world conquered by European explorers.

One of the distinctive characteristics of Ribero's maps is the detailed representation and description of astronomical and navigational instruments such as the quadrant, the astrolabe and circular declination tables. The depiction of instruments replaces the customary decorative icons of earlier maps and had the explicit purpose of providing evidence of the sophisticated technology used

## Chapter 6: The European Comprehension of the World

to prepare the map, its accuracy and its credibility. The map is not only a picture of the world; it also makes explicit the correct way such an image should be manufactured, even representing the mapmaker. Maps are at the same time windows or glass panes through which to gaze upon the world, but also mirrors in which the authority of the cartographer is represented.

This was not, of course, the first attempt to represent the world. We have examples of cartographic representation of the world from Babylonia, India, China, the Muslim world and Medieval Christendom. But it could be argued that the 16th century offered the first picture of the modern, that is to say, the Western, world.

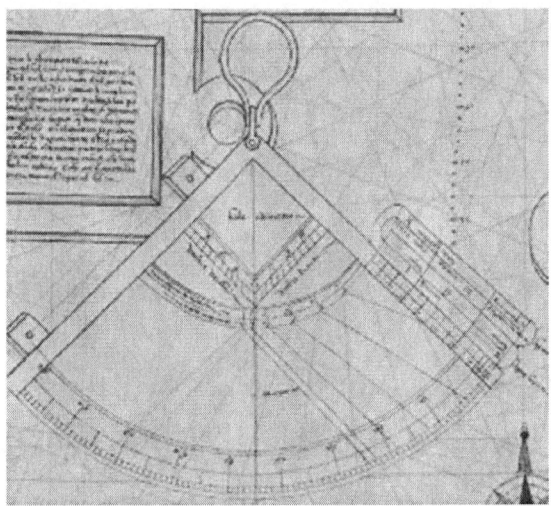

**Image 1.2**. Observational instruments are a notable feature of the map. This detail illustrates a quadrant, precisely drawn in order to illustrate its use. *Carta Universal de Diego Ribero, 1529*, detail.

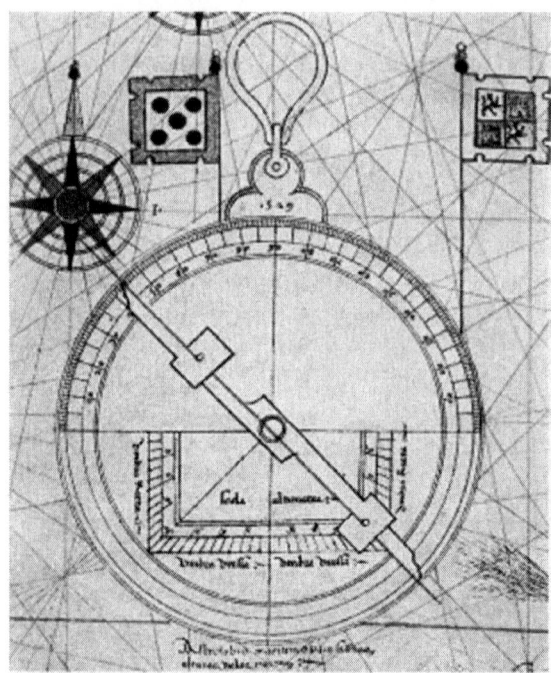

**Image 1.3.** Astrolabe. Carta Universal de Diego Ribero, 1529, detail

## 3.2. Natural History: a new world of plants and animals

The conquest of the New World did not end with the domination of the oceans. Arrival in the islands or the coasts of *Terra Firme* in the Indies was the beginning of a major new challenge. After the solitude of the sea and the confinement of the ships, the voyagers were now faced with lands of unexpected extent and a natural world that was exuberant, beautiful and hostile at the same time. The transatlantic route was a challenge replete of difficulties, but once they had landed the Christians were faced with territories that were already occupied. The conquest of the Americas was a violent invasion, which not only required overcoming the resistance of the natives, but also using their ancestral knowledge. The penetration of the continent presupposed the navigation of unknown and dangerous rivers, long days spent in tropical climates, jungles and deserts and traversing passes through interminable mountains.

## Chapter 6: The European Comprehension of the World 119

Despite the evident riches of the New World, the Europeans lacked sufficient knowledge to procure foodstuffs, to defend themselves against animals and to protect themselves from the climate. On land, many explorers, obsessed with gold, silver and other riches, were to lose their lives.

Explorers required new knowledge if they were to survive, but they had another mission that was even more difficult: they had to take these New World riches to Europe. In the Americas, Christians came face to face with parts of creation for which no testimonials known to them existed and which would require intense labor if they were to be controlled.

If the New World were to be brought under the dominion of Europe it was now necessary to register systematically and store information on access routes or the layout of the coasts and of every other thing that made up the natural world: the rivers, the mountains, the settlements and their inhabitants, the sources of valuable minerals, the plants and the animals.

In his *Historia general y natural de las Indias* Gonzalo Fernández de Oviedo describes very clearly the challenges posed by the extent and variation of nature found in the Americas:

> What moral inventiveness could comprehend such a diversity of lakes, of habits, of customs of these men of the Indies? Such variety of animals both domesticated and wild and savage? Such an indescribable multitude of trees, copiously laden with all kinds of fruit and others sterile—of the kinds of plant the Indians cultivate, and those that Nature on its own produces without the aid of mortal hands? How many useful plants and herbs, and beneficial to man? How many other uncountable varieties that are unknown to him and so many varieties of roses and flowers and perfumed fragrances? What variety of birds of prey and other kinds? So many soaring and fertile mountains? How many meadows and landscapes suitable for agriculture and such suitable riverbanks? How many admirable mountains and others as terrifying as Etna or Mongibel, or Vulcano and Estrongol; and all of them under the control of Your Majesty?[26]

The different cultures, the animals and plants of the New World represented a major challenge for the Europeans of the 16th Century. In the "Introduction to the King" of his *Historia General de las Indias,* López de Gómara justifies the description of the Indies as the "New World", saying:

---

[26] Oviedo, *Historia General,* op. cit., p. 8.

[...] and it is not so much that they call it new as newly found, but for its size: almost as large as the Old World, which contains Europe, Africa and Asia. It can also be called new because everything in it is totally different from the things in our world. The animals, in general, though there are few species, are of a different kind; the fish of the waters, the birds of the sky, the trees, the fruits, the herbs and the grains of the earth: which is no small consideration on the part of the Creator, the elements being one single thing both here and there.[27]

The animals of the New World did not accord with the personal knowledge of the voyagers and nor had they been classified by the ancient authorities; therefore, from the European perspective they had no names. The Bible taught that Adam had given names to all the animals according to their natures; now these animals apparently without name would have to be baptized and brought within the Christian order of Creation.

How should this New World be carried to Spain? How should it be described convincingly so that Europeans could gain a faithful idea of a world they had never before seen? Or better, how could Europe *comprehend* the New World. One obvious way was to compare the unknown species with familiar referents. Thus, many descriptions of American nature treated them as hybrids and combinations of animals and plants that were already familiar, like so many jigsaw puzzles made up of pieces of beings already known.[28] The first means of establishing connections was the use of analogy and comparison through which the unfamiliar shed its strangeness and appeared within a known frame of reference that made it possible for it to be named and classified. For Pedro Mártir de Anglería the opossum had the head of a fox, the tail and feet of a monkey, the ears of a bat and the hands of a man; Álvar Núñez Cabeza de Vaca referred to peccaries as wild pigs and called jaguars tigers; in Patagonia Pigaffeta described penguins as geese while a little later Urdaneta called them "wingless ducks"; Pedro Cieza de León described llamas as shaped like camels and of the size of a small donkey, while anteaters and sloths were both given the name "bear" (*oso hormiguero* or ant-eating bear and *oso perezoso*, lazy

---

[27] López de Gómara, Francisco. op. cit., "A Don Carlos, Emperador de Romanos, Rey de España, Señor de las Indias y el Nuevo Mundo". p. 5.
[28] De Asúa, and French, op. cit., p. 14.

## Chapter 6: The European Comprehension of the World

bear), bringing these exotic creatures into the realm of the familiar.[29]

Another example is provided by the pineapple ("piña" in Spanish), which was described as a hybrid between the familiar piña (pine cone) and an artichoke, while its properties were likened to those of common European fruits:

> The name piña was given by the Christians because they were similar to them in some way, though these are more beautiful and less robust than the pine cones that bear pine nuts in Castile; because those are made of wood, or almost, while these are cut with a knife like a melon or, better, into rounds after first removing the skin which has prominent scales making them resemble pinecones. But they do not open or divide at the point where these scales meet, as pinecones do (...) and it seems to me that a more suitable name would be artichoke, as it grows among thistle-like spines, though it resembles a pinecone more than it does an artichoke. In truth it is not different *totaliter* from an artichoke (...) its flavor is more unusual (...) like a peach and it smells like a mix between apricots and quinces; indeed, in the pineapple this smell is mixed with that of muscatel and, therefore, it tastes better than does a peach."[30]

A central element in this process of "comprehension" and domestication was the act of naming things in order to eliminate the ambiguity, variation and difference between local names. As in the case of the names of geographical features and places it is important in natural history classification for things to have only one name. As Oviedo explains: "...and as the Indians have many and diverse languages, so they name them many names". [31] Although the name pineapple is not entirely adequate, it was certainly preferable to the disorder and confusion that multiple local names generated.

Giving names, then, is a form of appropriation and translation. In order to possess the natural world the things in it must have only one name and the ambiguity and variety of local names be eliminated. European names such as "piña", "armadillo", "tigre",

---

[29] ibid, p. 33.
[30] De Oviedo, *Historia General... op. cit.*, vol. 1, libro VIII. cap. XIV. "of what the Christians call *piñas* because they resemble them; the fruit which the indians call *yayama*, and another kind of the same fruit *boniama*, and another kind *yayagua*, as will be said in this chapter although in other parts it has different names." pp. 241–242.
[31] loc. cit.

"perico ligero", "ave mosca", "tominejo" or "oso hormiguero"[32] make the unknown a part of a familiar world.

Closely related to the provision of descriptions and naming is the classification and incorporation of each creature within a pre-existing group or class. Describing and naming objects assumes the existence of some cataloguing system. Many American creatures resisted classification and it was by no means clear which of the categories established by Aristotle and implicit in Pliny were appropriate. The iguana, the manatee, the cactus and the American felines provide some examples of these difficulties. Indeed, the quantity and variety of animals and plants, of trees, reptiles, insects and serpents, appeared to make the task of naming and classifying impossible, and a long time was to elapse before apparent order was achieved under the Linnaean system in the 18th century.

The 16th century chroniclers narrate and describe "incredible" things but with pretensions to telling the truth, and it is precisely for this reason that they were required to create a new standard of credibility. This standard should be established, on the one hand, by incorporating the new into familiar frames of reference and, on the other, by asserting the power of direct, personal testimony that clearly distanced their words from works of fiction or the imagination.

Referring to the pineapple Oviedo writes:

> Some have been taken to Europe and very few have arrived there. And if they do arrive they cannot be perfect nor good because they have to be cut green and are seasoned by the sea air and in this way they lose value. (...) I have tried to take them and because of navigational errors, and many days' delay to the journey, all were lost and rotted, and I tried to take seedlings and these also were lost.[33]

The most efficient way to take living products across the sea and to show them to the Europeans was in words and images. On the advantages of painting to the field of natural history Oviedo comments: "...the eyes give a large part of the information on these

---

[32] *Perico ligero*: the three toed sloth (*perico* originally having a wide range of meanings in Spain, none related to animals) *ave mosca*: hummingbird ("bird" plus "fly"); *tominejo*: another word for hummingbird (from *tomín*, a very small measurement of weight, figuratively: something very small).

[33] loc. cit.

things since because they themselves cannot be seen or touched their image is of much help to the pen."³⁴

**Image 2.** Piña, Gonzalo Fernández de Oviedo, *Historia General*

Some of these strange creatures and objects were taken to Europe, and this was not the first time that such exotic exhibits had been seen in the courts of Europe, displayed as symbols of luxury and power. Collections of objects from distant lands became symbols of dominion and power over the alien. The creation of "cabinets of curiosities"—collections of natural objects and artifacts brought from remote places—grew fashionable amongst the powerful merchants and princes of Renaissance Europe.³⁵ The exotic, then, was a symbol of the power of mankind over nature—and the natural world formed a part of the world of property, a fact that was translated into private collections of strange objects and into spectacular, beautifully illustrated, publications that functioned as great catalogs of the unknown. |Through this process of mobilization, classification and translation of the natural objects

---

34 Quoted by José Rabasa, *op. cit.*, p. 146.
35 See Smith and Findlen (eds.), op. cit.

found in cabinets or publications the wild was domesticated and nature became property. Naturalists and collectors such as Athanasius Kircher, Conrad Gessner, Ulisse Androvandi, and Niccolò Serpetro provide examples of how the monstrous and savage of the New World had by the 17th century become a part of European culture.[36]

The exercise of ordering and classifying nature has always been closely linked to conquest and imperial expansion. Every such project requires mechanisms to appropriate the unknown and strategies to incorporate what is strange into familiar frameworks. The construction of an empire presupposes intense scientific activity by means of which it is possible to order nature and society under common codes. Thus, cosmography, maritime navigation, cartography and natural and political history should all be considered to be expressions of an overarching aim of control and dominion.

**Image 3**. The Museum of Ferrante Imperato in Naples, 1599

---

[36] Findlen "Inventing Nature. Commerce, Art, and Science in the Early Modern Cabinet of Curiosities" in Smith and Findlen (eds.), op. cit., pp. 297–323.

## 3.3. Translation and appropriation of non-Western knowledge and European's self image

The relationship that this chapter seeks to illustrate between European expansion and the history of Western science, and the skepticism it displays concerning both the diffusion model and the origin myth that a new and unique epistemology was born in Renaissance Europe, introduces another historiographical challenge of great interest: what was the role of non-European peoples and cultures in the construction of a new science? The European comprehension of the world also involved a process of translation and appropriation of human experience and knowledge. As has been argued by Kapil Raj, what we understand as Western science had roots beyond the West, and explains how British imperial science was also produced in the colonial periphery making apparent Europe's scientific debt to India. Raj's book deals with scientific practices in India from de 17th to the 19th centuries, but any attempt to understand the process by which Modern Europe was constructed has to take into account the earlier Christian expansion and the Iberian conquest of the New World in the 16th century.

The traditional narrative of the exploration of the non-European world and the parallel history of the diffusion of Western science ignores the complexity of cultural exchanges between European science and what has generally been described in the literature as local traditions.[37] Historians have been uncomfortable or remained completely silent about the relationship between European visitors and so-called local knowledge. The European appropriation and use of Native American knowledge is a fascinating and largely unexplored field of research.[38]

The creation of knowledge about new lands is not the result of a direct relationship between the explorer and nature. It is only possible through the mediation of cultural traditions in which complex relations between nature and society already exist.

It is absurd to assume that European explorers travelled across the empty American continent finding gold mines by accident, discovering—for example—tobacco and coca, testing plants and

---

[37] S. Irfan Habib, Dhruv Raina, and Zaheer Baber, 2007.
[38] Mundy, 1996. Nieto, 2000.

guessing at their possible uses; and it is a mistake to imagine a relationship between the explorer, naturalist, botanist, geographer or zoologist and a pure nature disconnected from the cultures and experiences of non-European populations. On the contrary, the only method that could be effective in understanding the medical virtues of plants, in dealing with strange animals, in conquering an unknown geography or in learning about the people themselves, was to listen to the natives. Therefore, in order fully to understand the nature of European science outside Europe the dynamics operating between Western knowledge and the knowledge of the inhabitants of conquered places must be explained. It is very important to pay attention to the appropriation, mobilization and translation not only of nature, but also of the knowledge of others.

Native American traditions played a determining role in the construction of European science, which in the early modern period distanced itself from classical authorities. Firstly, the knowledge of the other, though characterized as mere superstition or belief, was the starting point for the clear differentiation and confirmation of a more rational and legitimate body of knowledge. As it has been argued, the encounter and construction of the other, in this case uncivilized, superstitious and impious, constitutes a central part of the simultaneous construction of a European Subject, civilized, rational, and spokesman of religious and philosophical truth. It would be impossible to understand Europeans self-image without this subaltern other.

It may seem paradoxical that such native knowledge—described as irrational—was often incorporated into the chronicles and descriptions of the New World. Thus, the process by which subjects who presented themselves as genuine spokesmen of the natural order constructed their positions cannot be explained without attention to the ways in which the knowledge of others was translated and appropriated.

As Michel Callon argues, "To translate is to displace, but to translate is also to express in one's own language what others say and want, why they act in the way they do and how they associate with each other: it is to establish oneself as a spokesman. At the end of the process, if it is successful, only voices speaking in unison will be heard".[39] It is therefore important to study the ways in

---

[39] Callon, 1986, 196–233.

which the 'non enlightened' traditions, and the knowledge about nature held by the inhabitants of the Americas, were incorporated within Christian and humanist frames of reference that denied their local character and declared themselves 'universal.' This knowledge, once expressed in another language, under codes that were familiar to learned Europeans, was presented as the fruit of European discoveries and held to belong to Europe. This process helps to make sense of how a vast body of knowledge was constructed and accumulated as the property of a few, and how the traditions of others were silenced and their authority invalidated.

A quick glance at the great 16th century treatises on nature in the Americas shows a vast and complex process involving the translation of native knowledge. It is far from the scope of this essay to review the American contributions to the early modern natural history or medicine, however it is worth mentioning a couple of examples. In his *Historia natural de Nueva España*, Francisco Hernández compiled descriptions of nearly three thousand plants and more than three hundred animals. Many of these, including corn, the tomato, cacao, tobacco, coca and potatoes, were to transform Western culture and the history of the modern world. Francisco Hernández's work introduced the natural richness of New Spain to Europe, and at the same time, perhaps without meaning to, evidenced the complexity of American cultures.

Another interesting 16th century figure who promoted a project to comprehensively translate the knowledge of indigenous Mexican peoples in the fields of astronomy, history, religion, natural history and political organization was Friar Bernardino de Sahagún. Sahagún created a clearing house where native artists built up a colossal collection of images in which they registered their knowledge. Later, Sahagún devoted himself to the transcription of the material, producing a bilingual text that presented indigenous knowledge on geography, commerce, religion and politics in Spanish and in Nahuatl. The detailed manner in which plants and animals, medical practices and the natural order in general were described provided a clear example of the vastness of "local knowledge" on nature in the Americas and served to reveal mysterious and sophisticated cultures.[40]

---

[40] Bernardino de Sahagún, 2005.

One of the most prominent works published in Europe dealing with American plants with medical virtues was Nicolas Monardes, *La historia medicinal de las cosas que traen de nuestras Indias Occidentales* (1565); translated into English with the title *Joyful newes out of New Found World*. Once more the text presented a list of new vegetable remedies, presented as legitimate "European discoveries" taken or translated from indigenous practices.

## 4. Travelling knowledge, the science of distance control and standardization

The transatlantic transport of the geography, flora and fauna of the Americas presented obvious difficulties. The territory, its continents, the islands and most of their natural wealth could not be transported and stored in European cities. The task of taking wealth from the New World to Europe implies that numerous products were transported. Some of these, such as gold and silver and many other varieties of non-perishable merchandise were relatively easy to move, but the appropriation of living plants and animals required sophisticated techniques of representation and a great deal of work and organization. With some exceptions, plants and animals did not survive the passage or failed to adapt easily to European climates, so the process by which they were dominated had to be virtual. That is, Europe proclaimed its dominion over the vastness of nature through texts and images. Detailed descriptions that make use of domestic references, the employment of names drawn from the Christian tradition or other references familiar to Europeans and the elaboration of images were the principal strategies employed to incorporate wild and distant lands into a Christian order. Success in these forms of distance control required the creation of strong links, whose solidity depended on the degree of credibility and fidelity of the representations. A new code of legitimacy and truth was required, a point that returns us to the earlier assertion that the problem of domination is in many ways an epistemological one.

The information derived from sailors and explorers had to be systematized. Common rules therefore had to be devised to ensure that their experiences and observations could be compiled reliably. Essential projects for the Empire such as mapmaking would have been impossible without some way of normalizing experience; a mass of explorers and sailors with individual experiences and without stable codes for observation was useless to the imperial machine. For such a task of gathering, accumulating and organizing information to succeed many people had to be trained and employed in the powerful institutions of the empire.[41] Yet the requirement of complex technological products such as ships, navigation manuals, weapons and observation instruments were no less important. Particular human testimonies alone are not sufficiently reliable and steady to transmit accurate information, and they require new codes, disciplined observers and in the case of cartography a set of calibrated instruments to dissolve the local and the circumstantial. Such depersonalization not only eliminates the arbitrariness of sensation but also forges a homogenous discourse that makes it possible to compare and categorize experiences accumulated in different places and by different people. This entails the use of equivalent instruments as much as disciplined observers working under common rules.[42]

This was one of the main duties of the *Casa de Contratación* in Seville, which was gradually transformed into a center for data collection and for training sailors and cartographers, becoming the fulcrum of intense scientific debates and technological challenges.[43] The accumulation of such practices enabled safer navigation and more efficient commerce and also initiated an enormous scientific project that was to transform the *terra incognita* into *Spanish America*.

What is novel, unusual and interesting about the Spanish treatises on navigation, cosmography and natural history, and about the use made by them of classical traditions, is their dedication to resolving the practical problems associated with imperial expansion. The detailed registration of data, based on reliable information about the observed facts is not so very different from the tasks performed by a royal servant trained to record events or transactions in suitable legalese. Indeed the language employed when gathering scientific data bore important

---

[41] Barrera, 2010.
[42] Bourguet, Liccope and Sibum, eds., 2002.
[43] Barrera, 2010.

similarities to the legal rhetoric employed to register evidence,[44] was in harmony with the mission of the imperial emissaries and was shared across the fields of law, commerce, geography, medicine and natural history. That is to say that the history of the regulation of colonial rule is indissolubly intertwined with the history of science.

The *Casa de Contratación* was to be, rather than a warehouse, a center for compiling and accumulating information. Maintaining a "register" is an act of writing, it is the production of texts, lists, tables, maps or chronicles. It is apparent that serious efforts were made to formalize writing practices and to standardize visual representations of the world. The *Casa de Contratación* was, therefore, a place for the normalization and institutionalization of knowledge and practical techniques, articulated with the political interests of the Crown and of the merchant class.[45]

Thus, the *Casa de Contratación* emerges as a "Center of Calculation"[46], which not only required the acquisition and construction of artefacts but also the formalization of technical professions required to guarantee that trade and imperial expansion were well administered and efficient.

Clearly, then, matters related to bureaucracy, trade, navigation, the law, cartography and natural and moral history should be understood as elements of a single political, scientific and religious enterprise. The Imperial Catholic State was a scientific and technical organization, and science and technology were government responsibilities offered up to the service of God and the King.

There is a close relationship between religious and imperial expansion and the development of a science with equally global ambitions. The Spanish cosmographers and naturalists of the 16th century had a practical bent and their work was clearly intended to serve the Hapsburg Crown whose legitimacy, it should be remembered, was based on religion.

Imperial control may be reduced to the fundamental problem of how to mobilize people, goods and information. To ensure this task

---

[44] De Asúa and French, op. cit., p. 72.
[45] Barrera, 2010, op. cit. op. cit., p. 48.
[46] The notion of the Center of Calculation was introduced into the sociology of science by Bruno Latour, in reference to the sites or places where information is accumulated and knowledge is produced. See Latour, 1992.

of mobilizing, accumulating and organizing information was successful it was necessary to train many people in a wide range of roles and professions and to set them to work within powerful institutions. But in addition—and of no less importance—many, complex, products of technology such as ships, navigation manuals, firearms and observational instruments were also required. Human testimony on its own did not prove as reliable as human testimony produced with the aid of calibrated instruments, which did away with all that is local and circumstantial.

Standardization, it should be remembered, is central for any attempt to produce reliable knowledge. A piece of data or a measurement may be considered precise in as much as they are useful to others. Stable and universally accepted units of measurement are fundamental characteristics of contemporary science. This was one of the central problems facing shipbuilders and cartographers, complicating the measurement of geographical location on the high seas and the task of merchants and of the bureaucrats who were responsible for commercial oversight. Only in as far as there exists a science with global parameters is it possible to proclaim universality in the field of knowledge.

The origins of the mathematical view of the world, generally attributed to mechanical philosophy and thinkers like René Descartes, in fact lay in large part in the demands for control and order made by imperial administrators. In his study of the role of world trade in the 16th and 17th centuries, Harold J. Cook argues that the minute description of natural and medicinal products, the gathering of facts and the ordering of information concerning the natural world, alongside the accumulation and exchange of products from remote places, required robust networks and practices that turned out to be central to the consolidation of a new science. The economic transformations of the first era of world trade relied fundamentally on the careful accumulation of information, a process that shaped the ways in which the natural world was perceived.[47]

Thus, the two pillars of what has traditionally been known as modern science—empiricism, knowledge based on direct experience and the mathematical picture of the world—are present

---

[47] Cook, op. cit., pp. 3–4.

in the Iberian project to exercise imperial control over the New World.

## 5. Modern Science and Europe's self image

Up to this point, strong evidence has been provided that early antecedents of what is usually considered modern science were present in the Iberian Atlantic in the first half of the 16th century. It was clear that the main paradigms of antiquity, and classical notions concerning geography, natural history, and the patterns of world demography fell short when faced with the New World. However, explaining the significance of such process by referring to an "early scientific revolution"[48] or recognizing in it the "Iberian roots of the Scientific Revolution"[49] is also problematic.

The point argued is rather different: that European expansion was inseparable from the construction of science as we understand it and that the practices involved in the conquest of the world (the capacity to control processes at great distances) were at the same time central to the construction of a new kind of knowledge whose practice brought with it claims to global legitimacy.

It is no coincidence that Francis Bacon chose as the Frontispiece to the Great Instauration (preface to his *Novum Organum* of 1620) the picture of a ship passing through the Pillars of Hercules and that it should have borne the inscription: "Many will travel and knowledge will increase". As Bacon put it: "Nor should we ignore the fact that the distant voyages and overland travels which have become frequent in our day have opened up and revealed to us many things in nature which can throw new light on philosophy."[50]

---

[48] Barrera, 2010.
[49] Cañizares-Esguerra, 2006.
[50] Bacon, *Novum Organum*, quoted by Vogel, p. 839.

# Chapter 6: The European Comprehension of the World 133

**Image 4.** The frontispiece to Sir Francis Bacon's *Instauratio magna* (*Great Instauration*) of 1620 depicts a ship sailing through two classical columns into an open sea; it symbolizes moving beyond the limits of classical scholarship into a realm of potential unlimited natural knowledge.

The "discovery" of the New World and setting sail beyond the Pillars of Hercules symbolize the triumph of exploration and experience over ancient authority. This idea—of going beyond the limits imposed by the Ancients—was not limited to geographical exploration. It was a potent idea that defined the very character of modern philosophy and science, as an expression of human emancipation, which itself represented the confidence that it was possible to understand and control the whole of nature. The "Pillars of Hercules" do not exist only astride the Strait of Gibraltar but represent the boundaries of knowledge and of the arts and, in sum, the limits of human power over nature. In a classic study of Renaissance science W.P.D. Wightman suggest that if there is one defining characteristic of science in the period it is the changing conception of the relation between humanity and the cosmos.[51] Throughout, he provides startling examples drawn from art, magic and science in which a single guiding principle emerges: that "men can do all things if they will."[52]

For the Christians of the 16th century human emancipation had its limits, since it would always be subject to Divine Power and Wisdom. Though human pride is referred to in several places in the Bible as a sin, the very possibility of understanding the order of creation and the right to dominate nature have a theological justification. López de Gómara explains this with great clarity in the first paragraph of his *Historia General de las Indias*:

> The world is so large and beautiful, and has such a diversity of things in it that differ one from another, that it inspires admiration in those who contemplate and think about it. There are few men, unless they live like brutish animals, who have not at some point taken time to consider its marvels, because the desire to know is natural to everyone [...][53]

Quoting the words of King Solomon, López de Gómara goes on to remind us:

> [...] God created the world to serve man and He gave it to him in his power, and He placed it beneath his feet and, as Esdras says, those who inhabit the earth can understand what is in it; thus did God place the earth at our disposal and He made us capable and worthy of understanding it, and He gave us the voluntary and natural inclination of knowing; let us not lose our privileges and mercies.[54]

This view remained powerful throughout the Renaissance: the hermetic tradition, magic, art and science operated according to a central assumption—that it was possible to know the world because it obeyed the rules of a rational Creation. In this sense, God could

---

[51] Wightman, William P.D.,1962. "If there is any characteristic by which the Renaissance can be recognized it is (...) in the changing conception of Man's relation to the cosmos." p. 16.
[52] ibid, p. 18. Wightman recalls these words of Leon Battista Alberti.
[53] López de Gómara, op. cit.,"Primera parte de la Historia General de las Indias". p. 7.
[54] loc. cit.

Chapter 6: The European Comprehension of the World    135

be praised and understood through His word but also through His works.⁵⁵

A powerful image of Europe's self-perception in the early modern period was the series of engravings by Stradanus, known as Nova Reperta, which illustrate how 16th century Europeans considered themselves superior to the rest of the world. Major inventions of other cultures, such as printing, the use of the compass, artillery and the art of navigation and the discovery of America, were presented as European achievements.

**Image 5.** Stradanus (Jan van der Straet) Nova Reperta (New inventions and discoveries of modern times) c. 1599-1603.

---

55   On the hermetic tradition in the Renaissance, see Yates, Frances A., 1964.

**Image 6**. Stradanus (Jan van der Straet) Nova Reperta. The discovery of America

The image used by Stradanus to represent America is a patent image of European self-perception. Amerigo Vespucci, who gave his name to the New World, holds in his right hand a Christian crux and in his left an astrolabe, symbols of the true religion and of science and technology. Behind this properly dressed man lies a powerful sailing ship and the general tenor of the scene is celebratory of the European feat of long distance travel and discovery. America, by contrast, is represented by a passive, naked, woman resting and waiting in a hammock. The scene in the background shows an act of cannibalism and the whole picture is a contraposition of civilized and savage worlds.

Europeans viewed themselves as new men in command of nature, and of the world. At the end of the 15th century and during the early decades of the 16th, Iberian seamen circumnavigated Africa, discovered numerous islands in the Atlantic and the Pacific Oceans and a new and gigantic continent, navigated around the earth and encountered many unknown peoples, plants and animals; all of this in the name of God.

This constituted a major change in what Ancient and Medieval Europeans had held as certain, and the emergence of a new geography, a new cosmology and a new world order in which Christian Europeans presented themselves as legitimate rulers of the whole earth. Thus Christian Europeans had the right to conquer and the duty to enlighten and civilize the rest of the world.

This *New Order* that comprehends and creates associations between the familiar and the new was born of an expansive dogmatic culture that was defined by its determination and its success at domesticating the rest of the planet. If we take up again the idea that Eurocentrism involved the incorporation of the unknown into familiar frames of reference,[56] then the idea of *comprehension* allows us to understand the ways in which cartography and natural history contributed to the consolidation of Europe as the center of the modern world.

# References

De Asúa, M. & French, R. (2005). *A new world of animals: Early Modern Europeans On The Creatures Of Iberian America*. USA: Ashgate Pub Co.

Barrera, A. (2010). *Experiencing Nature: The Spanish American Empire and the Early Scientific Revolution*. USA: University of Texas Press.

Basalla, G. (1967). 'The Spread of Western Science.' *Science, 156 (3775),* 611–622.

Bourguet Marie, C. L. & Sibum, H. O. (eds). (2002). *Instruments, Travel and Science. Itineraries of Precision from the Seventeenth to the Twentieth Century*. London: Routledge.

Braudel, F. (1997). *El Mediterráneo y el mundo mediterráneo en la época de Felipe II*. México: Fondo de Cultura Económica.

Burtt, E. A. (1932). *The metaphysical Foundations of Modern Science*. USA: The University Chicago Press.

Butterfield, H. (1957). *The Origins of Modern Science*. London: G. Bell.

Callon, M. (1986). Some elements of a sociology of translation: domestication of the scallops and fishermen of St Brieuc Bay. In John Law (ed) *Power, Action and Belief: A New Sociology of Knowledge?* London: Routledge and Kegan Paul.

Cañizares-Esguerra, J. (2006). *Nature, Empire and Nation: Explorations of the History of Science in the Iberian World*. Carolina: Stanford University Press.

Cohen, I. B. (1985). *The Birth of a New Physics*. New York & London: W.W. Nortor & Company.

---

[56] Dirlik, 2002.

Cook, H. J. (2007). *Matters of Exchange: Commerce, Medicine, and Science in the Dutch Golden Age*. New Haven & London: Yale University Press.

Dackerman, S., Swan, C. & Karr Schmidt, S. (eds.) (2011). *Prints and the Pursuit of Knowledge in Early Modern Europe*. New Haven: Yale University Press.

De Sahagún, B. (2005). *Fauna de Nueva España*. México: Fondo de Cultura Económica.

Debus, A. G. (1972). *Science Medicine and Society in the Renaissance*. New York: Science History Publications.

De Greiff, A. & Nieto, M. (2006). What we still do not know about South-North technoscientific exchange: North-centrism, scientific difusion, and the social studies of Science. In Ronald E. Doel & Thomas Söderqvist (eds.) *The Historiography of Contemporary Science, Technology, and Medicine. Writing recent science*. London : Routledge.

Dijterhuis, E.J. (1950). *The Mechanization of the World Picture: Pythagoras to Newton*. New York: Oxford University Press.

Dirlik, A. (2002). History without a center? In: *Fuchs and Stuchtey (eds.) Across cultural borders. Historiography in Global Perspective*. USA: Rowman and Littlefield Publishers, Inc.

Dussel, E. (2000). Europa, modernidad y eurocentrismo. In Edgardo Lander (ed.) *La colonialidad del saber: eurocentrismo y ciencias sociales. Perspectivas latinoamericanas*. Buenos Aires: CLACSO.

Eisenstein, E. (1983). *The Printing Revolution in Early Modern Europe*. Cambridge & New York: Cambridge University Press.

Fernández de Oviedo, G. (1852). *Historia general y natural de las Indias, islas y tierra-firme del mar océano. Tomo primero de la segunda parte, segundo de la obra / por el Capitán Gonzalo Fernández de Oviedo y Valdés; publicala la Real Academia de la Historia; cotejada... enriquecida... por José Amador de los Ríos*. Madrid: Imprenta de la Real Academia de Historia.

Findlen, P. (2002). Inventing Nature. Commerce, Art, and Science in the Early Modern Cabinet of Curiosities.' In P. Smith & P. Findlen (eds.) *Merchants and Marvels: Commerce, Science and Art in Early Modern Europe*. New York and London: Routledge.

Gadamer, Hans-Georg, (1992). *Verdad y método*, Ediciones Sígueme, S.A., Salamanca.

Hall, A. R. (1962). *The Scientific Revolution, 1500-1800. The Formation of the Modern Scientific Attitude*. London: Longmans.

Harley, J. B. (2005). *La nueva naturaleza de los mapas. Ensayos sobre la historia de la cartografía*. México: Fondo de Cultura Económica.

Headrick, D. (2012). *Power over Peoples: Technologiy, Environments and Western Imperialism. 1400 to the present*. Princeton University Press.

Heidegger, M. (1983). *El ser y el tiempo*. Fondo de Cultura Económica,

Hobson, J. (2004). *The Eastern Origins of Western Civilisation.* Cambridge & New York: Cambridge University Press.

Johns, A. (2000). *The Nature of the Book: Print and Knowledge in the Making.* Chicago: University Of Chicago Press.

Koestler, A. (1959). *The Sleepwakers.* New York: Macmillan.

Koyré, A. (1961). *La révolution astronomique: Copernic, Kepler, Borelli.* Paris: Hermann.

Kuhn, T. S. (1957). *The Copernican Revolution.* New York: Vintage Books.

Lafuente, A., Elena, A. & Ortega, M. (eds.) (1993). Mundialización de la Ciencia y la Cultura Nacional. Madrid: Doce Calles.

Latour, B. (1992). Ciencia en Acción: cómo seguir a los científicos e ingenieros a través of the sociedad. Barcelona: Editorial Labor.

Latour, B. (1990). Drawing Things Together. In M. Lynch & S. Woolgar (eds.) *Representation in Scientific Practice.* Cambridge: The MIT Press.

López de Gómara, F. (1552). Historia General de las Indias, Barcelona, Iberia 1965.

Macleod, R. (1987). On Visiting the Moving Metropolis: Reflections on the Architecture of Imperial Science. In N. Reingold & M. Rothemberg (eds.) *Scientific Colonialism: a Cross-Cultural Comparison.* Washington: Smithsonian Institution Press.

Mundy, B. (1996). *The Mapping of New Spain: Indigenous Cartography and the Maps of the Relaciones Geográficas.* Chicago: The University of Chicago Press.

Nieto, M. (2000). *Remedios para el Imperio: Historia Natural y la Apropiación del Nuevo Mundo.* Bogotá: ICANH.

Olby, R.C., Cantor, G. N., Christie, J. R. R. & Hodge, M. J. S. (eds.) (1990). *Companion to the History of Modern Science (Routledge Companion Encyclopedias).* London: Routledge.

Sloterdijk, P. (2009). *God's Zeal: The Battle of the Three Monotheisms.* Cambridge: Polity Press.

Porter, R. & Teich, M. (1992). *The Scientific Revolution in National Context.* Cambridge: Cambridge University Press.

Rabasa, J. (1993). *Inventing America.* USA: University of Oklahoma Press.

Raj, K. (2007). *Relocating Modern Science: Circulation and the Construction of Knowledge in South Asia and Europe, 1650-1900.* Hampshire & New York: Palgrave Macmillan.

S. Irfan Habib, Raina, D. & Baber, Z. (2007). *Social History of Science in Colonial India, Oxford in India Readings. Themes in Indian History.* New Delhi: Oxford University Press.

Shapin, S. (1996). *The Scientific Revolution.* Chicago: University of Chicago Press.

Smith, P. & Findlen, P. (eds.) (2002). *Merchants and Marvels: Commerce, Science and Art in Early Modern Europe.* New York and London: Routledge.

Vogel, K. A. (2006). European Expansion and Self-Definition. In K. Park and L.Daston. *The Cambridge History of Sciene. Early Modern Science*. England: Cambridge University Press.

Webster, C. (1982). *From Paracelsus to Newton: Magic and the Making of Modern Science*. Cambridge: Cambridge University Press.

Westfall, R. S. (1977). *The Construction of Modern Science: Mechanisms and Mechanics (Cambridge Studies in the History of Science)*. Cambridge: Cambridge University Press.

Wightman, W. P.D. (1962). *Science and the Renaissance*, 2 Vol. Edinburgh : Oliver and Boyd, New York: Hafner Pub. Co.

Yates, F. A. (1964) *Giordano Bruno and the Hermetic Tradition*. Chicago: The University of Chicago Press.

# Chapter 7:
# Institutional Re-structuring in the Social Science World: Seeds of Change

Hebe Vessuri and Carmen Bueno

## Introduction

In this paper we engage with the dominant debates about globalization of the social sciences exploring novel aspects in institutional infrastructure, and develop an account that is sensitive to changing historical forms. We take globalization as those processes of change, "which underpin a transformation in the organization of human affairs by linking together and expanding human activity across regions and continents" (Held et al., 1999, 67). Universality, when seen as synonym of globality, is often associated to homogenization and identified with Western-Northern imposed forms of thought. The set of norms, values and practices that characterizes the social sciences, while deemed to be universally valid and applicable in different contexts, faces a growing clamor for recognition from other knowledge forms under the charge that the supposedly general theory largely neglects or distorts the experience of the majority of mankind living in places distant from the centres as well as the theory production in those spaces. Variegated manifestations of social reality in different parts of the world, either unthinkingly or consciously, have often been subsumed under unwarranted knowledge claims produced in the West-North.

Our argument, to anticipate, is fivefold:

First, despite the long history of several national social science communities, inter and intra-regional inequalities persist, and invisibility and marginality of knowledge production in the south continues to be accepted as a fact of life. Clearly dominant cultural flows and institutions have deep historical roots and are closely entwined with the resulting social science production. In time, however, with different aims, regional and transnational associations were created, as part of the dreams of alliances and collaboration across national boundaries. Some of them endure and have acquired momentum, representing a vivid expression of today's fashionable transnational networks.

Second, the massification of higher education, that is to say, the huge growth in the number of people that independently of age group get access to higher education institutions has ultimately affected the identity of universities. For a long time the key educational institution for science production and reproduction and for educating the elites, more recently the university has been forced to compete with other institutions and social agents more aligned with corporate cultures and policy-making. The new "market" setting constitutes a renovated milieu for social science production. What the identity of universities will be in the future is difficult to predict.

Third, new initiatives and trajectories have emerged that have started to reconfigure the topography of knowledge production and diffusion. A series of technological and institutional novelties are once again altering the balance. New technologies and telecommunications, among other factors, generate global cultural flows whose stretch, intensity, diversity and rapid diffusion exceed those of earlier eras. Accordingly, the centrality of national cultures, national identity and their institutions is being challenged.

Fourth, original aspects in organizational infrastructure pave the way for an unprecedented transformation in the governance of knowledge production and diffusion of the social sciences. International agendas, "politics" in scientific organizations, tailored research for public policy, funding priorities and other channels of knowledge production are immersed in contradictory forces that challenge the purposes and aspiration of national academic systems and national social science traditions. Although these were never self contained universes but were always embedded in transnational relations of various kinds, today's interdependencies and new developments on a more global scale are also affecting the understanding of the social sciences and their contributions worldwide.

Fifth, given the dominant "inevitabilist" discourse, developing and emergent countries face new and difficult challenges to generate and use new knowledge, even social knowledge according to social or economic goals defined with varying forms of autonomy. We perceive a growing willingness for new discourses aiming to break with the stratified power structures that have prefigured the dichotomies between North-South, core-periphery, East-West. Signs of this is the involvement of scientific communities arising from the margins with different modalities of operation, such as open access to knowledge production, and forms of virtual collaboration. All the above might result in a richer and diversified social science world system. So far, however, the asymmetric geography of knowledge seems to persist, although some of the players have altered their strength.

These five arguments move us to explore the impact of contemporary sociocultural globalization that undoubtedly is transforming the contexts in which and the means through which social sciences produce knowledge and are legitimated.

## Local/National Underpinnings of Transnational Regional Integration of the Social Sciences

Within the United Nations System that emerged after the second World War, the idea of international and regional organizations for the natural and the social sciences acquired renewed impetus. At the first World Congress of Sociology in September 1950, an independent resolution was passed urging the development of the International Council for Social Research. The 6th General Conference of UNESCO followed this up by passing the resolution which formally led to the founding of the ISSC, authorising the Director General to establish an International Social Science Research Council and an International Social Science Research Centre for the study of the implications of technological change, as well as to survey existing social-science research institutes "with a view to the subsequent examination of the contribution these institutions might make to the scientific solution of the most important problems of the present age and for the purpose of aiding their development and cooperation" (Platt, 1998). So it was clear from the start that the motive for interest in the social sciences was the expectation that they would contribute directly to solving social problems in the world that emerged from the ashes of the Second World War and the end of colonialism.

In 1954, the ISSC in cooperation with UNESCO's Social Science Department (SSD) held a meeting of Representatives of National Science Councils and Similar Bodies. This meeting facilitated the exchange of ideas and experiences between various country-based social science councils. Similar meetings were organized in 1965 and in the early 1970s. To this day, little has changed in organizational terms. The ISSC still works with the mission of advancing the social sciences for solving global problems. International organizations, with an increasingly large constituency of countries and individual members, added to more dense transnational connections, "while simultaneously contributing to the formation of an international disciplinary canon and an international hierarchy, dominated by scholars and scholarship from the U.S." (Heilbron, 2014: 690). Their explicit aim is to combat the fragmentation of knowledge production, to disseminate knowledge more effectively, discuss specificities in development processes strengthening the institutional bases, cooperation and collaboration.[1] Nevertheless, actual collaboration across national borders remained infrequent. International organizations were more important for diffusion of information from the centre to the peripheries and for intellectual diplomacy than in effective transnational collaboration. Gigantic disparities persisted in research capacities in social science communities, not only the historical difference between the north Atlantic basin and the rest of the world, but also among peripheral spaces. For decades transregional associations have tried to attenuate these gaps.

In 1973, the ISSC established a Standing Committee for Cooperation with National Councils (SCCNC) to sustain its international efforts, which was the origin of the International Federation of Social Science Organizations (IFFSO). IFFSO's membership then consisted of national and regional bodies and later on this was expanded to include academies. The case of the

---

[1] In 2002, for example, The International Council for Science (ICSU) decided to establish four Regional Offices for Developing Countries to replace the ICSU Committee on Science and Technology for Developing Countries (COSTED).

social sciences in Europe has been described as representing "the most advanced case of transnational regionalization" (Heilbron, 2014:693). Since the 1980s a systematic European science policy came into being, and the several 'Framework Programmes' served to further stimulate transnational collaboration, serving as models for research funding in other regions. For some disciplines, the persistence of national structures in the largest European countries, frequently translates in situations in which they have a larger membership than the European association, evidence that the European space is still relatively weak. In other parts of the world there was a conscious push to promote transnational regional structures, as part of the spread of the social sciences beyond the west, accompanying development programs and attempts at modernization. A Pan-African research organization titled Council for the Development of Social Science Research in Africa (CODESRIA) where five regions of Africa are represented appeared on 1973. Later on, another association in this same region emerged, the Organization for Social Science Research in Eastern and Southern Africa (OSSREA). In 2010 the Arab Council for Social Sciences (ACSS) was founded, having its central office in Lebanon. All these associations have in common that they have strong ties with UNESCO through the ISSC.

Despite the general lack of strength of most such experiences, it seems worthwhile to elaborate a little on one of them, the Consejo Latinoamericano de Ciencias Sociales (CLACSO), created in 1967. It currenty gathers more than 300 research centres and graduate programs (Masters and Doctoral ones) in several fields of the Social Sciences and Humanities, located in 25 countries of Latin America and the Caribbean, in the US and Europe. Its headquarters are in Buenos Aires, Argentina. From a cursory review of the activities of transnational regional associations, CLACSO offers a model allowing to think of it as a "seed of change" because compared to other regional associations, it has diversified its activities, having a deliberative inclusion policy, sharing resources with universities located in marginal areas, using technological platforms to offer open access to scientific knowledge, promoting online courses, and providing information about scholarships and graduate programs. It also has a virtual library where not only academics may consult publications produced in other countries but also gives the possibility to widen the visibility of what is produced in the region. Despite the leadership of Argentina, Colombia, Mexico, and Brazil among the 371 member centres, CLACSO has aimed at having a truly regional coverage, seeking to close the gap between countries with special initiatives geared to the poorest ones in the region.

Its dynamic expansion and diversification of activities is supported by an informational technological platform, that none of the other above-mentioned regional associations has. CLACSO includes 25 thematic working groups, mostly oriented to issues "in vogue" in the region: social conflicts, social movements, citizenship, climate change, decolonization, feminism, education, pro-poor public policy, security, violence, none of them related to discussions around grand-theory. CLACSO also organizes virtual seminars and online graduate courses that include topics related to south-south relations with Africa or South-East Asia. Its open source virtual Social Science library provides more than a million requests and downloads per month. Through agreements with different governments and other donors it grants scholarships to graduate students and promotes mobility in the region.

After more than fifty years of existence CLACSO is a clear expression of a transnationally organized social and cultural network emerged alongside the reorganization of global science, accompanying the changes of finance and production. This transnational network is also a kind of "globalization from below", with its emphasis more on challenge than adaptation. It is an effort to build different understandings, through the formation of transnational working groups and networks. But it is good to remember that the persistence of local organizing after the groups had been formed was essential to achieving its goals. Acting regionally/globally enables local organizing that would otherwise be impossible; but it does not replace local organizing. Transnational groups and networks are not a substitute for local action, but a catalyst that enables local efforts to become more efficacious. This is a case showing that building transnational networks may give local organizing new prospects of success, and local mobilization is an essential element changing the balance of myriad local initiatives but also in facilitating more progressive institutional arrangements and accomplishments.

## Institutional Re-structuring in Cultural Globalization

It has been argued that the university is the best institution for the production of universal knowledge. However, when one gets down to concrete reality one observes people and perspectives whose absence has made the university's claim to universality a mere illusion. In Fuller's words "the result [...] is a form of knowledge – the concrete universal- that is rather different from what both the original ideologues and the newly included others had envisaged" (Fuller, 2003). Today the university's institutional integrity is at risk as it is competing on a levelled playing field with other institutions that attempt to fulfil only one or another of the university's many traditional functions, such as science parks (for research) and online degree courses (for teaching) and when the attack of corporate culture on the university seems unstoppable. When teaching is being reduced to the dispensation of credentials while research is being privatized as intellectual property, one can envisage the end of the university as we know it, for it is being pulled apart by alternative pursuits, which effectively disaggregate teaching from the research function and redefine both. What will follow from the present predicament, whether the university will be reborn from its contemporary ashes as an institution explicitly focused on second-order issues, and what shape it will assume, cannot be predicted today. Nevertheless we can foresee that knowledge production and diffusion are shaping a new socio-spatial canvas. Mass higher education has become a core element of national education systems. Universities and other higher education institutions and research centers are immersed in organizational restructuring and new systemic arrangements, breaking down boundaries and enhancing collaboration. There is a proliferation and diversification of traditional ritual (congresses, workshops, colloquia) all over the academic world, geared towards the building of supra-national networked scientific communities. Most of the time, this academic ritual complies with the agendas of private and public funding organizations for global scientific research or the strategic global plans of powerful National Science Councils.

In the past decade global rankings have transformed research universities into a single world market. The big game changers, emptying out the political economy of higher education, come from outside academia or from non-traditional initiatives in the academic milieu, like Moocs (Massive Open Online Courses). According to *The New York Times*, 2012 became "the year of the MOOC" as several well-financed providers, associated with top universities, emerged, including Coursera, Udacity, and edX. The larger non-profit organizations include the Bill & Melinda Gates Foundation, the MacArthur Foundation, the National Science Foundation and the American Council on Education. University pioneers include Stanford, Harvard, MIT, the University of Pennsylvania, CalTech, University of Texas at Austin, the University of California at Berkeley, San Jose State University, and the Indian Institute of Technology, Bombay IIT Bombay. This might be the point at which mass higher education slips off the leash. Some would say this is a good thing, while many others are less enthusiastic about it. Powerful emerging movements like MOOC come to strengthen the currently dominant academic culture, perhaps making it more difficult for alternative voices to be heard:

> A combination of powerful academic cultures, the location of the main creators and disseminators of MOOCs, and the orientation of most of those creating and teaching MOOCs ensures the domination of the largely English-speaking academic systems. The millions of students choosing to participate in MOOCs from all over the world do not seem to be concerned about the nature of the knowledge or the philosophy of pedagogy that they are studying. Universities in the middle-income and developing world do not seem concerned about the origins or orientations of the knowledge provided by the MOOCs or the educational philosophies behind MOOC pedagogy. (Altbach, 2014)

Universities still have the control of traditional tracks of knowledge production despite the challenges from more flexible knowledge production and reproduction spaces of multiple organizational infrastructures both institutionalized and non-institutionalized in a "market" that demands urgent and practical problem-solving abilities. However, a myriad grassroots' initiatives look in different directions toward multiple local realities that go by other rules. Most often they operate outside academia, and are rarely legitimized in university settings. This alternative knowledge production spaces are rapidly expanding, and increasing numbers of researchers with or without institutional affiliation support expertise production and perform as independent agents.

The American educational landscape is no less subject to deep changes. The "Ivy Plus" (the members of the Ivy League plus Stanford University and Massachussetts Institute of Technology) have long flourished as elite institutions, both socially and academically. Increasingly, though, their predominance is defined by the great magnitude of their wealth relative to their modest size and to the rest of the higher-education universe (Bianco, 2007). This reflects the contemporary American tendency of the rich to get much richer. Will this trend lead to scientific breakthroughs that otherwise would not have been possible? Or will it mainly serve to accelerate the deterioration of many other schools that have a vital role to play in training the next generation? The author of the note says that the infusion of riches at the Ivy Plus schools has dramatically extended their lead over everyone else, especially the public colleges and universities that collectively serve the vast majority of American students. This dominance-and the inequalities it fosters- are likely only to grow.

## Continuities and Changes in the Topography of Knowledge Production and Dissemination

Networking has become a big issue in current academic life. Not that this is a new phenomenon. Among its earliest precedents is the notion of 'invisible college' related to the precursor group of the Royal Society in the 17$^{th}$ century (Westfall, 1971). In modern times, this idea has been extended from Diana Crane's study of networks of collaborating scientists through co-citations, which in turned was based on Derek de Solla Price's work on citation networks, to the global network of communications of Caroline Wagner's *The New Invisible College: Science for Development* (2008). Other related concepts are that of 'epistemic communities' (Haas, 1992), 'community of practice' (Wenger, 1998), 'knowledge as a commons' (Hess & Ostrom, 2006), 'open collaborative science' (Chan & Okune, 2014). The idea of worldwide scientific networking today emphasizes the expansion of talents in the pool of scientific knowledge, among other things as a result of more students from the peripheries getting scholarships to study abroad and also the more frequent circulation and inter-national interaction of larger numbers of scholars.

In the first global century (1820–1913) migration flows were intense in the world, particularly in the Atlantic basin. After an interwar backlash, globalization was resumed after World War II, although migrations were less impressive than in the previous period, while commodity trade intensified (Williamson, 2002). Whereas the 'brain drain' was originally a concept addressed to migration from Europe (specifically the United Kingdom) to North America in the 1960s, it has been used more frequently to describe the net loss of highly skilled labor from developing countries (Collier, et al, 2004). In sending countries of the developing world, the problems caused by brain drain have been great in connection with migrants who are generally more likely to stay in the host country than migrants from advanced countries.[2]

More recently, other approaches have given a more positive meaning to the international circulation of the highly skilled, even in connection to developing countries. The *2010 World Social Science Report* argues that the mobility of scholars stimulates strong network relations between north and south. It states that mobility has had a positive impact because scholars that do not return to their countries keep nonetheless strong ties with universities in their place of origin, turning into brokers and strengthening long-distance collaboration. Information and resources flowing through these networks are said to allow an upgrade in material and social infrastructure in the periphery. However, countries, regions, cities, universities, research centers and firms worldwide are today competing to maintain their attraction for highly skilled personnel in the various professional areas, and the expression of brain drain fear is no longer confined to developing countries.[3]

New forms of networking mediated by information technologies are reconfiguring knowledge production hotspots impacting

---

[2] Survey evidence on the share of foreign PhD graduates in science and technology who stayed abroad show that 79% of 1990–91 doctoral recipients from India and 88% of those from China were still working in the United States in 1995. In contrast, only 11% of Koreans and 15% of Japanese who earned science and engineering (S&E) doctorates from US universities in 1990–91 were working in the United States in 1995. Cervantes and Guellec, 2002.

[3] For an illuminating analysis of the international migration of human capital on the verge of the century, see Mahroum, 1999.

diverse knowledge flows.[4] The latter constitute the material and intellectual infrastructure that most affects knowledge production and knowledge consumption in the 21st century. In Appadurai's (2001) terms, in this new "academic technoscape", self-contained institutions that used to be centered in their own faculties, even isolated from the rest of society, have a chance to redefine their every-day activities and transform themselves into open organizations where knowledge resources of different kinds flow, overcoming geographic barriers. The use of different devices and applications (internet, skype, data bases, dropbox, @cloud) expand rapidly, becoming a key component in everyday routines of academic life. Access to these informational devices can be considered a seed of change as they contribute to facilitate virtual connectivity. Besides, knowledge production spaces (institutionalized and non-institutionalized) broaden their social capital and access to international scientific production in a more open and practical way. No doubt, there are material infrastructural disparities and regulations that explain variable accessibility, but scholars who work in marginal places state that information technology is having an interesting impact on the dynamics of their work and stimulates cross-national collaboration.

Collective initiatives and a multiplicity of open access databases[5] are the offspring of the era of information technology. They encourage intensive communication and diffusion of knowledge, and tear down obstacles and construct bridges. "*Knowmads*," for example, circulate simultaneously between networks and institutions. A new framework with nodes of different sizes, barriers, hatches, also strainers that help or restrain scholars moving along this labyrinth and where research teams form, mutate, dissolve, and reform, is already in place.

---

[4] Changes mentioned above experienced by CLACSO, associated to the modern institutionalization of the social sciences in Latin America illustrate the possibilities of enhanced collaboration and growth of scientific capacity for academic communities wherever there is access to virtual technologies

[5] *Knowmads* is an internet platform connecting students, partners, staff, advisory board and a wide network of professional and volunteer experts/contributors who share talents, creative ideas and inspiration trying to initiate positive change. See http://www.knowmads.nl

Almost twenty years ago Appadurai (2001:187) argued that these new forms of communication contributed to change social practices and networking, shaping a new socio-spatial canvas. Space, in his argument, is conceived as relational and contextual, bringing together scholars from diverse backgrounds that comply with institutional norms and regulations and at the same time navigate through self-organizing networks. Twenty-years on, we witness dramatic changes in publishing practices. Transformation of many journals into an electronic format and the development of large databases give way to the open access (OA) to worldwide scientific production. Intellectual and cultural commons are organized around shared intellectual and cultural resources (Nonini, 2008). Since its launch in 2001 Wikipedia is one of the most ambitious attempts of knowledge production in the present time, demonstrating that scientific concepts, theories, methods, data, technologies and research devices can be created and regenerated through social exchange and sociability.

There have been rapid changes in the short evolution of OA journals. Non-hegemonic regions are increasingly turning to large-scale non-commercial OA publishing portals. Latin American journals are using the OA publishing model to a far greater extent than other world regions. The inclusion of regional initiatives such as Scielo and RedALyC in the academic evaluation system of many universities and national R&D systems in the region has helped to give weight to these databases. The region is making a great effort to build the reputation of journals that meet accepted "international" editorial standards and employ open source software solutions, principally Open Journal Systems, to manage their publishing processes online. This arises out of both the sense of public mission among Latin American universities and OA's effectiveness for sharing knowledge, and there is reason to believe that this is contributing to an increased presence and impact of this literature.

These current initiatives speak encouragingly about the region's growing contribution to a global knowledge exchange and the research literature's standing as a public good. Since one of the traditional claims of Latin American researchers has been the need to get greater access and visibility, it was only natural for them to be among the early users of the possibilities opened up by Internet (Vessuri et al. 2014). The result has been that Latin American OA initiatives (even before the movement came into existence) have been common in most research-intensive universities and national science evaluation systems and have begun to alter the way local research is perceived. The percentage shares of OA in all indexed journals for Latin America are clear evidence of how fast already established high quality Latin American journals made their e-versions openly available.[6]

The inclusion of other regions of the global south in this OA system needs social and institutional shifts that encourage better access and visibility in the virtual academic world. Nevertheless, it cannot be ignored that this development is largely a response to the behaviour of international commercial databases that continue to capture only a minimum percentage of the production from developing regions. Looking at South America as a whole, for example, Scopus only has 726 of the journals from the region (15% of the 4,882 listed in the Latindex Catalog (http://www.latindex.unam.mx/latindex/catalogo.html). Commenting on this fact, Alperin, in a recent letter to Nature writes "more than half of South America's research output is hidden from Scopus because it takes place in regional journals that are excluded from the index. It is possible and even likely, that there is an "impact gap", but as long as commercial databases continue to capture such a small percentage of all the output from developing regions like South America, we will not know for sure (Alperin, 2014).

## Transforming the Framework of the Worldwide Governance of the Social Sciences

The overall system is integrated by institutions and networks embedded in multiple scales of governance. Higher education and scientific activities mingle with political interests and financial support. Universities have become political and scientific organizations. The complexity of decision-making systems and the

---

[6] Journals from Latin America are the ones with the fastest growth in DOAJ (Lund's initiative of the Directory of OA Journals, the biggest and most qualitative directory of OA journals). A recent study has shown that of the roughly 15,000 peer-reviewed journals indexed in 2010 in the Scopus database, 74% of OA journals are Latin American, 5% North American and 7% European.

endemic priority of "politics" in scientific organization, means that science is important only when it justifies the course of action that politicians wish to pursue. There is a compromise of social research with vested interests. Politicians react to particular interpretations of reality, dragging out the reports provided by their advisors and brandishing the scientific findings when politically convenient. It can be stated then that knowledge hierarchies are predicated upon hierarchies of social and political power.

The challenge is greatest for countries that started to build their academic institutions and scientific communities during the second half of the 20$^{th}$ century. Academic infrastructure in the non-OECD world has evolved rapidly but it is still in a maturing process. An entanglement of contradictory forces persists due to the emergence of new issues identified with national sovereignty that confront traditional ones, and also owing to the centrality on national interest of some nations in the construction of international development agendas. In the current shift from a relatively nationally centered scientific system to a global one, it often appears as if international organizations, not national authorities, set the rules, while representatives of the most advanced countries continue to exert control of the international organizations and programs. Thus the national and the international or the global are played with new language but maintaining old habits.

The globalization of markets is a strongly promoted idea in the academic domain by the main dominant economic and political agents in the international setting. Multinational agencies and firms proliferate at the present time in the funding of science. The agendas of supra-national organizations, funding institutions and national research councils build and reconfigure boundaries and bridges, impacting the ability of traditional institutions such as universities to cope with programs aimed at a global reach. [7]

---

[7] An interesting example is that of *Future Earth*, sponsored by the members of the Science and Technology Alliance for Global Sustainability, "an informal international partnership that is committed to making full use of science and technology to inform equitable, sustainable solutions to the most pressing issues currently confronting humankind." Its members envision a sustainable world where decision-making is informed by the best available scientific evidence and knowledge. By working together, the Alliance members will fulfil this mission by promoting interdisciplinary research and facilitating

Science is increasingly perceived to be an integral part of the business establishment and the business–oriented state.

We witness the overpowering profit motive of the new knowledge market. The augmented importance of privately funded research targets some social science fields that allow a greater applicability and commercialization. The *World Social Science Report 2010* offers an inkling of just a particular kind of global picture of the strengths and weaknesses of the main disciplines that integrate the social sciences in today's globality, one particular version of the global. Considering publications registered in the Social Science Citation Index (SSCI), Economics and Administration have leading positions after Psychology[8] (Jonkers, 2010). The reason is not unexpected: Economics and Management have a quantitative, pragmatic approach. These two disciplines are leaders in public policy design, instrumentation and evaluations, as well as in prefiguring international standards about productivity. Thus they are more involved in government programs and productivity, being functional to the current setting. On the other hand, Communication Studies and Anthropology have experienced a sustained reduced stand. This may come as a surprise in a world that is so variegated from a cultural and ethnic point of view and where intercultural communication seems so urgent. But it can be explained in view of the pressing homogenising trends.

This type of disciplinary analysis says nothing about a form of intellectual activity that is constantly growing, feeding into and overcoming disciplinary boundaries, and even those of interdisciplinarity and multidisciplinarity. The intensified boundary crossing between disciplines and the entanglement of knowledge traditions characteristic of current research goes a long way to explain transformations in the way of producing knowledge. The changing research landscape promotes knowledge production that attempts to solve real-world problems through "a context specific negotiation of knowledge," very different from the

---

partnerships between the scientific community, political bodies, business sector and civil society." Its members are the International Council for Science (ICSU), the International Social Science Council (ISSC), the Belmont Forum of Funding Agencies, UNESCO, UNEP, UNU and the World Meteorological Organization as an observer.

[8] This is a very large umbrella discipline covering a multiplicity of fields and which may be today considered very close to the natural sciences.

"generalizing, decontextualizing and reductionist" approach that has traditionally characterized disciplinary approaches to knowledge generation. Problem focused, contextualized, and consultative research, with an evolving methodology and active collaboration of stakeholders, which is characteristic of transdisciplinary research, is seen by many knowledge analysts as incompatible with the disciplinary framing of research problems and the institutional structures and processes that support, regulate and promote disciplinarity (Wickson et al., 2006: 1048–1052).

To the extent that the social and natural sciences have an important interface with public policy, their knowledge production does not take place within the frame of classical disciplines nor in their interdisciplinary version. Neither is it the case that the expertise of theoretically mature disciplines is used to solve more practical problems in interdisciplinary collaboration (Böhme and Schäffer, 1983). Transdisciplinary or integrated research is a result of current political, commercial or other type of forces. It emerges from the very practice of science (Fuller, 1993; Huutoniemi et al. 2010; Vessuri, 2014). Researchers embark with genuine scientific interest in transient combinations, for the achievement of scientific aims that are recomposed through time as a function of the changing agendas that society poses to them.

At the core of the academic world, however, there is a lot of resistance to these new formats. Resistance is a principled one (concerns about standards, quality, evaluation, etc.), but it is also inertial, for it is rooted in practice, in the form of the typical disciplinary institutionalization of topics, the control of work posts and of recompense systems. Among the obstacles still faced by the new forms of research that need to be adjusted to the new knowledge regime are key aspects such as the predominant evaluation, recognition and recompense system, but it is most likely that they will be overcome by the sheer numbers of new practitioners and practice forms. Many countries are trying to change the hierarchical structure and give birth to a variegated / diverse academic governance that serves to counterbalance an increasingly disfunctional system.

## Division of Labour in a Sincle Stratified System or Multiple Dialogues in the Social Science World System?

The structuring role of privatization and marketization of research observable in many places, but particularly in American universities since the 1980s has intensified in recent years. This affects not only the conditions of funding of University research but also the production of scientific work in the universities as well as university careers. This may be observed in the process by which managerial fashions today become accepted as scientific theses, in marked contrast with the traditional curves of popularity enjoyed by management technologies until they were dismissed by American academics according to the norm that envisaged its rejection in the short or medium term. The institutionalization of a management technology such as "lean production" since the 1990s is running a very different course, after becoming omnipresent in all factories of world car builders first, then in other industries, in the services, and more recently in administration. University faculty that would have been expected to engage in de-mystifying this managerial fashion as in the past, "have on the contrary enthroned it as a scientific thesis" (Pardi, 2015). Privatization and commercialization of this knowledge production leaned on the side of the promoters of lean production, contributing to marginalise and even neutralize criticism and resistance against the process, be it in the firms, the unions and the universities.

Besides, there are new demands on the social sciences: a compulsory engagement with different social actors; an intensification of regional and international collaboration; attention to novel or previously disregarded problems, increasing access to knowledge of immediate local relevance; empowerment of the population through this knowledge, as well as a reconfiguration of the "geography of knowledge" and the power relations that continue to shape it. The complexity of global phenomena urges a reflexive complementation of multiple interpretations of the social, beyond the simplistic ones derived from the death of positivism.

Some schools of thought in the North Atlantic basin still promote the grand narrative of universalism and homogeneization, with scholars still conceiving of international social science as synonym of North American. General social theory as it exists today produces statements, concepts and notions that disregard particular contexts, ignoring the experience of the majority of mankind, those living in the global south as well as the production of general theories in the south. Southern social reality seems unduly subsumed under / assimilated to the claims produced in the North.

What prevails is a deeply-rooted separation between a North Atlantic- oriented academia concerned with the progress of grand theories aimed at extending the knowledge frontier, and the rest of the world supposed to approach Social Science issues and priorities in a manner more directly attuned with local societal needs. In the recent history of the social sciences in non-OECD countries, however, multiple theories have emerged in response to Euro-centric theories. To mention some of them since the late 1970s, we have Edward Said and his de-construction of Orientalism (1978); Samir Amin's criticism against Euro-centrism (1989), Anibal Quijano's analysis of the coloniality of knowledge and its epistemic hegemony (2001); Walter Mignolo's emphasis on local histories and global designs (2000), Dipesh Chakrabarty (2000) and his "provincializing" Europe to find out how and in what sense European ideas that were universal were also, at one and the same time, drawn from very particular intellectual and historical traditions that could not claim any universal validity; David Turnbull's argument that all cultures have messy, spatial local ways of producing knowledge, including science (2000), Pankaj Mishra's tale of the Asian renaissance from the ruins of empire in the last two centuries (Mishra 2012).

This "non-western" theory production has had some impact in North-South relations. No doubt, the various contributions can be considered inspiring milestones that have stimulated diverse voices in the international scientific scene and have fostered fresh ideas and methods. These theories were born in the margins of knowledge production paving their way against the tide, and contributing to a kind of renaissance of social thought beyond the usual mainstream theoretical consensus. They confirm Archer's argument that "as our subject matter changes because of its human constitution, this needs to be matched by theoretical reformulations which explain these unpredictable re-patternings.

The [social] production of a new variety of theory is always entailed by the social production of new variety in the real world" (1991: 133).

On the other hand, many difficult obstacles still remain. Open access publications that superficially seem to break with the North-South knowledge production dichotomy, often replicate hegemonic-peripheral asymmetric relations. In the Latin America region, there has been a recent explosion of portals. This has produced an illusion among students and many young scholars that their writings are present on the web, regardless of their doubtful quality, although it is likely that nobody will ever consult them. Meanwhile mainstream databases that are highly regarded media of scientific production diffusion, such as the Social Science Citation Index (SSCI), SCOPUS and related indexes have never given equal coverage to disciplines and regions.

These international databases, keen on standardization, dominate the evaluation system cross-nationally and are still the canonical referents in the selection and admission of publications. That is to say, they provide the criteria for defining acceptance in the international context irrespective of issues of local or national relevance. Uniformity and standardization are achieved with quite narrow forms of control that are pervasive and increasingly streamlined. There is better access to worldwide knowledge production, but still the scheme remains unchallenged because entrenched cultural patterns shape the behavior of the user's consultation and appropriation of knowledge in the center as well as in the peripheries, reinforcing established asymmetries.

Besides, a language barrier holds back the possibility that what is being researched in a native language in the periphery captures the interest of the center. For example only 13 out of the 113 Mexican Social Science journals credited by the Mexican National Council of Science and Technology due to their high quality standards, are indexed by the Thompson Reuters Science Web. Even if this global network is an international system that offers opportunities to new entrants, unwritten rules, norms and mechanisms govern participation. The intensification of knowledge production in non-hegemonic places reflects a very limited participation in mainstream academic circuits or is invisible to scholars in hegemonic centers, except the ones translated into English and put into circulation by prestigious open access journals. This means that even if OA expansion is exponential, it often accounts for a selective inclusiveness that fails to overcome the barriers to the interactions in hegemonic nodes where academic cultural and social capital converge.

When we move from the academic domain to other spheres of society, the era of globalization evidences an increased demand for shared and inclusive knowledge, diversifying the channels of knowledge production. Non-academic organizations such as non-governmental organizations (NGO's), think-tanks or lobbies operate with flexible structures, responding to *á la carte*, fast-track knowledge production. They pave the way, reacting to the parameters of efficiency of the global era, being more successful in connecting "light" science with urgent problem-solving, building bridges between science and government, science and business, science and civil society. Alternative knowledge production and reproduction are oblivious of the need of defining themselves in terms of hegemonic science and grand theoretical references, for they respond to a different logic. In these domains, the need for academic quality assurance of science gets in contradiction with contemporary social processes of knowledge production and use.

Another intervening factor is the growth of the interactions between science and policy. The realization that science rarely translates directly into policy because of competing forces in the policy arenas –ideology, economic and political interests, prior information and institutional constraints- has made it clear that policy-making is part of politics and not the strictly rational enterprise that some people would like it to be. As public decision-making came to be perceived as a form of 'pluralistic accommodation', scientific research started to lose much of its earlier aura and authority. In policy-making, power relations in the 'negotiation' process are the rule, rather than seeking an unequivocally 'best' solution for the social group involved.

No doubt, this alternative domain of applying science has, for better or for worse a social impact in localized spaces. Communication practices also differ from traditional scientific production. Visibility in mainstream knowledge dissemination channels is not important here. This alternative knowledge production is invisible in the *World Social Science Report 2010*, and we are unable to measure its impact in global knowledge production; neither can we perceive whether a new knowledge topography is being designed. We need to have more information related to the possible links, kinds of praxis between the production of problem-solving outputs and long-term accumulation of knowledge and theorization.

As said before, evaluation parameters in academia have to cope with an international standardized agenda. By contrast, hands-on social science projects whose results are the property of governments, communities, or business, seem to be unconcerned with building meeting points between these two domains. Are we wasting the opportunity to enrich both domains, urging academia to redefine its purposes for the sake of society? Dialogue seems more demanding than a parade a social pluralism worldwide. It entails a second kind of information flow, one which develops in the periphery' itself and generates its own concepts to capture regional tendencies and trajectories.

## Final Remarks

We may now synthesize the dominant features and trends of the social sciences in the contemporary scene. Current patterns display unparalleled qualitative differences, in terms of organization and reproduction, with regard to the recent past. These differences are part and parcel of historically unprecedented levels of global interconnectedness and a unique confluence of changes in the domains of politics, law and governance, military affairs, and new forms of economic and social organization that transcend national boundaries. It was in Europe where the rise of nations and nationalism originally developed and it was partially through the twines of European empire that this idea spread to Asia, Africa, the Middle East and the Americas. Not only modes of organizations but also modes of thought and ideologies were spread from Europe to the rest of the world, modes with a claim to universal applicability. Science, together with socialism and liberalism were some of those novelties.

The potency of these ideas and the new mode of social organization was not lost on the rest of the world and contributed to the intensity and power of anticolonial movements in the twentieth century. In today's context, the relationships between sovereignty, territoriality and state power, which resulted in the emergence of nation-states as distinctive collective social actors in the long nineteenth century, have begun to erode.

> Science was diffused in conjunction with a whole set of institutional organizations and practices... [often] as part and parcel of the diffusion of new technologies and industries, of medical techniques and practices and of agricultural innovations... The spread of a Western scientific worldview, though global in its extent, has been slow to percolate beyond the elite stratum of scientists, technologists and educationalists intimately involved in its disciplines (Held et al., 1999, 339)

The social sciences were part of the science enterprise and shared its main features. But in their case, the language issue introduced a number of contradictions, *non sequiturs* and tensions that could be disregarded in the 'hard' sciences. Although English stands at the very centre of the global language system in science and academia, it is also true that the social sciences became institutionalized in the context of modern nation-building in the non-OECD world, where myriad of other languages of limited reach prevail for cultural communication and interaction, and are generally restricted to national or regional boundaries. Thus they became both a tool and a critical weapon in the construction of modern nation-states, following European molds but more closely intertwined with local realities and problems.

Particularly since mid-twentieth century new networks of global communications have crossed national borders with impunity, although the infrastructure is not evenly placed around the globe. The vast majority of international cables, both old and new, lie across the North Atlantic, North Pacific and the Mediterranean. The number of lines between Latin America and Africa across the South Atlantic, for example, is much smaller. Similarly, ownership and use of satellite technology is very heavily skewed towards the West and the states of the former Soviet Union. In addition, if in modern time, intellectual and cultural flows were primarily from West to the rest following lines of imperial control, in the contemporary world the flows continue to be generated primarily in the West and its cultural institutions –universities, research councils, scientific journals, congresses, etc. However, flows have begun to change direction, primarily through migration but also through other forms, shifting South to North and East to West. Concepts, ideas, beliefs and literature from the South and East have been percolating into the Western academic culture, creating new lines of theoretical interconnectedness and fracture.

Academic social science cultures, while obviously making use of these technologies, and occasionally featuring as content within them, are drowned in the high seas of business information systems and commercialised popular culture. No historic parallel exists for such intensive and extensive forms of cultural flows that are primarily of commercial enrichment and entertainment. There can be little doubt that above local and national social science developments, a group of large associations and vested interests that have their home base in OECD countries, dominate global academic markets and have acquired a very large significant institutional and ideological presence on nearly every continent. The social sciences risk becoming part of the business information systems and commercialized popular culture as well as an instrument of global domination and control.

There have been and continue to be a multiplicity of ways of conceiving the shape of the world. But today's experience of the world seems to be going beyond the European Enlightenment thought of the world as a unique generic humankind, above and beyond distinctions of biological, social or spiritual nature, while re-centring humanity. In the wise words of the Nigerian scholar Akiwowo (1988) "We all share the impacts of the capitalist systems –good and bad. We should, with open minds, establish a reciprocity of scholarly traditions...But in the final analysis there is but one social science, but many societies and cultures: many languages, intelligences, but one mind, the human mind" (cited by Archer, 1991).

Whereas the vast majority of social science academic interactions in previous eras were elite to elite, since the postwar the demographic growth of the social sciences in the most disparate countries has coincided with interactions taking place increasingly through popular cultural media and artifacts, accompanying the emergence of transnational media corporations. These have some precedents in the modern era's publishing houses and international journals, but their reach, diversity and power are now of a different order. Reverberations of these changes have been registered in other domains. We have witnessed the massification of higher education, the growth of distance education and borderless programs and more recently the initiatives at the internationalization of universities.

The various regional social science communities can help explore the impact of global trends in spaces not confined to the boundaries of nation-states. Social science governance has an internal component –ruled by its own members- but it also relates to interactions with real societies. Which types of research are carried out, which are not, who decides with respect to priorities, how are the agendas built, how is knowledge produced, what happens to research results, to new knowledge are some of the questions with regard to social science in our time. The new conditions are already here while the understanding of social science as a social activity is lagging behind.

Clearly, there is pressure for more diversity. In earlier eras when territory and sovereignty were less closely linked, core and periphery, metropole and colony were useful models for describing political space. As such, many interregional and global flows transformed and extended those areas rather than necessarily crossing boundaries. Today, historically unprecedented levels of global flows and interconnections cross a world that is almost universally made up of nation-states. However, the enmeshment of different states and different social groups within those nation-states and their relative levels of control over those flows, remains highly uneven. The intensity of global flows and interconnections relative to national and local networks remain variable across domains and states.

The social sciences do not exist in a cultural vacuum, but develop in specific social and cultural contexts. The processes involved have great complexity, given the interactions and creativity they engender. However, it is by no means clear whether the transnational social science communities and social science thought that begins to emerge have affected significantly mainstream social sciences and national and regional identities. It seems, though, that contemporary patterns begin to configure a distinctive historical form that is itself a product of a unique juncture of social, political, economic and technological forms.

# References

Alperin, J.P. (2014). *South America's impact is largely hidden.* Letter to *Nature*: http//www.nature.com/nature/journal/v511/n7508/full/511155c.html

Altbach, P. (2014). MOOCs as Neocolonialism: Who controls knowledge? *International Higher Education, Number 75, Spring.*

Amin, S. (1989). *El eurocentrismo. Crítica de una ideología.* México: Siglo XXI Editores.

Appadurai, A. (2001). *La Modernidad Desbordada.* Argentina: Ediciones Trilce/FCE.

Arab Council for the Social Sciences (n.d.). http://www.arabsocialscience.org

Archer, M. S. (1991). Presidential Address. Sociology for one world: Unity and diversity. *International Sociology*, 6(2), 121–147.

Bianco, A. (2007). The dangerous welath of the Ivy League. *Business Week*, December 10: 38–44.

Böhme, G. & Schäffer, W. (1983). *Finalization in Science. The Social Orientation of Scientific Progress.* Reidel, Dordrecht.

Cervantes, M. & Guellec, D. (2002). The brain drain. Old myths, new realities. *OECD Observer, No. 230, January.*

Chakrabarty, D. (2000). *Provincializing Europe. Postcolonial Thought and Historical Difference.* Princeton and Oxford: Princeton University Press.

Chan, L. & Okune, A. (2014). Opportunities of Open and Collaborative Science for Development in the Global South. *Centre for Critical Development Studies, 43 pp.* University of Toronto-Scarborough and Innovation Hub (iHub), Nairobi,

Collier, P., Hoeffler, H. & Pattillo, C. (2004). Africa's exodus: capital flight and the brain drain as portfolio decisions. *Journal of African Economics*, 13(2), 1115–1154.

Consejo Latinoamericano de Ciencias Sociales (n.d.). http://www.clacso.org.ar

Council for the Development of Social Science Research in Africa (n.d.). http://www.codesria.org

The International Federation of Social Science Organizations (n.d.). http://www.ifsso.net

Crane, D. (1975). *Invisible Colleges: Diffusion of Knowledge in Scientific Communities.* University of Chicago Press.

Fuller, S. (1993). *Philosophy, Rhetoric and the End of Knowledge. The Coming of Science and Technology Studies.* Madison, WI: University of Wisconsin Press.

Haas, P.M. (1992). Epistemic Communities and International Policy Coordination. *International Organization, 46(1)*, 1–35.

Heilbron, J. (2014). The social sciences as an emerging global field. *Current Sociology*, oroginally published online 10 October 2013, DOI: 10.1177/0011392113499739

Held, D., McGrew, A., Goldblatt, D. & Perraton, J. (1999). *Global Transformations. Politics, Economics and Culture.* Stanford : Stanford University Press.

Hess, C. and Ostrom, E. (2006). *Understanding Knowledge as a Commons: From Theory Practice.* Cambridge, Mass :MIT Press.

Huutoniemi, K. et al. (2010). Analyzing interdiscipinarity: Typology and indicators. *Research Policy. 39:* 79–88.

ISSC (2010). *World Social Science Report (2010)* www.unesco.org/.../resources/reports/world-social-science-report

Keim, W. (2010). The Internationalization of Social Sciences: Distortions, Dominations and Prospects. In: *World Social Science Report 2010.* Paris : ISSC-UNESCO.

Kuhn, M. (2013). "Academic Dependence: The WorldSocial Science Arena- a Battlefield among Parochial Thought". In M. Kuhn & K. Okamoto (eds.) *Spatial Social Thought. Local Knowledge in Global Science Encounters,* Stuttgart: ibidem-Verlag.

Lins Ribeiro, G. & Escobar, A. (eds.) (2006). *World Anthropologies. Disciplinary Transformations Within Systems of Power.* The Wenner-Gren Foundation/Berg. Oxford and New York.

Lyotard, J. F. (1979). *La condition postmoderne: Rapport sur le savoir.* Paris, Éditions de Minuit.

Lomnitz, C. (1998). Modernidad Indiana. *Nueve ensayos sobre nación y mediación en México.* Planeta, México.

Mahroum, S. (1999). Highly skilled globetrotters: The international migration of human capital. *DSTI/STP/TIP (99) 2/Final.* OECD.

Mignolo, W. (2000). *Local Histories/Global Designs. Coloniality, Subaltern Knowledges, and Border Thinking.* Princeton, N.J: Princeton University Press.

Mishra, P. (2012). *From the Ruins of Empire. The Revolt Against the West and the Remaking of Asia.* Milton Keynes: Penguin Books.

Mudimbe, V. Y. (1988). *The Invention of Africa. Gnosis, Philosophy, and the Order of Knowledge.* Indiana and Bloomington: Indiana University Press.

Neave, G. (ed.) (2006). *Knowledge, Power and Dissent Critical Perspectives on Higher Education in Knowledge Society. Education on the Move.* Paris :UNESCO Publishing.

Nonini, D. (2008). *The Global Idea of the Commons,* Inglaterra: Berghahn Books.

Organization for Social Science Research in Eastern and Southern Africa (n.d.). http://www.ossrea.net

Platt, J. (1998). *A Brief History of the International Sociological Association.* Madrid : ISA.

Price, D. de S. (1963). *Little Science, Big Science.* New York: Columbia University Press.

Quijano, A. (2001). *Capitalismo y geopolítica del conocimiento,* Buenos Aires: Ediciones del Siglo.

Rodriguez Medina, L. (2013). *Centers and Peripheries in Knowledge Production.* New York and London: Routledge.

Said, E. (1978). *Orientalism,* New York: Pantheon Books.

Turnbull, D. (2000). *Masons, Tricksters and Cartographers. Comparative Studies in the Sociology of Scientific and Indigenous Knowledge.* New York and London: Routledge.

Vessuri, H. (1998). La movilidad científica desde la perspectiva de América Latina. In J.B. Meyer and J. Charum (eds.) *El nuevo nomadismo científico. La perspectiva latinoamericana.* Bogotá Bogotá: Escuela Superior de Administración Pública.

Vessuri, H. (2013). Who is the Social Scientist in the Twenty-First Century. Commentaries from academic and applied contexts and from the mainstream and the periphery. In M. Kuhn and S. Yazawa (eds.) *Theories about and Strategies Against Hegemonic Social Sciences.* Tokyo : Center for Glocal Studies, Seijo University.

Vessuri, H. (2013). The Transformation Process in Global Social Knowledge. In M. Kuhn & K. Okamoto (eds.) *Spatial Social Thought. Local Knowledge in Global Science Encounters,* Suttgart: ibidem-Verlag.

Vessuri, H. (2014). Los límites del conocimiento disciplinario. Nuevas formas de producción del conocimiento científico. In P. Kremier, H. Vessuri, L. Velho and A. Arellano (eds.) *Perspectivas latinoamericanas en el estudio social de la ciencia, la tecnología y la sociedad 2014.* Buenos Aires : Siglo XXI Editores.

Vessuri, H., Guédon, J. C. & Cetto, A. M. (2014). Excellence or quality? Impact of the current competition regime on science and scientific publishing in Latin America and its implications for development. *Current Sociology, 62(5),* 647–665.

Wagner, C. (2008). *The New Invisible College, Science for Development.* USA: Brooklyn Institution.

Wenger, E. (1998). *Communities of Practice: Learning, Meaning and Identity.* Cambridge University Press.

Westfall, R. (1971). *The construction of modern science.* Cambridge University Press.

Wickson, F., Carew, A. L. & Russell, A. W. (2006). Transdisciplinary research: characteristics, quandaries and quality. *Futures, 38:* 146–159.

Williamson, J.G. (2002). Winners and Losers over Two Centuries of Globalization. Paper delivered at the 2002 WIDER Annual Lecture, Copenhagen.

# Chapter 8:
# What happened to the spread of universal ideas?

Reiner Grundmann

In this chapter I will ask the question how the relation between Western Science and other forms of knowledge has been conceptualised, and what role one specific form of knowledge production, the university, has played in this process. I will examine the contributions from two different research traditions that usually have not much contact with each other, the diffusionist framework in the history of science, and the neo-institutionalist analysis in organizational sociology. I will also look at the role and visibility of non-Western scientists and social scientists in the current academic landscape.

## Western and indigenous knowledge: diffusion, translation, circulation

In the social science literature the term Western Science is frequently accompanied by the term Indigenous Knowledge, not least since George Basalla in 1967 proposed an influential three phase model of the world wide diffusion of science from Western Europe to the rest of the world.

Basalla (1967:611) identified three overlapping phases or stages: 'during "phase 1" the non-scientific society or nation provides a source for European science. The word nonscientific refers to the absence of modern Western science and not to a lack of ancient, indigenous scientific thought of the sort to be found in India or China... "Phase 2" is marked by a period of colonial science [where indigenous researchers start working with the Western rules and frameworks, RG], and "phase 3" completes the process of transplantation with a struggle to achieve an independent scientific tradition (or culture).'

The model was met with several criticisms. It was said that Basalla shares with other scholars (such as Needham) the fundamental idea that science is universal and based on certain principles and truths which are then spread across the globe, thus helping the rest of the world see the 'truth' (see Raj 2013 and Lipphardt & Ludwig, 2011 for a summary). The criticism came from two different angles, from Post-colonial and post-structural scholarship (Said, Foucault) and from new approaches in the history and sociology of science. The first rejected the implied universalism for political and moral reasons, the second pointed to the situated and negotiated nature of scientific knowledge.

However, it should be noted that while Basalla speaks of 'transplantation' at the same time he grants the previously developed indigenous knowledge the status of 'science'. He does not assume an inferior position of non-Western knowledge (in phase 1 or even before), or of non-western scientists as they emerge in phase 2 and 3. He argues that cultural and organizational factors hinder an even development.

His argument is more precise in that he suggests the following. The knowledge created by Western scientists in the 'new lands' during phase 1 is re-imported to the Western colonial powers, stimulating knowledge development there (many zoological and botanic observations give rise, for example, to the theory of evolution). The emerging colonial scientists are restricted in terms of access to informal networks, which are maintained and populated by western scientists. They also lack the critical mass to establish their own organisations of knowledge production. The asymmetry is not cognitive, but organizational, financial, and institutional.

Thus when Raj (2013) says 'that being colonized and having agency are not antithetical it is in the asymmetry in negotiation processes that the power relationship resides, and it can be brought to light in its specificity only through a rigorous analysis of these processes, instead of being raised to the status of an explanatory category'—this is not in contradiction to Basalla's framework.

Raj maintains that while the diffusionist model suffers from deficiencies, the new approaches are not without problems either. With regard to critical scholarship a la Foucault and Said he thinks that they share with Basalla the same epistemological position, i.e. that there is a Western science that has spread to the rest of the world. As Raj put it, 'they share with the more optimistic earlier

## Chapter 8: What happened to the spread of universal ideas?

positions the widely accepted idea that there is something essential and unified called modern science that, like modernity itself, originated in Western Europe and subsequently spread to the rest of the world.'

This is where the social studies of science literature is useful. They propose to move away '... from a conception of science as a system of formal propositions or discoveries', understanding it as the

> 'Construction, maintenance, extension, and reconfiguration of knowledge, focusing equally on its material, instrumental, corporeal, practical, social, political, and cognitive aspects. Systematically opting for detailed case studies of the processes through which knowledge and associated skills, practices, procedures, methods, and instruments are created in preference to "big picture" accounts, they have investigated the negotiated, contingent, and situated nature of the sciences. This new scholarship has convincingly shown that scientific research is not based on logical step-by-step reasoning but on pragmatic judgment, much like that involved in practical crafts, and is thus historically and geographically situated' (Raj 2013:341).

But also this newer strand of critique of diffusionist approaches and views of science as universal has its shortcomings, as Raj explains:

> 'They still share with earlier traditions and with postcolonial critiques of modern science the dogma of its Western origins, a significant pointer being the absence of case studies from anywhere but Europe and America, knowledge production in non-European spaces of modernity being left largely to anthropologists and area studies specialists. They also implicitly share with them a belief in the "center/periphery" model for the spread of the sciences as well as in the use of the dichotomous vocabulary of "metropolitan" versus "colonial" science, although they do endeavor to bring to light the mechanisms that make diffusion possible instead of simply taking the phenomenon for granted. It is thus worth remarking that ... postpositivist historians have acquiesced willy-nilly to the obdurate Eurocentric postulate that modern science is "distinctly Western in its inception—although no longer in its pursuit or execution."'(Raj 2012:342).

It seems as if Basalla's paper left a long shadow. Two waves of criticism did not overcome some basic assumptions—first, the assumption of a universal science; the second, the assumption of a centre periphery divide with knowledge emanating from the former and being taken up by the latter.

Raj suggests a new conceptualisation that is supposed to overcome the weaknesses of the diffusionist model and its critics by using the term *circulation*. This is based on the insight that there is movement of ideas, expertise and practices around the world, from one place to another. In the process of moving they encounter each other and interact. The interactions 'are themselves a locus of knowledge construction and reconfiguration. In other words, I shall focus on the unanimously acknowledged centrality of circulation to analyze its consequences for the sciences and their history on a global scale.' (Raj 2012:343).

In so doing he hopes to address several shortcomings of postpositivism and postcolonialism. By science we should not understand 'free-floating ideas, but the production of knowledge, practices, instruments, techniques, and services; and by circulation ... not the "dissemination," "transmission," or "communication" of ideas, but the processes of encounter, power and resistance, negotiation, and reconfiguration that occur in cross-cultural interaction.'(Raj 2012:342).

Positing 'circulation itself as a "site" of knowledge formation constitutes a major change in approach with respect to science studies orthodoxy. ... social studies of science have so far, albeit implicitly, separated three moments in the making of knowledge: the collection of information or objects; their accumulation and processing within the local, segregated space of the laboratory; and, finally, the spread—and eventual universal acceptance—of the knowledge thus engendered. However, it is precisely the *mutable* nature of the knowledge makers themselves, as much as of the knowledges and skills that they embodied, their transformations and reconfigurations in the course of their geographical and social displacements, that the focus on circulation helps bring to the fore.' (Raj 2012:343-4).

This position advocates an approach that focuses on contingencies in history, thus carrying further an impetus from the field of social studies of science. It thus replaces the question of why Western science has become dominant historically with a more general question about the reconfiguration of knowledge through circulation.

## Institutions and organisations

It is sociological commonplace that knowledge production and knowledge consumption cannot be understood in isolation, without the social environment in which they operate. Interests, norms and values play an important role and their influence is greater if they are stabilized over time and in space. This is achieved through institutions that provide the formal and informal rules that govern expectations and actions of members of organisations. In what follows I will present a critical appraisal of neo-institutionalist theory with regard to the development of the university and global knowledge production.

## The role of isomorphism

Joo & Halx (2011) present a critical discussion of the usefulness of neo-institutional theory for the analysis of the university sector (their case being performance related pay in South Korean higher education (HE) institutions).

Institutional isomorphism can be defined as a process by which one institution or organization takes on the same structures which are considered rational and legitimate by others (Di Maggio & Powell, 1983; Meyer & Rowan, 1977; Scott, 2001). The unit of analysis is not individual organizations, but a sector comprising many organizations.

Scholars in this tradition distinguish three mechanisms of institutional isomorphism: coercive, mimetic, and normative. Coercive isomorphism "results from both formal and informal pressures exerted on organizations by other organizations upon which they are dependent and by cultural expectations in the society within which organizations function" (DiMaggio and Powell 1983: 150). Mimetic isomorphism results "from standard responses to uncertainty" and leads to copying of practices from one organization (or more) by another (see Tarde, 1903 for the original formulation). 'Best practices' and 'benchmarking' are concepts used often by managers when referring to this kind of isomorphic pressure. Normative isomorphism results from the social norms, values, and standards. Professional organisations are often in a position to drive or shape such normative expectations.

Neo-institutionalist theory has been rightly criticized for its bias towards uniformity. It is good at explaining convergence of practices in a sector, but not when one seeks to account for innovation or diversity (Ash 2006; Beckert 2010).

Looking at the expansion of the university globally, it seems obvious that a strong trend of homogenization has occurred with regard to several key features (Kiuppis and Waldow 2008; Drori et al. 2003; ). There is still national diversity, and differentiation within countries. When it comes to identifying common features and convergence, neo-institutional theory can provide some insights.

Frank & Meyer (2007) claim that the university is a unique institution that is global, expanding, relatively unified, and that rests on universal values. Much of the expansion has taken place in the social sciences. 'Fields such as sociology, economics, political science, and psychology, which once had no place at all in the university, are now found almost everywhere... The emergence of the knowledge society after WWII has led to a change in the role of the university.' As Frank and Meyer explain (2007:295),

> In several dramatic ways, the emergence of the "knowledge society" after World War II indicated a change in this older vision of the societal context—beyond merely adding complexity requiring more training. A globalized and individualized society began to surface in the post-war era, offering enhanced centrality to the university and increasing the pace of its expansion (and all but burying the concept of over-education). This means first that to an increasing extent it came to be understood that university education could actively create the kinds of knowledge and personnel that could produce—not just adapt to—societal development. For example in the economy, the idea took hold that human capital (viz., education) could directly lead to innovations, new occupations, and increased prosperity. Similar ideas arose vis-à-vis political and social development. Overall, it became accepted that higher education could initiate, not simply respond to, a future golden age ...

Note the argument made here refers very much to the skills of graduates, and the volume of graduates produced by the higher education sector. It does not mention the word 'skill', but 'knowledge' and 'personnel'. And it makes the case for economic prosperity as an effect of increased production of knowledge workers. Essentially this is an argument suggesting that increased levels of supply will create their own markets. The rationale for this supply side argument is the promise that increased investment in universities will yield economic prosperity.[1]

The authors oppose a view which is common, namely that the university is a place for the instruction and training of citizens which are made to function according to the (scientific and technical) demands of modern society. Frank and Meyer argue that if it

---

[1] This supply side argument as applied to the labour market has been advanced by several other scholars, such as Bell (1973); Drucker (1968); Stehr (2002).

were true we would see different responses to these demands in different countries. What we see instead is a set of uniform trends. Universities increase in number, the course offerings multiply, the number of students grows, the influence of certified experts grows in society, as does the influence of societal groups on universities (interest and pressure groups of all sorts).

## The impact of the university on society

> Much of the role-activity of present day society, that is, is not merely served by the educational system but is literally constituted by it.... Much of this value is educationally constructed without regard to the delivery of verifiable services. Therapy adds value to the GDP even when the patient fails to get better, whereas solace from friends is economically valueless even when the person improves dramatically (Frank and Meyer 2007:296).

However, the evidence that is presented to support this claim does not seem to derive from systematic empirical studies. The authors are candid in their admission:

> Illustrations of all these changes—both in the theory of knowledge and in the theories of students and pedagogy—are easy to accumulate. More systematic work is obviously required, however, before we can empirically ground generalizations about the university's transformations. (Frank and Meyer 2007:306).

It is therefore an open question if universities produce a useful service to society or if they just follow their own aspirations. The authors indication from above, that there is more pressure from different social groups on the university would suggest that considerations of utility and social service are on the rise.

## The impact of society on the university

As more and more citizens went through university education, the universities opened up to ever more social strata.

> With so few cultural materials remaining outside the university orbit and with wide-open access to the student role, the post-war university began to enmesh with society as never before, undercutting the ivory-tower-style isolation that had been celebrated earlier as a measure of purity. Critics of this process see the university's penetration by society (and by its commercial and market elements in particular) as representing the destruction of academic values. But they tend to grossly understate the countervailing trend—the rising extent to

which academic values, perspectives, expertise, and knowledge come to transform and in many senses dominate society. (Frank and Meyer 2007:298-9).[2]

A clear picture emerges here. Universities are imprinting their values on society, propelled by a tailwind of universalistic norms and meritocratic promises, reshaping the society around it, while at the same time being shaped by powerful interest groups. For the university to have such an influence, there is a price to pay: it cannot exist in isolation, or be 'autonomous' from societal interests.

## Fragmentation and inequality

Despite its grandiose claims, the neo-institutional narrative presented above should perhaps be regarded as just one story: partly plausible, partly wishful thinking, but not supported by much systematic evidence.

It is therefore a good idea to examine what empirical studies on the subject have concluded. Among the sources that are heavily quoted (also by Frank and Meyer, and by other Neo-institutionalists such as Drori and Krücken) are the works by Philip Altbach (Drori et al. 2003).

In the introduction to his book *Comparative Higher Education: Knowledge, the University, and Development,* Altbach (1998) describes the historical background and current trends in higher education. The currently dominant university model has its roots in Medieval European forerunners, most notably the University of Paris. This institution was from the beginning international in character, attracting scholars and students from various countries who communicated in a lingua franca, which was Latin then, and is English now. Today, universities world-wide are hugely influenced in their structure by the United States model which represents a combination of the English collegiate idea, the German ideal of combining research and teaching, and the American idea of providing a service to society.

Enumerating these different sources makes clear that there were, and still are, national differences that distinguish the way universities operate across the globe. On the level of guiding norms

---

[2] For a critique of 'neoliberal tendencies' within higher education, see Mirowski (2011).

and ideals it appears that the United States model has become dominant but is itself a hybrid of at least three different traditions. For neo-institutional theory to be convincing it would need to demonstrate how isomorphic pressure has led to an assimilation of different models to one.[3]

Altbach suggests that universities in the Medieval epoch and in the current post-colonial period are truly international, a trait which was only suppressed during the 19th century with the rise of the nation state and nationalistic tendencies in society.

Nevertheless, it seems to be the case that even today there is difference within unity. While different countries pursue different science policy options, governments are keen to exploit the universities' potential for purposes of economic competitiveness. Universities also offer career prospects and keep parts of the population out of the labour market for several years. This means that on the one hand a nation needs to provide HE opportunities or else its brightest talents move abroad. On the other hand university graduates need appropriate jobs, which means that societies are likely to expand their knowledge intensive sectors.

No matter how successful nations are in this respect, there is still considerable mobility across the globe with large numbers of students moving to countries hosting 'the best' universities (BritishCouncil 2012; Leung 2013; Oleksiyenko 2013).

Status hierarchies are reflected on many levels of academic life, from the epistemological status of disciplines to the visibility, reputation, and influence of specific paradigms or authors. So when we talk about the question of how 'Western science' has become, or is becoming universal we always must ask the question about the level on which this phenomenon is occurring.

Is Western science becoming universal because universities are expanding their student numbers and degree courses, as Frank and Meyer seem to suggest? Or because there is a university model with a specific structure which diffuses from one centre to the rest of the world? Because governments have developed similar policies of how to capture the knowledge base for economic benefit? Or is it

---

[3] Frank and Meyer (2007:299) note that within the European Union, 'the 1999 Bologna Declaration seeks unprecedented organizational homogeneity among the historically distinct universities of Europe'. However, this may be limited to the degree structure, there are still large differences with regard to organizational features of the universities in different EU countries (see Ash 2006).

because specific contributions from specific scientific fields in the West have become influential in non-Western regions of the globe? These question lie beyond the scope of this paper. Here I will limit myself to the aspect of visibility of non-western research.

## Hegemonic paradigms and scholars

In a recent Nature article, it was pointed out that

> Despite many good intentions and initiatives, gender inequality is still rife in science. Although there are more female than male undergraduate and graduate students in many countries, there are relatively few female full professors, and gender inequalities in hiring, earnings, funding, satisfaction and patenting persist. (Larivière et al. 2013).

We could without much difficulty, replace the gender aspect with a developmental aspect and say:

> Despite many good intentions and initiatives, global inequality is still rife in science. Although there are many more undergraduate and graduate students (and scholars) in non-Western countries, there are relatively few visible scientists, and many inequalities with regard to scientific output and impact across the globe persist.

Within the social sciences, as with the sciences in general, there are highly visible or hegemonic paradigms at any given period in time. Within the social sciences, and especially within social theory, these are approaches associated with labels like Post-structuralism, critical theory, rational choice theory, cultural theory or institutional theory.

If we look at influential authors, names such as Foucault, Habermas, Giddens, Bourdieu or Castells come to mind. In fact, different lists have been produced to show the most cited social science scholars. In 2009 the *Times Higher Education Supplement* published such a list of most cited authors in the social sciences and humanities (SSH), based on their book publications (see table 1).

## Chapter 8: What happened to the spread of universal ideas?

| Field | Citations to books in 2007 |
|---|---|
| Michel Foucault (1926-1984) Philosophy, sociology, criticism | 2,521 |
| Pierre Bourdieu (1930-2002) Sociology | 2,465 |
| Jacques Derrida (1930-2004) Philosophy | 1,874 |
| Albert Bandura (1925- ) Psychology | 1,536 |
| Anthony Giddens (1938- ) Sociology | 1,303 |
| Erving Goffman (1922-1982) Sociology | 1,066 |
| Jurgen Habermas (1929- ) Philosophy, sociology | 1,049 |
| Max Weber (1864-1920) Sociology | 971 |
| Judith Butler (1956- ) Philosophy | 960 |
| Bruno Latour (1947- ) Sociology, anthropology | 944 |
| Sigmund Freud (1856-1939) Psychoanalysis | 903 |
| Gilles Deleuze (1925-1995) Philosophy | 897 |
| Immanuel Kant (1724-1804) Philosophy | 882 |
| Martin Heidegger (1889-1976) Philosophy | 874 |
| Noam Chomsky (1928- ) Linguistics, philosophy | 812 |
| Ulrich Beck (1944- ) Sociology | 733 |
| Jean Piaget (1896-1980) Philosophy | 725 |
| David Harvey (1935- ) Geography | 723 |
| John Rawls (1921-2002) Philosophy | 708 |
| Geert Hofstede (1928- ) Cultural studies | 700 |
| Edward W. Said (1935-2003) Criticism | 694 |
| Emile Durkheim (1858-1917) Sociology | 662 |
| Roland Barthes (1915-1980) Criticism, philosophy | 631 |
| Clifford Geertz (1926-2006) Anthropology | 596 |
| Hannah Arendt (1906-1975) Political theory | 593 |
| Walter Benjamin (1892-1940) Criticism, philosophy | 583 |
| Henri Tajfel (1919-1982) Social psychology | 583 |
| Ludwig Wittgenstein (1889-1951) Philosophy | 583 |
| Barney G. Glaser (1930- ) Sociology | 577 |

| | |
|---|---|
| George Lakoff (1941- ) Linguistics | 577 |
| John Dewey (1859-1952) Philosophy, psychology, education | 575 |
| Benedict Anderson (1936- ) International studies | 573 |
| Emmanuel Levinas (1906-1995) Philosophy | 566 |
| Jacques Lacan (1901-1981) Psychoanalysis, philosophy, criticism | 526 |
| Thomas S. Kuhn (1922-1996) History and philosophy of science | 519 |
| Karl Marx (1818-1883) Political theory, economics, sociology | 501 |
| Friedrich Nietzsche (1844-1900) Philosophy | 501 |

**Table 1**: Visible SSH Authors (source: http://www.timeshighereducation.co.uk/405956.article

This is a list of eminent scholars, mostly male, white and western (dominated by French, German and American authors). Edward Said is an exception in that he originated from Palestine, but even he shot to fame through his presence in a prestigious US university. To be sure, we could add some more highly visible female scholars, such as Margaret Mead, Mary Douglas or Donna Haraway—the fact remains that these are Western scholars (see also Heilbron 2013).

If we look back at Basalla's three phases model, it might be argued that the rise of science in non-western countries has led to an independent scientific tradition or culture. Phase 1 started in the 16th century and has led to new scientific cultures in the USA, Australia. Japan, Russia, China, Brazil, among others. But what about SSH? To be sure, Western scientists (mainly European ethnographers and anthropologists in the 19th and 20th century) visited indigenous cultures, described their practices and re-imported them to their home countries. At the same time, the rise of SSH in these countries has started, but with much delay. Phase 3 has not come to fruition yet if we give ponder the citation count of visible authors.

It is ironic that the SSH, a field where critical reflection is part and parcel of much ongoing work, has not succeeded in initiating a movement of successful post-colonial SSH. Thus when Raj states with regard to the sciences that '... it is precisely the *mutable* nature of the knowledge makers themselves, as much as of the knowledges and skills that they embodied, their transfor-

# Chapter 8: What happened to the spread of universal ideas?

mations and reconfigurations in the course of their geographical and social displacements, that the focus on circulation helps bring to the fore'—one has to be sceptical with regard to SSH.

Rather, one is reminded of C.P. Snow's two cultures (of humanities and science) where the requirements of the former make it much harder to attract students from non-elites compared to the latter (Snow 2012). The theoretically oriented and demanding language games of SSH may have cemented the monopoly position of their founders and their heirs, who occupy the same geographical and social places. Western social theory seems to have established a firm grip and cemented a monopoly position that has proven impossible to break. It seems a deep irony that those approaches most critical in theory about colonialism and its legacy have achieved so little in their own fields.

The above table is based on book publications but a similar picture emerges when looking at journal papers and their impact, according to data obtained through the Web of Science (WoS) database (Thomson Reuter's ESI database). I compare SSH and science publications/citations across several countries. Tables 2 and 3 show data for the top 20 countries, using as examples the field of social science, defined as 'Social Sciences-General' (which includes disciplines like Philosophy); and 'Chemistry and Molecular Biology'. There are about 20 subject areas listed in the ESI database total so my sample cannot be representative).

As many bibliometric studies have pointed out, the emphasis on English language publications introduces a bias to WoS (Mosbah-Natanson and Gingras 2013). However, as English has become the *Lingua franca* of the sciences globally, this bias allows to trace the visibility of different countries in different disciplines. As Heilbron points out, 'English, furthermore, has become the global language in the social sciences. In the 1950s and 1960s nearly half of the publications registered in the International Bibliography of the Social Sciences were in English, by 2005 this share had gone up to over 75%. The proportion of all other languages declined, for the most important other languages, German and French, to a level of about 7%.' (Heilbron 2013:691).

Much depends on which criterion to apply for country classification. According to Basalla's original typology, USA, Canada, Australia or Japan would count as non-Western science nations as they have gone through a process of colonization by European countries.

However, for the present purpose it seems more appropriate to adopt a shorter timescale which comprises the post World War II period only. I thus include developing nations such as China, Korea, Brazil, Taiwan, or South Africa (I included also Russia, which might be regarded as problematic. However, in terms of output it seems to be a very marginal country, as 'the production of articles books has increased almost everywhere [with] the Russian Federation being the only exception (Heilbron 2013:691).

**Social Sciences**

| Country/Territory | Papers | Citations | Citations Per Paper |
|---|---|---|---|
| USA | 280,359 | 2,168,861 | 7.74 |
| ENGLAND | 78,164 | 566,835 | 7.25 |
| CANADA | 38,883 | 278,431 | 7.16 |
| AUSTRALIA | 36,182 | 209,203 | 5.78 |
| NETHERLANDS | 23,109 | 193,744 | 8.38 |
| GERMANY (FRG) | 26,357 | 149,336 | 5.67 |
| SWEDEN | 13,575 | 105,194 | 7.75 |
| FRANCE | 15,535 | 97,137 | 6.25 |
| SWITZERLAND | 8,391 | 79,139 | 9.43 |
| SPAIN | 18,312 | 74,984 | 4.09 |
| ITALY | 11,637 | 73,881 | 6.35 |
| SCOTLAND | 9,998 | 71,424 | 7.14 |
| DENMARK | 7,326 | 64,692 | 8.83 |
| NORWAY | 8,290 | 60,055 | 7.24 |
| BELGIUM | 8,417 | 54,595 | 6.49 |
| FINLAND | 6,365 | 50,315 | 7.9 |
| JAPAN | 8,190 | 48,567 | 5.93 |
| AVG | 35,241 | 255,670 | 7 |
| CHINA MAINLAND | 15,769 | 80,909 | 5.13 |
| BRAZIL | 13,172 | 46,557 | 3.53 |
| SOUTH AFRICA | 9,038 | 43,865 | 4.85 |
| AVG | 12,660 | 57,110 | 5 |

**Table 2**: Social Sciences journal articles, source Essential Science Indicators, Thomson Reuter (accessed 15 March 2014).

## Chemistry

| Country/Territory | Papers | Citations | Citations Per Paper |
|---|---|---|---|
| USA | 245,849 | 4,729,738 | 19.24 |
| GERMANY (FRG) | 104,447 | 1,601,310 | 15.33 |
| JAPAN | 117,872 | 1,501,042 | 12.73 |
| FRANCE | 71,496 | 1,015,304 | 14.2 |
| ENGLAND | 56,396 | 940,934 | 16.68 |
| SPAIN | 55,278 | 784,248 | 14.19 |
| ITALY | 47,431 | 660,762 | 13.93 |
| CANADA | 37,940 | 561,384 | 14.8 |
| SWITZERLAND | 21,275 | 390,836 | 18.37 |
| NETHERLANDS | 19,448 | 370,403 | 19.05 |
| AUSTRALIA | 23,880 | 330,747 | 13.85 |
| POLAND | 33,768 | 257,778 | 7.63 |
| SWEDEN | 15,335 | 242,444 | 15.81 |
| BELGIUM | 15,360 | 223,457 | 14.55 |
| **AVG** | **61,841** | **972,171** | **15** |
| CHINA MAINLAND | 275,693 | 2,467,582 | 8.95 |
| INDIA | 87,928 | 709,119 | 8.06 |
| SOUTH KOREA | 48,883 | 538,219 | 11.01 |
| TAIWAN | 25,550 | 277,836 | 10.87 |
| RUSSIA | 64,706 | 263,750 | 4.08 |
| BRAZIL | 26,326 | 220,462 | 8.37 |
| **AVG** | **88,181** | **746,161** | **9** |

**Table 3**: Chemistry journal articles, source Essential Science Indicators, Thomson Reuter (accessed 15 March 2014).

If we look at this sample and the output of peer reviewed journal articles and their citations per country it is striking that in Chemistry six non-western countries are represented in the top 20 nations, publishing 38% of papers. This compares to just three countries in the Social Sciences (with 6% share of output). In chemistry, China is science nation number one in terms of paper output, number two in citations, although the citations per paper are much lower compared to other countries.

Looking at the impact of research papers it is obvious that non-western countries are below the average of citations per paper. The performance of non-Western social science nations is especially poor in the Social Sciences where the best nation (Denmark) with 8.9 compares with 3.5 for the lowest (Brazil).

However, there is still a much bigger discrepancy if we look at table 1. SSH scholars listed here typically do not publish journal papers but seek the book as the prestige publication. The book format favors narrators of grand stories, including those who reject grand narratives. Authors who work more empirically make their career through peer review paper publishing and this seems to create a more equal playing field across countries—a feature that applies across the sciences.

## Conclusion

In this paper I have examined two different strands of literature, the diffusionist framework and its critics on the one hand, and the neo-institutionalist analysis of the spread of one typical site of knowledge production, i.e. the modern university.

The upshot of my discussion is that the various critiques of the diffusionist framework have led to an abandonment of the notion of universal science, of linear transfer, and hence of the very concept of Western science. Sociologists and historians of science favour particularistic accounts with no appetite for generalizations.

In contrast, researchers in the Neo-institutionalist framework invoke the existence of universalist norms when it comes to knowledge production. The expansion of the universities on a global scale is explained through the appeal of a universal ideal, that of truth and universal validity. There are reasons to be skeptical towards this interpretation and to advance a more pragmatic reading in terms of isomorphism in that societies have become convinced of the value of universities for knowledge creation that is instrumental in the search for efficacy. Governments support science in a global competitive market for talent, and individuals try to enhance their life chances by entering higher education.

If we, for the sake of the argument, apply Basalla's three phases to the present case, we can probably identify phase three in the data: there is still an absolute dominance of Western authors in the field of social theory and 'grand narratives'. This could be due to the fact that Western HE institutions are still an obligatory passage point for global elites and their offspring, that the Western legacy is too esoteric for new generations across the globe, or that it has become irrelevant.

Brazil, South Korea or China are rising science nations but their performance lags still behind Western nations, especially in the Social Sciences and Humanities. It looks as if SSH have not received the attention or funding which would enable them to embark on their path to a national academic culture that competes on a par with Western scholars. Further research is required to assess to what extent this is unique to SSH.

# References

Altbach, P. G. (1998). *Comparative Higher Education: Knowledge, the University, and Development* (Google eBook). Greenwood Publishing Group.

Ash, M. G. (2006). Bachelor of What, Master of Whom? The Humboldt Myth and Historical Transformations of Higher Education in German-Speaking Europe and the US1. *European Journal of Education, 41(2)*, 245–67.

Basalla, G. (1967). The Spread of Western Science. *Science, 156(3775)*, 611–22.

Beckert, J. (2010). Institutional Isomorphism Revisited: Convergence and Divergence in Institutional Change *. *Sociological Theory, 28(2)*, 150–66.

Bell, D. (1973). *The Coming Of Post-Industrial Society*. New York: Basic Books.

British Council. (2012). *The Shape of Things to Come: Higher Education Global Trends and Emerging Opportunities to 2020*.

Drori, G. S., Meyer, J. W., Ramirez, F. O. & Schofer, E. (2003). *Science in the Modern World Polity: Institutionalization and Globalization*. Stanford University Press.

Drucker, P. (1968). *The Age of Discontinuity: Guidelines to Our Changing Society*. New Brunswick, New Jersey: Transaction Publishers.

Frank, D. J. & Meyer, J. W. (2007). University Expansion and the Knowledge Society. *Theory and Society, 36*, 287–311.

Heilbron, J. (2013). The Social Sciences as an Emerging Global Field. *Current Sociology, 62(5)*, 685–703.

Joo, Y. H. & Halx, M. D. (2011). The Power of Institutional Isomorphism: An Analysis of the Institutionalization of Performance-Based Pay Systems in Korean National Universities. *Asia Pacific Education Review, 13(2)*, 281–97.

Kiuppis, F. & Waldow, F. (2008). 'Institute University' Meets Bologna Process: The German System of Higher Education in Transition. In D. Palomba (ed.) *Changing universities in Europe and the Bologna process: a seven country study*. (pp. 73–99) Rome: Aracne.

Larivière, V., Ni, C., Gingras, Y., Cronin, B. & Sugimoto, C. R. (2013). Bibliometrics: Global Gender Disparities in Science. *Nature, 504(7479)*, 211–13.

Leung, M. (2013). Unraveling the Skilled Mobility for Sustainable Development Mantra: An Analysis of China-EU Academic Mobility. *Sustainability, 5(6)*, 2644–63.

Lipphardt, V. & Ludwig, D. (2011). "Knowledge Transfer and Science Transfer Knowledge Transfer and Science Transfer."

Di Maggio, P. J. & Powell, W. W. (1983). The Iron Cage Revisited. *American Sociological Review, 48(2)*, 147–60.

Meyer, J. W. & Rowan, B. (1977). Institutionalized Organizations: Formal Structure as Myth and Ceremony. *The American Journal of Sociology, 83(2)*, 340–63.

Mosbah-Natanson, S. & Gingras, Y. (2013). The Globalization of Social Sciences? Evidence from a Quantitative Analysis of 30 Years of Production, Collaboration and Citations in the Social Sciences (1980-2009). *Current Sociology, 62(5)*, 626–46.

Oleksiyenko, A. (2013). Opportunity Structures and Higher Learning in a Globally-Connected Place: Tensions and Ties between Outbound and Upward Mobility. *Higher Education, 66(3)*, 341–56.

Raj, K. (2013). Beyond Postcolonialism ... and Postpositivism: Circulation and the Global History of Science. *Isis, 104(2)*, 337–47.

Scott, W. R. (2001). *Institutions and Organizations (2nd Ed.)*. SAGE Publications.

Snow, C. P. (2012). *The Two Cultures (reprint)*. Cambridge University Press.

Stehr, N. (2002). *Knowledge and Economic Conduct: The Social Foundations of the Modern Economy*. University of Toronto Press.

Tarde, G. (1903). *The Laws of Imitation*. New York: Henry Holt & Company.

# Section III:
# The social science world under the 'European' universalism and beyond

# Chapter 9:
# Intervening in the Geopolitics of Travelling Theory: Constraints, Limitations and Possibilities

Sujata Patel

Three concerns drive the arguments presented in this chapter. First, the paper starts off with the assumption that in today's globalizing environment it becomes important to confront and contest the universalizing episteme promoted in 19th and early 20th century—known in social theory as Eurocentric methodology (Wallerstein, 1997, 2006) or coloniality of power (Quijano, 1993, 2000, 2007). Second, it discusses and deliberates the methodological options and interventionist strategies available today that challenge it, such as provincialism (Chakrabarty, 2008), endogeneity (Houtondji, 1995, 1997) and the transmodern perspective (Dussel, 1993, 2000, 2002 and Mignolo, 2003). Third, I argue that these options and strategies need to be contextualized-for these are related to one's institutional, disciplinary and geopolitical location in the global order. For, while the globalizing world has created challenges that allow a more complex theoretical reframing of the world, institutional and geographical inequalities have not disappeared. Merely intervening in the world of knowledge will not displace Eurocentric knowledge; intervening in the practices that structure knowledge will. The last section will outline the issues regarding the politics of these practices[1].

## Colonial modernity, Eurocentrism and its binaries

Samir Amin (2008) is the first theorist who presents an historical claim regarding the growth of the Eurocentric episteme in the 18th

---

[1] This paper is based on earlier published work. See Patel, 2006, 2007, 2010, 2010a, 2010b, 2011, 2011a, 2013, 2013a.

century when he argues that this episteme is entwined in the twin processes of crystallisation of the European society and Europe's conquest of the world. Eurocentrism, Amin argues, clothe these twin processes by emphasizing the first and disregarding the significance of the latter in the formation of the first.

Amin's argument is presented at three levels: First, he contends that Europe was the periphery of the Mediterranean tributary states (the other being that of the Afro-Asiatic region) whose centre was at its eastern edge. Scholastic and metaphysical culture of these tributary systems created four systems of scholastic metaphysics: Hellinistic, Eastern Christian, Islamic and Western Christian. While all of these contributed to the formation of culture and consciousness of Europe, it was the contribution of Egypt and later of medieval Islamic scholastics which was decisive in changing Europe's culture from being metaphysical to scientific (Amin, 2008:38). Second, he shows how since the Renaissance period, this history of Europe has been distilled and diluted, to be replaced with another history that narrated its growth as being the sole consequence of its birth within the Hellinic-Roman civilisation. Third, through the means of what the Latin American philosopher, Enrique Dussel (2000:465) has called 'semantic slippages', Amin argues that the European narrative made Europe the centre of the world and of modern 'civilisation', the distinctive characteristic of which was science and 'universal reason'. The rest of the world was constructed to be its peripheries, which, it was argued could not or did not have the means to become modern.

Immanuel Wallerstein (1997, 2006) has extended this perspective to suggest that Eurocentrism defines the theory and practices of social science. In the nineteenth century social sciences naturalized the distinctions between 'scientific universalism against essential particulars' when it elaborated a theory of progress. It used the tropes of historiography, an analysis of (Western) civilization, and Orientalism(Wallerstein, 1997:94) to create an 'original epistemology' (Wallerstein, 2006:48). Consequently, this epistemology became 'a key element' in comprehending and legitimizing the project of modernity.

This rationale is further extended by Enrique Dussel and Anibal Quijano when they assert what Amin had said earlier-that Eurocentrism was a theory of constructing a self-defined ethnocentric theory of history, that of 'I'. They also affirm, in a manner similar

# Chapter 9: Intervening in the Geopolitics of Travelling Theory

to Amin, that the European narrative and thus its theory of history simultaneously makes invisible and silences events, processes and actions of violence against the rest of the world, without which Europe could not have become modern. They extend this thesis to suggest that Eurocentrism is not only a theory of history but an episteme, a theory of power/knowledge. If this epieteme theorised the 'I', it also theorized the 'other', the 'periphery'. Thus Dussel argues:

> ...Modernity is, in fact, a European phenomena, but one constituted in a dialectical relation with a non-modern alterity that is its ultimate content. Modernity appears when Europe appears itself as the 'centre' of *World* history that it inaugurates; the periphery that surrounds this centre is consequently part of its self-definition. The occlusion of this periphery ... leads the major thinkers of the centre into a Eurocentric fallacy in their understanding of modernity (Dussel 1993: 65).

Second, this episteme now termed 'categorical imperative,' simultaneously creates the knowledge of the 'I' (Europe, the moderns, the West) against the 'other' (as the peripheral, non-modern, and the East). This perspective legitimizes a theory of the separate and divided nature of the knowledge of the West and the East. It divides the attributes of the West and the East by giving value to the two divisions; while one is universal, superior and 'emancipatory', the other is particular, and non-emancipatory and thus inferior. Dussel quotes Immanuel Kant who argued that while European 'Enlightenment is the exodus of humanity by its own efforts from the state of guilty immaturity'...'laziness and cowardice are the reasons why the great part of humanity remains pleasurably in the state of immaturity' (Dussel, 1993: 68). This inferiority, a condition of its not becoming modern, in turn further legitimates the need to emulate the 'moderns' and to accept the colonising process as a 'civilizing' process. This was the myth of modernity and led, according to Dussel to the management of the world-system's 'centrality':

> If one understands Europe's modernity—a long process of five centuries—as the unfolding of new possibilities derived from its centrality in world history and the corollary constitution of all other cultures as its periphery, it becomes clear that, even though all cultures are ethnocentric, modern European ethnocentrism is the only one that might pretend to claim universality for itself. Modernity's Eurocentrism lies in the confusion between abstract universality and the concrete world hegemony derived from Europe's position as center (Dussel, 2002:222).

Third, as mentioned above, Eurocentric knowledge is based on the construction of multiple and repeated divisions or oppositions which gets constructed as hierarchies. These oppositions, Anibal Quijano (2000) argues, are based on a racial classification of the world population. This principle becomes the assumption to further divide the peoples of the world in geo cultural terms, with which are attached further oppositions, such as reason and body, science and religion, subject and object, culture and nature, masculine and feminine, modern and traditional. While European modernity conceptualized its growth in terms of linear time, it sequestered the (various) East(s) divided between two cultural groups, the 'primitives'/barbarians and the civilized as being enclosed in their (own) spaces. No wonder this episteme could not provide the resources to elaborate a theory of space, affirming Karl Marx's insightful statement of 'annihilation of space by time'.

The consolidation of these attributes across the West-East axis and its subsequent hierarchisation across spatial regions in the world allow for social science to discover the 'nature' of the various peoples, nations and ethnic groups in the world in terms of the attributes of the binaries. This structure of power, control, and hegemony termed by Quijano as 'coloniality of power' is founded on two myths:

> ...first, the idea of the history of human civilization as a trajectory that departed from a state of nature and culminated in Europe; second, a view of the differences between Europe and non-Europe as natural (racial) differences and not consequences of a history of power. Both myths can be unequivocally recognized in the foundations of evolutionism and dualism, two of the nuclear elements of Eurocentrism (Quijano, 2000:542).

These seminal assumptions were embodied in the framing of the disciplines of sociology and anthropology in late nineteenth century. Sociology became the study of modern (European-later to be extended to western) society while anthropology was the study of (non-European and non-western) traditional societies. Thus sociologists studied how the new societies evolved from the deadwood of the old; a notion of time and history were embedded in its discourse. By contrast, anthropologists studied how space/place organised 'static' culture that could not transcend its internal structures to become modern. These frames constructed the academic knowledge of ex-colonial countries such as India, Egypt or Indonesia as colonial administrators and anthropologists further divided the East that they were studying in separate geo-spatial territories with each territory given an overarching cultural value.

Fourth, this classificatory scheme, that of use of the attribute of race to divide the peoples of the world found its own 'local' legitimation, its own articulation and a 'voice', once colonial authorities had imposed these to divide the 'natives'. Thus this project found an expression (ironically and paradoxically) in the work of indigenous intellectuals in the subcontinent searching to find an identity against colonialism. For them, the immediate necessity was to locate 'our modernities'. Thus unlike the Europeans for whom, "the present was the site of one's escape from the past", for the indigenous Eastern intellectual "it is precisely the present [given the colonial experience] from which we feel we must escape". As a result the desire to be creative and search for a new modernity is transposed to the past, a past ironically constructed by orientalist colonial modernity. Thus Partha Chatterjee, the subaltern historian, argues 'we construct a picture of 'those days' when there was beauty, prosperity and healthy sociability. This makes the very modality of our coping with modernity radically different from the historically evolved modes of Western modernity' (Chatterjee, 1997:19). This past was now rarefied to understand the present and the future; an orientalist imagination came to define the so called indigenous expression.

Obviously racial constructions of 'difference' found a new legitimacy within an elitist indigenous ideology as these two overlapped each other to organise the study of social sciences. Eurocentric episteme' thus became part of the 'background understandings' and 'beliefs' and have obfuscated a critical look at knowledge production of social sciences in most ex-colonial countries. In this paper, I am arguing that in ex-colonial countries this knowledge 1) was produced as part of colonial politics of rule; 2) was expressed and organised in terms of values that were in opposition to modernity; 3) used disciplinary practices such as Indology[2], Orientalism and ethnography to elaborate the politics of rule; 4) was codified with the help of native elite intelligentsia; 5) reflected the social order as represented by the native intelligentsia both in its expressed articulations (in anthropology and later social anthropology) and in its silences (in economics); 6) and mitigated an examination of the way classification systems of the state organized new forms of inequalities in the colonial territory.

## Endogenous critique of colonial social sciences

The legacy of Eurocentrism was thus not only in creating a global hierarchy of knowledge divisions in terms of universal and particular but to ensure that this episteme is diffused across the colonial space and through this process obfuscate an analysis of the principles organizing the transition process across the colonized globe.

Partha Chatterjee (1997:19) has reminded us that "...(t)here is no promised land of modernity outside the network of power" and one may add, outside its discourse. Modernity brought together for the once colonised two promises: the struggle for 'dreams of freedom' and at the same time, the experience of being "victims of modernity'; its episteme organised both the 'desire for power' and the 'resistance of power'. No wonder the discussion on modernity in most ex-colonial countries has been steeped in ambiguity given colonialism's framing of modernity, as a discourse simultaneously of freedom and of subjugation. Nationalism structured an understanding of being both unfree and free to change the world. In so doing it now reconstructed the colonial binary in a new context, that of the nation-state. How did this ambiguity play itself out in framing of nationalist social sciences?

In most ex-colonial countries social science disciplines were moored in the project of nationalism. Below, I give an example of India and elaborate how nationalism related itself with social sciences. Nationalist thought in India had three currents: the modernists, the traditionalists and modern-traditionalists (Parekh,

---

[2] In India Orientalist thought was defined as Indology, a field that laid out the theory and methodology of the study of language, religion and history of India's past through textual sources.

1995). While all three agreed that colonialism, domination by the British, the extraction and control for imperialist purposes of India's rich material resources and the destruction of its vitality and ideas by the colonial elite were the key components of the problems that structured the country, there were differences regarding the possible solutions.

The 'modernists' wanted India to identify with the future and with progress. They argued that the problem was with the past, with Indian culture that had made the 'Indian' people passive, lifeless and non-productive. They advocated the path set by Europe earlier and wanted India to have a new industrial economy, free from agrarian dependencies. It is no coincidence that these ideas became the source for building a new discipline of economics and helped to chart the knowledge regarding planning and developmental in independent India.

The modernist perspective was countered by the 'real traditionalists'. The latter argued for a need to draw out concepts and theories from the past-from that of India's rich histories and its civilisation. Though this civilisation had suffered a decline, it was essentially and fundamentally sound and was embodied with much strength. These strengths had kept the 'Indian' people together over centuries and these ideas will continue to bind them together in the future. Indians and its social sciences needed to mobilise their society's creative resources for its regeneration without losing its coherence and inner balance. They also cautioned Indians not to imitate the West, take its language and its values. India has to work out its own salvation in its own terms-its temperaments, traditions and circumstances. This set of ideas framed sociological language in India and can be best seen in the work of G.S.Ghurye[3] who was Head of the Department of Sociology at the University of Bombay, for thirty five long years and who trained most of the next generation of sociologists in India. He used an Orientalist methodology to discuss indigenous concepts that organised Indian traditions: such as caste, tribe and family system and Hinduism[4] (Patel, 2013, 2013a).

---

3   Ghurye's addresses the question of civilization in his magnus opus, *Caste and Race in India* (1932).
4   The traditional nationalists suggested that India was a civilisation and thereby borrowed and reinterpreted orientalist knowledge to articulate an

For Ghurye, culture and civilisation were understood as being the same: as a complex of ideas, beliefs, values and social practices (Upadhyay, 2002: 44). His work rarely mentions any material practices. He eschews any discussion on livelihoods, control over resources or classes. Briefly, Ghurye argued that India was a civilisation. He suggested that Indian civilisation drew its unity from Hinduism and that Brahminism and its ideas and values provided the core values of this Hindu civilisation. Brahmins were considered 'natural' leaders, the torch bearers and bearers of this civilisation and its 'moral guides'. As a result, sociology in India was initiated with the Orientalist idea that the territory of the nation state is equivalent with its culture.

The third trend, the 'modern-traditionalists' framed the ideas of syncretism. The goal of modern-traditionalists was to understand the present and construct a social science language best suited to bring in transformation of the specific culture that they were studying: India. Unlike the traditionalists they did not advocate the necessity to go back to the golden age, some of them even suggested that democracy has an indigenous moorings.

A focused critique to the 'real traditionalist' argument emerged in the work of the historian D.D. Kosambi[5] who critiqued the Indological assumption that India did not have a continuous history, that its history was a series of episodes, that the sources of this history can be located within the written texts rather than non-written sources and that culture and religion organise the unity of India's territory, rather than its diverse material and ecological experiences. He inaugurated a paradigm shift from colonial and nationalist frameworks and the centrality of dynastic history to a

---

Indian version. The notion of civilisation has a long history in orientalism. In the late 18th and early 19th century, Orientalists generalised on the basis of the Greek and Egyptian civilisations. Later with the discovery of 'Indian' civilisation the study of India was absorbed into the existing discourse about antique civilizations. Early British orientalists used Sanskrit texts to study this civilization and to place it within the linear theories of history. Some even argued that the high culture of Hindu civilization emerged from Greek influence. However the traditional nationalists inverted this argument to suggest that Greek culture has learnt its science from India.

5   Kosambi (1907–1966) was a mathematician who was an historian by choice. Contemporary historians have argued that he has reframed Indian historiography (Gurukkal, 2008).

## Chapter 9: Intervening in the Geopolitics of Travelling Theory

new framework integrating social and economic history that related the cultural dimensions of the past to these investigations. Kosambi's theories displaced the episteme of colonial modernity that coupled place/territory with cultural identity (India as civilisation). This position together with his assertion that India had a long history allowed contemporary Marxists (henceforth) to wholly disregard the 'culturist' language that structured colonial and nationalist discourse.

For Kosambi the history of ancient India cannot be extracted from texts written by 'brahmins' and reconstructed during the colonial period as part of its project to codify 'ancient Indian civilisation'. Rather what was needed was the use of combined methods inputting linguistics, archaeology, anthropology and sociology together in the perspective of the materialistic social theory of history (Thapar, 2008). Third, Marxism was thus seen as a tool to assess and understand the material and environmental history. It was not perceived as an all-pervasive ideology or a positivist theory that structured the debates of historical sociology. Given the phenomenal diversity of India, Kosambi completely rejected any unilinear sequence of "modes of production" and argued for the simultaneous presence of several modes of production at any given time in India's long history (Thapar, 2008).

Kosambi argues that this 'diversity' is part of a collective memory of the people of India. Oftentimes this is legitimised by using scriptures that elaborate theories of this 'diversity' and thereby allowed certain classes and the elite to relive these precepts as values and ideals. Instead as a Marxist historian, he would argue that material conditions organising ancient Indian civilization stagnated and died out, leaving only its 'culturist' memories in place. A society, according to Kosambi, is held together by bonds of production. The philosophic individual cannot reshape a mechanized world nearer to heart's desire by the 'eternal' ideologies developed over two thousand years ago in a bullock-cart country". (Kosambi, 1956: xiii). Following him historians of ancient India have tried to demystify the ways in which the past was constructed by indologists and then used as political ideologies.

## The Politics of Travelling Theory

Since the late 1970s and particularly after the 1990s, the dynamics of the world have changed. At one level, the world has contracted. It has opened up possibilities of diverse kinds of trans-border flows and movements, of capital and labour and of signs and symbols, organised oftentimes in intersecting spatial circuits. It is no longer north to south and space no longer encapsulates culture at all points of time. While in some contexts and moments these attributes cooperate, at other times, these are in conflict and contest each other. Thus even though we all live in one global capitalist world with a dominant form of modernity, inequalities and hierarchies are increasing and so are fragmented identities. Lack of access to livelihoods, infrastructure, and political citizenship now blends with exclusions relating to cultural and group identity and are organised in varied spatial and temporal zones. Fluidity of identities and their continuous expression in unstable social manifestations and in new geographical regions demand a fresh perspective to assess and examine them. Not only do contemporary social processes, sociabilities and structures need to be perceived through new and novel spaces, prisms and perspectives but it is increasingly clear that these need to be seen through new methodological protocols. As a consequence, should we not be in search of a new framework that moves beyond the 19$^{th}$ and early 20$^{th}$century social science language and addresses the new challenges posed by contemporary processes?

Some social scientists have argued that the best way out of this epistemic and methodological difficulty is to particularise the universals of European thought. Dipesh Chakrabarty, the historian of subaltern studies has made a similar argument. He coined a new methodology called, 'provincialisation', and suggested that its quest was the following:

> To "provincialize" Europe was precisely to find out how and in what sense European ideas that were universal were also, at one and the same time, drawn from the very particular intellectual and historical traditions that could not claim universal validity (Chakarbarty, 2008:xiii).

I would argue that we have to evolve a twofold strategy. On one hand there is a need to deconstruct and provincialise Eurocentrism and make discrete its entanglements with casteist and patriarchal ideologies, imageries, and dispositions in social science theories and practices. This is what Hountondji (1997) means when he advocates the need for endogenising social science. Suggesting that all nationalist knowledges remain particularistic, (he calls it 'ethnoscience') and thus part of the colonial and neo-colonial binaries of the universal-particular and the global-national, he presents a new alternative that he calls endogeneity. The latter appropriates and assimilates through a critical mind all international heritage available including the very process of scientific and technological innovation and then interface it with a critical assessment and re-appropriation of one's heritage recognising its adaptability and creativity. "This is not traditionalism, but the exact opposite" (Hountondji, 1995:9).

Much the same is suggested by Enrique Dussel through his conception of 'transmodernity'. Dussel suggests a need for a new theory of modernity that simultaneously comprehends the dialectic of exploitation together with the epistemic subjugation and which excavates and builds new versions as these manifest themselves through an exterior reading of its history. "Trans"-modernity affirms "from *without*" the essential components of modernity's own excluded cultures in order to develop a new civilization for the twenty-first century. In the context of ex-colonial countries, this perspective implies a necessity to explore not only the pre modern but also the way colonialism and later nationalism mobilised elite western patriarchal visions together with social science practices which self-consciously absented an analysis of inequities and exclusions since the late 19th century.

This implies secondly a need to go beyond the 'content' of the social sciences as it is practised in the Global North, that is the explanations they offer and the narratives they construct shaped as they are by a genealogy that is both European and colonial. Rather, we need to analyse their very 'form,' that is, the concepts through which explanations become possible, including the very idea of what counts as an explanation. Obviously, it is not possible to suggest that the social sciences are purely and simply European and are, therefore, 'wrong'. Such an argument has little relevance given the fact that we are and remain within one world capitalist system. We cannot dispense with many of these categories, but it is important to recognise that they often provide only partial and often times flawed understandings. We need not reinvent the wheel;

however there is a necessity to generate explanations that are relevant for different contexts.

## Constraints, Limitations and Possibilities

Till now, the paper has suggested that the Eurocentrism was an episteme 'that needed to be contested and indicated the various strategies that can used to displace this episteme'. However, Eurocentrism is not only an episteme, it is also a way to organize the production, distribution, consumption and reproduction of knowledge unequally across the different parts of the world. The Malaysian thinker Syed Hussein Alatas (1972) and the African philosopher, Paulin Hountondji (1997) have discussed these as the 'captive mind' and 'extraversion' (or externally oriented knowledge) respectively. They argue that the syndrome of 'captive mind' and 'extraversion' can be seen in the teaching and learning processes, in the way the curriculum and syllabus is framed; in the processes of research: the designing of research questions and in the methods and methodologies being used; in the formulation of criteria adopted for accepting articles for journals and books, and ultimately in defining what and where one publishes and what is academic excellence. The argument here is that the trenches of this episteme' are deep and layered. Thus this episteme cannot be merely replaced through cognitive supplants of concepts, theories and methods, which was what the best of nationalist social science in ex-colonial countries attempted to do.

This is its history in many newly independent countries such as Nigeria, Brazil or South Africa. Scholars have noted some positive outcomes of this strategy, e.g. the growth of nationally oriented intellectual infrastructures that include not only universities, research institutes and laboratories but also journals, publishing houses together with professional norms and ethics. However it has also promoted varied but uneven intellectual traditions within different nation states and their professional orientation is very limited. More importantly this strategy has not been able to question Eurocentrism as an episteme. Institutionalisation under the aegis of the elite nationalist orientation has reproduced practices in place across the Global North.

The consequence of this dependence has been the 'infantilisation' of scientific practices within the Global South regions[6]. Not only are these at an incipient stage of growth but this very condition encourages brain drain and further intellectual dependencies. Additionally, an intellectual culture defined by northern social science is held out as a model for the rest of the world. It is backed by the sheer size of its intellectual, human, physical, and capital resources together with the infrastructure that is necessary for its reproduction. This includes not only equipment, but archives, libraries, publishing houses, and journals; an evolution of a professional culture of intellectual commitment and engagement which connects the producers and consumers of knowledge; institutions such as universities and students having links with others based in northern nation-states and global knowledge production agencies. Farid Alatas has called this academic dependency[7].

The question that we need to address is how do we confront it? How is this possible? How should we move forward? Obviously we need to move out of truth claims that are universal and assert those that are contextual to make the social science market competitive rather than monopolistic as it is now. One tactic is to 'open' up the market of production, distribution and consumption of knowledge to new audiences, institutions, and processes. Social science needs to articulate itself in many expressions at different sites (other than academic) and engage with the ways these define their distinctive culturist oeuvres, epistemologies, theoretical frames, cultures of science and languages of reflection, as well as sites of knowledge production and transmission. In addition to classrooms and departments, together with syllabus formulations and protocol of professional codes, this type of move can also include campaigns, movements, and advocacies. Thus, its production involves a creative dialectic within and between activists, scholars, and communities assessing, reflecting, and elucidating immediate events and

---

[6] See the UNESCO report on the social science production in the Global North versus the Global South, 2010.

[7] Farid Alatas (2003) defines academic dependencies as having six attributes: a) dependence on ideas; b) dependence on the media of ideas; c) dependence on the technology of education; d) dependence on aid for research as well as teaching; e) dependence on investment in education; and f) dependence of Third World social scientists on demand in the West for their skills

issues which intervene to define the research process, as well as the organising and systematising knowledge of the discipline in long-term institutionalised processes central for teaching and learning.

The second tactic is to build intellectual networks across institutions and scholarship among and between scholars of the non-Atlantic region. Horizontal linkages between localities, regions, and nation-states of the non-Atlantic regions can substitute for existing vertical hierarchical linkages between imperialist and ex-colonial countries or between that of core and periphery in production, distribution, and consumption of knowledge. This type of initiative will help to reflect collectively on common and relevant themes that structure the experience of being part of the 'south'. Through this type of process and intent, it will be possible to outline a 'south' perspective to define contemporary social science.

# References

Chatterjee, P. (1997). *Our Modernity*, Rotterdam & Dakar : Sephis, Codesria Publication, 1–20.

Chakrabarty, D. (2008). *Provincializing Europe. Post-colonial thought and Historical Difference,* Princeton: Princeton University Press.

Dussel, E. (1993). Eurocentrism and Modernity. *Boundary 2 (3):* 65–76.

Dussel, E. (2000). Europe, Modernity and Eurocentrism, Nepantla: *Views from South 1(3):* 465–478.

Dussel, E. (2002). World-System and "Trans"-Modernity, *Nepantla: Views from South* 3 (2): 221–244.

Ghurye, G. S. (1932). *Caste and Race in India*, Bombay: Popular Prakashan.

Gurukkal, R. (2008). The Kosambi Effect. The Hermeneutic Turn that Shook Indian Historiography, Special Issue, D.D. Kosambi. The Man and his Work, *Economic and Political Weekly,* 43 (30) 89–96

Hountondji, P. (1995). Producing Knowledge in Africa Today, *African Studies Review,* 38 (3), 1–10.

Hountondji, P (1997). Introduction in P Hountondji (ed.) *Endogenous Knowledge. Research Trails*, Dakar: Codesria.

Kosambi, D.D. (1956). *An Introduction to the Study of Indian History.* Bombay: Popular Prakashan.

Mignolo, W. D. (2002). The Geopolitics of Knowledge and the Colonial Difference. *The South Atlantic Quarterly,* 101 (1): 57–96.

Patel, S. (2006). Beyond Binaries. A Case for Self Reflexive Sociologies, *Current Sociology, 54 (3),* 381–395

Patel, S. (2007). Sociological Study of Religion: Colonial Modernity and Nineteenth Century Majoritarianism, *Economic and Political Weekly, 42 (13)*, 1089–1094.

Patel, S. (2010). The Imperative and the Challenge of Diversity. Reconstructing Sociological Traditions in an Unequal World. In M. Burawoy et al (ed.s) *Facing an Unequal World, Challenges for a Global Sociology Vol.1*, Taiwan : Academia Sinica, 48–62.

Patel, S. (2010a). Sociology's 'Other'. The Debate on European Universals in the *The Encyclopaedia of Life Support Systems (Social Sciences and Humanities)*, UNESCO. http://www.eolss.net.

Patel, S. (2010b). Introduction. Diversities of Sociological Traditions in Sujata Patel, (ed) *The ISA Handbook of Diverse Sociological Traditions*, London : Sage, 1–18.

Patel, S. (2011). Ruminating on Sociological Traditions in India in S. Patel (ed.), *Doing Sociology in India: Genealogies, Locations, and Practices,* New Delhi: Oxford University Press. xi–xxxviii.

Patel, S. (2011a). Sociology in India: Trajectories and Challenges. *Contributions to Indian Sociology, 45 (3)* 427–435.

Patel, S. (2013). Orientalist-Eurocentric framing of sociology in India: A discussion on three Twentieth-century sociologists. *Political Power and Social Theory: A Research Annual*, Bingley, UK: Emerald Books, Volume 25, 107–130.

Patel, S. (2013a). Are the theories of Multiple Modernities Eurocentric? The Problem of Colonialism and its Knowledge(s). In S. Arjomand & E. Reis (eds.) *Worlds of Difference*, London : Sage Studies in International Sociology, 28–45.

Parekh, B. (1995). Jawaharlal Nehru and the Crisis of Modernisation. In U. Baxi and B. Parekh (eds.) *Crisis and Change in Contemporary India*, New Delhi: Sage.

Quijano, A. (1993). Modernity, Identity, and Utopia in Latin America, *Boundary 2, 20 (3)* 140–155.

Quijano, A. (2000). Coloniality of Power, Eurocentrism and Latin America, *Nepantla: Views from South 1:* 553–800.

Quijano, A. (2007). Coloniality and Modernity/Rationality, *Cultural Studies. 21 (2–3)* 168–178.

UNESCO (2010). *World Social Science Report. Knowledge Divides,* Paris.

Upadhya, C. (2007). The Idea of Indian Society: G.S. Ghurye and the Making of Indian Sociology. In P. Uberoi, N. Sundar & S. Deshpande (eds.) *Anthropology in the East. Founders if Indian Sociology and Anthropology*, Delhi: Permanent Black, 194–255.

Wallerstein, I. (1997). Eurocentrism and its Avatars: The Dilemmas of Social Science', *New Left Review* 226:93–107.

Wallerstein, I. (2006) *European Universalism: The Rhetoric of Power.* London: New Press.

# Chapter 10:
# The Impact of Internationalization on Post-Soviet Social Sciences and Humanities

Igor Yegorov and Pal Tamas

Since the collapse of the Soviet Union, social sciences and humanities in that part of the world have passed through a painful period of transformation, which is far from completion. On the one hand, the 'old' system of organizations and interactions that had successfully formed and maintained scholars and researchers during Soviet times has significantly deteriorated. On the other hand, new structures and sources of funding have been established during the last quarter of the century with significant foreign influence, mainly by Western institutions. Scholars during the Soviet period were faced with ideological strictures, inefficiencies, and substantial isolation from the West. In the past twenty-five years, they have been forced to confront a wide range of other problems that threaten to destroy what had been the mainstay of research and training in the region—thriving intellectual communities.

The problems confronting the social sciences and humanities in the former Soviet Union (FSU) and those facing the research community today can be divided into four broad categories: infrastructural, methodological (intellectual), cultural (personal), and politically-related. These categories are linked, but are also distinct. Each must be considered in turn before we proceed to consider existing models and outcomes of the latest transformations.

## Infrastructural Problems

Here, the problem is quite clear: the institutional infrastructure for supporting research in the social sciences and the humanities has largely deteriorated throughout the region after the collapse of political systems in the post-Soviet states. While it is true that there are islands of success and of excellence, the overall picture is mixed. To put it in the sharpest terms, the formal institutions (research centers, universities, state research programs) for supporting scholars have crumbled. Some authors remarked that the new international boundaries dividing what was once the Soviet Union have inhibited the maintenance of previously long-standing ties (Kolodiy, 2006).

In the first decade after the collapse of the Soviet Union the region's general economic degradation eroded salaries, often impoverishing scholars and institutions. Some individuals and institutions have found non-academic means of support. This is not surprising. In such countries like Georgia or Ukraine, where the salary for a top University professor or academician was only $50 per month in the first half of 1990s, it was no wonder that scholars began to search in other fields for sustenance (Khromov, 1996). However fortuitous and creative such funding might be, non-scholarly income necessarily pulls scholars and institutions away from their research activities. The 'internal brain drain' in many of these societies away from academic life, broadly defined, is often greater than the 'external brain drain' abroad.

Economic decline has also eroded investment in the institutional infrastructure for social science and humanities' research. Libraries and archival repositories find themselves in especially difficult positions. The financial situation has forced governments to reduce expenditures on subscription and even to completely eliminate access to some government documents, manuscripts, and cultural artifacts. Many archives recently have been allocated little or no funds beyond wages and funds to cover the most basic operations. As a result, they have had to become self-supporting through fees. Libraries in the majority of the post- Soviet states were in a similar position, faced with declining budgets, lack of funds for international journal subscriptions, and delays in inter-library loan exchanges force them into ad hoc short-term arrangements. Even now libraries in many post-Soviet countries continue to be confronted with the almost insoluble problem of book preservation at the same time that they struggle to catch up with advances made in digital equipment and databases. The situation is worsening along with the growing price of a subscription, especially in the periods of sharpening economic crisis, as has taken place in the modern Ukraine in 2014-2015.

In addition to the crisis facing libraries and archives, journals, key publishers, and various databases have suffered as well. While specific journals, libraries, and archives are doing better than the norm, the general trend has been one of institutional decline and degradation. The impact of all of these trends has been hardest felt in provincial centers. On the other hand, some provincial research centres and universities have started to publish their own journals thanks to the introduction of educational fees for students or other sources of income. However, the level of the bulk of publications remains relatively low, and they are not included in the corresponding international databases.

Of equal importance, the ability of scholars and institutions to remain in contact with one another has declined as transportation and communication costs have risen. The Internet has provided something of a counterweight to the overall decline in scholarly infrastructure, although access to important sources is limited due to financial constraints.

Collapsing institutions have not necessarily prompted new managerial strategies in academic institutions. The record is mixed: there are some examples of successful academic entrepreneurs pulling their institutions into a new era, including such research centres, as the Higher School of Economics in Russia or Kyiv-Mohyla Academy in the Ukraine. Yet, overall, administrative and bureaucratic expectations often remain strikingly inflexible, old style managers prove increasingly ineffectual in a changing environment, and corruption degrades many otherwise worthy endeavors. In addition, the process of accreditation for new programs, institutions, and degrees is difficult. Barriers to the interconnection of research and teaching remain high in many institutions, as research is mainly concentrated in special research institutes, while universities are predominantly learning centres with a very high teaching burden established for professors. In the largest post-Soviet states, the Ukraine and Russia, expenditures on R&D in the university sector did not exceed 10% of GERD in the last 20 years (Gokhberg, 2014). Scholars also complain about restrictive teaching loads that relegate research and professional development to a second-rate priority (Mirskaya and Rabkin, 2004).

Some of the worst inefficiencies of the old system remain while new systems are slow to evolve. The simultaneous devaluation of old knowledge fields and assertion of new disciplines, research strategies, and methods creates a number of additional organizational and institutional issues that simply cannot be managed effectively. While these shifts in disciplinary focus and methodology are inevitable, they only exacerbate the structural constraints hindering the development of the social sciences and humanities in the region.

## Methodological (intellectual) problems

There are, of course, many positive aspects of the changes for the social sciences and humanities in the region over the past two decades and a half. For example, the region's academic community is more open to the broader international community than ever before. What one studies, how one studies it, and what one says about one's research are now freer decisions in a manner that could never have been possible under the Soviet regime. Moreover, a number of private research and training institutions have broken the monopoly of the Soviet state over the social science and humanities enterprise.

At the same time, it is worth stressing that the research agenda generated by the post-Soviet transition offers an opportunity to study some of the most fundamental issues of many social science and humanities disciplines. Economic theory will eventually be challenged in myriad ways by the economic transition; historians need to come to terms with a past that is more complex now that Soviet interpretations are no longer the model; and the study of politics has become a new discipline as well. Some subfields, such as opinion polling, have taken on new life. On the other hand, new types of control over interpretation of research results on behalf of university administration have emerged. So, for example, centers of so-called 'liberal' orientation have emerged, which do not tolerate other approaches within their walls. In history, more nationalistic and aggressive theories have started to dominate, while alternative views on historical events are not supported by state institutions.

As an example, let us consider interesting transformations, which are observed in economic sciences. In the largest countries of the region, Ukraine and Russia, two dominant trends are evident. One of them is associated with utilization of Western – oriented approaches. It includes representatives of such institutions as the Higher School of Economics, Gaidar Institute (Russia), Kyiv-Mohila Academy, Kyiv School of Economics (Ukraine), and numerous private think-tanks in both countries. Scholars from these research centres are following mainstream economic theories, they are trying to use econometrics and other mathematical methods widely to support their arguments. It is even possible to say that they are integrated into key networks in the economics discipline, which studies transformation processes from the 'orthodox' positions (see, for example, Kuzminov and others, 2005, Tambovtsev, ed., 2009, Oleinik, 2011). On the other hand, there are a large group of scholars, who are trying to develop alternative approaches to economic research, and first of all, to studies of development processes in the post- Soviet states. Partially, their approaches are based on traditional Marxian theory of reproduction, but they cannot be reduced to it (Geets, 2012, Gritsenko, 2008). As Sukharev notes, the main difference between the two camps lies in their assessment of the role of the state in the modern economy (Sukharev, 2013). 'Market-oriented' pro-Western scholars follow the mainstream paradigm of the need to reduce state intervention, while the other group stresses the leading and even growing role of the state in social and economic processes. Of course, there are a number of researchers who remain in intermediary positions, and whose views could be described as a mixture of the two extremes. The division between the two positions is especially evident in Russia. This is because, as Backhouse and Fontaine noted, economic theory is a combination of science and ideology (Backhouse and Fontaine, 2010). Russian rulers are trying to assert their country as a self-sufficient political actor with a certain economic power and X huge potential. And this position is reflected in the research of scholars, who continue the tradition of studies, which was initiated in Soviet times. It is worth mentioning that Soviet economists have developed a number of interesting ideas, such as the so-called SOFE – System of Optimal Functioning of the Economy (Fedorenko, 1968, in regard to planning largescale systems. Achievements of Soviet authors in mathematical modeling are also widely recognized (see, for instance, publications of the Nobel Prize winner L. Kantorovich (1960) or the author of methods of sub-gradient optimization N. Shor (1998)). Bibliometric analysis shows that substantial contribution was made on the general equilibrium theory too. Several economics journals were translated and still are translated completely into English by the leading publishing houses in the West (Malkov, 2014). However, now the main focus is on practical problems of economic development. Some authors are trying to justify return to the planning–type economy. At the same time, they make substantial amendments in classical Marxian analysis of the modern economy by attempting to tie up some well-known postulates with modern approaches to assessments of production factors (Mayevsky, Malkov, 2014, Voronin, Labzunov, 2014). Important contributions have been made into relatively new areas of economics research, notably evolutionary economics (Avotnomov, 1998, Kirdina, 2013, Kleiner, 2014).

However, now special attention has to be paid to the contribution of post-Soviet scholars to the development of the theory of neo-industrialization. This theory has emerged as a 'natural' reaction to the domination of mainstream economic theory in the post-Soviet states and to destruction of the industrial potential in many of them. These studies are a vivid example of neo-Marxian reflection on the negative tendencies in Russian economy, primitivisation and the decline of industrial structures (Glaziev, 1998, Gubanov, 2014, Arkhangelsky, 2014, Amosov, 2014).

'Pro-market' researchers, on the contrary, stress that the post-Soviet countries have 'standard' problems, which are common to all countries in transition (Rusinova, 2010). The difference in funding of the two directions of research is also clear. If the 'pro-state' researchers receive modest support from exclusive state funds, 'pro-market' scholars can also rely on lavish foreign grants.

Yet some challenges have emerged against a backdrop of a general devaluation of the academic enterprise throughout the region. While many social science disciplines prosper, humanities fields that may be less integral to the reform process -many smaller fields in which Soviet scholars have always performed at world level such as sanskritology, iconography, and various subfields of philology— are in decline. Recent gains in archival access, international contacts, and free publication are themselves threatened by the structural impediments mentioned above. As a result, an often private struggle for survival inhibits the capacity of scholars and institutions to respond to long-term research programs.

## Cultural (and Personal) Barriers

This is the point at which personal considerations similarly impinge on intellectual endeavors. Very often individual scholars face impoverishment, a sharp decline in status, a deterioration of collegial interaction, and growing personal isolation. Ironically, those who are successful in receiving support from abroad to make up for these deficiencies are faced with the jealousy of colleagues left behind. In one case, a talented specialist in international law from Kiev National Shevchenko University who received a grant to go to the United States as a Fulbright scholar found his dean and department unwelcoming upon his return, forcing him to move to another university, in spite of the fact that his academic credentials were much higher than those of his colleagues. This example is not unique; even some vice-rectors could not come back to their positions after staying abroad for one or two semesters[1].

On a more personal level, previous belief systems have collapsed, early optimism has turned to disillusionment, and wrenching social change undermines life and career strategies. The evolving position of women in the Caucasus and Central Asia, for example, has the potential of threatening professional opportunities for women scholars in the social sciences and humanities. After gaining independence, some norms of Central Asian societies have received strong support from authorities. Women have started to play more 'traditional' roles in Muslim societies. This is described as a return to the 'roots' and 'national traditions'. In practice, this means that women could (You seem to mean the present, but what you are communicating here is the past. If that is what you mean, fine, if not, this needs to be changed to "can" or change it to "it is difficult for women to reach...") hardly reach high positions in any sphere of public life, including research institutions.

In Russia, a psychology of "us vs. them" is interjecting itself into the small world of the social sciences and humanities. Russia's continuing difficulty to come to terms with the outside world wreaks havoc on a range of disciplines often identified as being inherently "Western." This is especially true for behavioral sciences and some

---

[1]   This information is a result of one of the author's works in the joint Ukrainian –American Commission on Selection of scholars for the Fulbright Program in the 2000s.

areas of sociology, including the studies of situations of persons with non-traditional sexual orientation.

Finally, and perhaps most critical, professional interaction has diminished, contributing to the lack of a sense of belonging to a group. In some areas, younger scholars are left without mentors as senior scholars have left academia or are virtually unavailable as they pursue other endeavors. This leaves even dedicated younger intellectuals without critical support and guidance. As the status of intellectuals declines, there is a corresponding diminished sense of mission for those engaged in intellectual pursuits.

## Politically-related obstacles.

Domestic and international politics in the FSU also pose obstacles that can threaten intellectual pursuits and Western efforts to provide support. The challenges posed by international relations are significant and threaten to become increasingly problematic, particularly in Russia. Growing anti-Western sentiment in Russia and in Belarus creates new obstacles for Western agencies attempting to stimulate mutual co-operation. On another front, the continued functioning of a Soviet-style academic bureaucracy in many places makes engagement with institutional structures problematic at best (Shulga, 2015). There were substantial changes in the institutional structures of the social sciences and humanities in the post-Soviet states.

First, the sizes of many research institutes were reduced. Now the average number of researchers in academic institutes is approximately 2-4 lower than in Soviet times.

Second, an observable trend is the creation of new research centres and institutes within the national academies of sciences. These institutes are oriented to the areas of economics, ethnic studies, demography and so on, which are of special importance for new countries. At the same time, some countries like Georgia have abolished institutes of the Academy of sciences completely.

Third, a sign of change is associated with the creation of independent think-tanks, especially in politology, sociology and economic studies. The problem is that in many cases these institutions are not officially registered as scientific organizations, according to official procedures. Thus, their activities are properly reflected in the state statistics.

Fourth, universities have started to play a more active role in research. It should be mentioned that the university sector is the only one in the largest post-Soviet states, where the number of professionals with doctoral degrees has grown during the last twenty years. However, the problem of scientific productivity in the university sector remains relatively low. University staff is overwhelmed with teaching duties (Balatsky, Yekimova, 2013). Another problem is a growing commercialization of universities (Balatsky, Sergeeva, 2014).

No less of a challenge are highly centralized regimes in some Central Asian states and the nationalist tendencies in some countries, which have politicized the study of history, politics, and many other disciplines.

## Western Influence

Over the past two and a half decades, there have been many efforts to confront the adversities described above. Hundreds of millions of dollars have been spent by public and private funding agencies from the USA and the EU. These efforts have certainly had an impact in redressing some problems and there are many examples of promising initiatives. However, as some experts have noted about the Russian case, 'reformers failed to anticipate the deepening financial and administrative crises in post-communist education and their Western allies were guided more by idealized Western models than by an accurate sense of Russian needs and capacities. It is difficult to assess what have existing programs accomplished and what can Western scholars learn in their efforts to design an alternative model for revitalizing the "invisible college" in the FSU' (The Humanities..., 1999)

In fact, the majority of initiatives have attempted to support a self-sustaining system of higher education. They can be separated into two broad categories: those that operate at the institutional level and those that operate on the individual level. The institutional level programs focus on systemic reform and target the structural problems that hinder institutional change. Individual-level programs target individuals as the building blocks of academia and focus on addressing the intellectual and personal challenges outlined above.

There is a range of institution-level programs that fall within this broad category of activity. One notable approach has been the creation or support of entirely new institutions of higher education. Another important and popular approach is university partnerships between institutions in the former Soviet Union and institutions in the West. There are also partnership programs that seek to foster ties between institutions in the region. Finally, there is a range of curriculum and higher education reform programs that fall into the category of institution-level programs and there are prominent success stories among them[2]. At the same time, the story of programs geared at creating and/or reforming institutions is a complex one facing many obstacles.

The creation of new institutions attempts to avoid the structural problem of institutional inertia by creating entirely new structures that will attract the most progressive scholars and students. This requires a significant, long-term financial commitment on the part of donors. Perhaps, the most far-reaching of such projects are the Moscow School of Social and Economic Sciences, the European University at St. Petersburg, the American University of Armenia, and the European Humanities University in Minsk. All of these institutions can be counted as successes, as they have excellent reputations both at home and abroad.

University partnership programs, on the other hand, often focus on a particular discipline, such as public administration or economics, and try to use long-term contacts with Western counterparts to counteract structural barriers to reform. They usually include faculty training and curriculum development, and sometimes include resource development such as libraries and computer facilities. There are many examples of American partnerships with universities in the region funded by USIA and USAID. Partnerships are also one of the primary vehicles for the reform of higher education in the region by the Europeans. The main European partnership initiative has been the EU TACIS Program, a European Union initiative designed to contribute to the development of the higher education systems of the post- Soviet states and Mongolia. The program supports the process of transformation to market econo-

---

[2] See, for instance, the Master's program on economics "EERC" on Kiev-Mohyla Academy base. Information on the program, teachers, grants. http://dir.meta.ua/ru/siteinfo/139166

mies and democratic societies through curriculum development, reform of higher education structures, and the development of training programs. Although fields designated for funding vary by country, the primary areas include economics, law, engineering and applied technologies, and teacher training. Another large partnership program is the British Know How Fund's Regional Academic Partnerships Scheme (REAP). REAP supports over 100 bilateral partnerships between institutions from the Former Soviet Union and UK higher education institutions in such sectors as health management, environment, and good government. Germany, primarily through the Deutscher Akademischer Austauschdienst (DAAD), has also invested millions of euros in university partnerships.

One type of partnership program was the new provincial partnership program that was part of the Open Society Institute's (OSI) Megaproject in Russia. The provincial partnerships pair such resource-rich institutions, like the New Economic School in Moscow, with progressive provincial universities. The resource-rich schools choose their partners, but it is also possible that the provincial universities choose their partners in an open competition. The partnerships included such activities as seminars, exchanges, curricular development, visiting lectureships, and library assistance.

Finally, there are the institution-level programs that aim to reform curricula or train higher education management and staff. The Salzburg Seminar's Universities Project, for example, targets the structural obstacles to reform by convening conferences where university professionals meet with their Western counterparts to discuss issues of higher education reform. Another example is the Civic Education Project, which administers two programs: one sends Western scholars to universities in the former Soviet Union and Eastern Europe to teach and act as catalysts for curriculum reform; the other helps provide positions and technical support to scholars trained in the West when they return to their home country. In the fields of the natural and physical sciences, the US Civilian Research and Development Foundation's Basic Research and Higher Education Program works at the institutional level as well. It seeks to establish Research and Education Centers within existing universities through a cooperative agreement with the Ministry of Education of the Russian Federation in order to promote permanent links between the university and other research institutions.

## New role of social scientists in the newly created states

From the early 1990s on, important groups of the social science intelligentsia got involved in practical social reforms or even parliamentary politics. Those activities engaged the most pragmatic part of the research communities, the people who in other circumstances would or could be the organizational leaders of academic renewal. Starting in the mid-1990s, the majority of these enthusiasts of practical social reforms usually left the political scene, but the power structure already stabilized by that time made it almost impossible for them to get involved in academic reforms.

Some representatives of research communities used foreign grants and research contracts to leave the region during post- Soviet years, especially in the 1992-2000 period (Zayonchkovskaya, 2004). It is important to stress that groups of potential institution-builders and founders of scientific schools are overrepresented in migration flows. With low academic incomes and the low attractiveness for many academics of better-paid local jobs in the market-oriented applied research centers, many fine researchers saw work abroad as a quality-of-life and professional alternative. Fewer groups in the social sciences than in the natural sciences were involved in this process. But the losses were significant, especially in the younger age groups and in some post-Soviet countries more deeply affected by socio-economic crises. This is reflected in the emigration, internal outflow of specialists to other sectors of the economy and deterioration of the age structure of the research community. As data from the largest post-Soviet states show, in some social sciences, the average age of doctors of science is well over 60. Under the cumulative impact of these factors, political reformers forgot the old academic sector for almost two decades, especially in countries where the positions of the old academic elite were more strongly defended, and limited resources were redistributed from the state budgets. The new, ambitious, dynamic groups of social researchers and projects concentrated in other places and organizations.

At the same time, as it was mentioned above, the new centres and educational programs emerging beyond the traditional academic sector are usually dependent on ongoing fragmented funding from different projects, rather than being integrated into larger systems, and do not provide security for professional careers.

A different model was developed in the more successful reform countries of Eastern and Central Europe, i.e., in Poland and Hungary. Here the intellectual and organizational modernization of the available infrastructure, i.e., of state-supported or state-financed institutions, became the mainstream. Thus, in these countries, there has been no serious dualization, no isolation of old and new research in separate networks, as it takes place in the majority of the post-Soviet states. After some compromises, modern social research was integrated in the major academic institutions.

## Transformation of scientific schools

In the Soviet Union, the scientific schools remained central elements of the organizational landscape of the social sciences. The situation has started to change in the last two decades with the emergence of alternative sources of financing. Old political institutions disappeared, and many intellectuals who in the communist years believed that the research system was the only safe place to survive and to defend their personal autonomy in a hostile environment now left it and started to discover zones of intellectual and professional existence outside of research. So the remaining centres of excellence in research and education started to be based on informal contacts, intergenerational alliances and networks. They saw the role of scientific schools where they still existed, mainly in economics, but also in sociology and political science, as especially important. But the structure of these schools changed significantly. Formally, they were patriarchal institutions centred on strong father-like personalities. The professional concepts and scientific worldview of the respective Great Old Men were transferred to the young through the school's middle-aged generations. With minor changes, this basic structure remains almost intact in the humanities, but began to change dramatically in the 1990s in the 'hard' social sciences. The force of international research contacts seems to have been central in this process.

The structure of schools whose founders possessed international merit was modernized, but not totally transformed. In most cases, even if he was a brilliant scholar, the Maestro, the central personality, was not really involved in international networking, and in the 1970s-1980s, this factor was not yet a major chunk of institution building in the internationally isolated 'socialist' social sciences. Consequently, in the new internationalized order of social research, the Great Old Men lost important portions of their organizational power to the middle-aged strata, who were usually better prepared for international networking than the founder of the school. The really young entering the research enterprise usually searched for integrators to help incorporate them into networks with resources available to them. They often considered middle-aged scholars more capable of integrating them and therefore as having more organizational power than the Maestros.

In some cases, members of that middle-aged generation were unable to make the necessary compromises in the internal power game, and their schools soon collapsed. But others pursued their interests and were able to stabilize their schools in new environments. The new school concept, however, was no longer centred on continuing or further elaborating the master's thoughts, but sought a discursive framework that allowed maximizing the availability of grants. In this respect, the school could be understood as a framing institution capable of packaging available intellectual resources for international and, in very special cases, for national trade as well. Naturally, schools in these situations usually did conserve the disciplines. Especially in resource-intensive research areas, the availability of grants was really limited to young scientists with approaches, methods, and views different from those of the established centre. At the same time, international research careers channeling the central personalities of existing or would-be centres to academic positions in the West had negative impacts on the established scientific schools in the region. Students were usually unable to follow their Masters to world centres. The Internet has improved that situation in the last few years to a certain degree, but has not changed it dramatically. Only very few new schools with distinct international merits emerged in the region.

## Social scientists as experts and advisors

In Soviet times, before the transition started, economists used to have more experience than sociologists or political scientists in policy consulting. Experts in collecting and interpreting data for policy decision-making were better established in their sectors than in areas directly related to ideology, where other social scientists could be used. Overpolitization of decision-making played a role here as well, but formally, the policy community tried to follow international patterns in many sectors of macroeconomics. The available roles of sociologists were more variegated. Sociologists broadly used and interpreted social statistics, but policy makers understood or interpreted their independent intellectual role in a much narrower way. Critical sociologists investigating substantial questions of transformation were not put in expert roles either before or after the changes started. On the one hand, the social policy administrators, former partners of sociologists in expert positions, did not disappear after 1992. Established contacts survived in personal communication. On the other hand, practical advisory roles for political scientists at existing centres are new. Behind the scene, ideologists of the late state socialism were already frequently using research data and other sorts of social science information formatted in accordance with international standards. However, they have to share their power and influence with the new politicians and experts. In some countries, like Armenia, Georgia and the Ukraine, representatives of diasporas have started to play an important role both in political processes and in the social sciences. Very few enlightened party apparatchiks of that time have occupied important positions, even in those countries where strong socialist parties dominated the political landscape of the 1990s. The majority of them, especially the 'party communicators', whose social science concepts were once in relatively high demand, simply disappeared from public view in most countries. Something similar also happened to their former advisors, the political science experts, but with more compromises. In the opinions of the new political class, segments of the research community that were closer to the pre-1992 power structure were therefore illegitimate. Elements of personal trust play an important role everywhere in this business, but the advisory roles around the former communist elite were especially removed from the public eye and based on personal relations. So the new political clients were not interested in the services of those who served the former rulers, despite the qualifications of some people in that circle. Later, in the 2000s, these experts were usually very successful in marketing research and other areas of expertise outside of politics.

During the transformation, new policy makers and new experts emerged on the scene. Both groups were just learning their roles, and in such a turbulent situation the communication between two inexperienced entities has been especially complicated. Former dissident intellectuals occupied important niches in some countries and political movements until the mid-1990s, but that did not generate genuine demand for closer relations between reformers and social researchers. Some of the new policy makers had once been researchers, and they considered themselves and their former professional careers as part of the contemporary social science community and therefore as 'experts' in their respective sectors. In fact, they were not interested in other experts, much less advisors from the community, except for the purpose of buying fresh social data.

The dynamics of the relationships between politicians and social science in public opinion and the media followed another trajectory. In comparison with the 1980s, the role of the political analyst, commentator, or chronist on the TV screen became much larger, or at least more visible. Popular opinion usually overestimated the impact on decision-making of the social scientists who were presented to the public in these programs. With significant delay, in the late 1990s and in 2000s, politicians used this particular mode of perception as well. Those social scientists with high public visibility were often presented to the audience as partners or allies of given political movements or governments, but they were used neither in forming broader concepts of reform, nor in supplying new social data. A new expert model of 'virtual advisors' has emerged. Because this group is highly visible to potential voters, decision-makers want to demonstrate its availability to politics as a further source of their legitimacy, though they are not interested in its concrete advice or knowledge.

However, social scientists produced remarkable changes by using concrete knowledge in the 1990s and 2000s in some countries. At the beginning of transformation in the leading post- Soviet countries (Ukraine and Russia, first of all), many intellectuals and of course many social scientists took personal part in campaign planning and in political communication. Of course, the people involved in these activities were not professional political technologists. Most of the concrete tasks were performed by researchers from the academic sectors, paid case by case for their performances. But the major organizational problem of the 2000s in this area was the growing discrepancy between the step-by-step, systematized or accumulated 'technological' skills of involved researchers as individuals, on the one hand, and the limited efforts in infrastructure building for them, on the other. The creation of organizational frameworks for knowledge generation usually lagged behind the accumulated personal experience of would-be political technologists formally still occupying academic jobs. The political system in most countries of the region in the late 2000s started to suffer from the low effectiveness of such practice. In those years, the policy intellectuals without proper infrastructure started to be marginalized on the markets of political expertise. At the end, they were replaced by consulting firms more or less similar to their Western functional counterparts. This change had two consequences. The first is connected to the structure of research, the second is related to the self-images of the social science elite. At the very end, the upper strata of academic social researchers enjoyed the dual job market of the 1990s and 2000s. On the one hand, they used to receive higher consulting fees as experts, but on the other hand, they continued to play the high-status roles of academic gurus. Also, their informal or only poorly formalized contacts with the political elite could be understood, both by the public and in their own role interpretations, as continuous involvement in the reforms and a kind of direct personal impact on the process of change in society. The latter was especially important for those social scientists that continued to be prisoners of the old role models of the Russian intelligentsia. For these public intellectuals, the availability of advisory positions was interpreted as an organic role or as a continuation of Russian tradition (Fortov, 2002). They were ready to accept them as part of their illusory involvement in political decisions. They continued to perceive these illusions as reality, even in indefensible situations. But in the late 1990s, they were forced to choose. Either they became practical consultants with real job descriptions and real income, accepting the asymmetries of service professions, or they continued to serve in the academic sector, while being quickly marginalized by professional policy consultants. Academic incomes in most countries continued to grow during the 2000s, but even where they did, this replacement meant financial losses for these 'dual' professionals.

Politicians also interpreted the new professional structure of experts as being quite ambivalent. On the one hand, the services offered by the new commercial consulting sector may have been more professional than the previous ones. But in the absence of academic interference, they were less stimulated for building concepts. Cooperation was more hierarchical, based on clear dependencies between services and their clients; the tasks were formulated in a more simple language; and the asymmetries grew rapidly.

But the neo-statist politicians of the 2000s and especially in the 2010s in some countries were not interested in legitimizing themselves by taking the intellectual's side anymore, and in general terms they were afraid of multifunctional players on the political scene (including the dual role of academic advisors), who make that scene more complex to calculate.

Most social researchers do not take part in guiding the change individually, but are rather integrated in various think tanks, searching for access to policy communities to inject new ideas into current debates. A policy community is all potential actors who share a common 'policy' focus and, sooner or later, succeed in shaping policy. In these networks, think tanks provide organizational and communication links between the different audiences. Participating as an active player in the processes of transformation, the social scientist may play two traditional roles: that of judge or that of historian. These roles cannot be confronted simply as being active or passive, near or distant, present- or future-oriented. The affinities imply convergence as well as divergence. In the classical tradition, historical writing had to vividly present characters and situations. The historian, like the judge, was expected to make a convincing argument by communicating the illusion of reality, exhibiting evidence he or someone else adduced. The tradition based on moral and political court speeches, followed by condemnations, has gone on for a long time and has been integrated in social researcher's modern role sets. A sort of judicial model is deeply incorporated not only in sociology, but also in historiography. In the last two decades, everywhere, and not only in Post-Soviet countries, words like PROOF or even TRUTH have acquired an unfashionable ring in the social sciences. This extreme anti-positivist attitude turns out to be a sort of inverted positivism.

The processes of institution building and problems of communication between different groups of scholars had significant impact on professional languages. We do not think primarily about the transformation of discourse or the change in semantics, but about basic structural problems like fragmentation and eclecticism. Those new professional languages of the social sciences in the post-communist world are mixtures of technical terms, fragments of Western theories that were fashionable 15-20 years ago, and Marxist terms isolated from their original intellectual or theoretical environments.

## Conclusion

The social sciences and humanities in the post-Soviet countries have developed in a completely new environment in the past two and a half decades. Four major problems reflecting this situation are:

1. Many of the projects (practically all of them in the beginning, in the early 1990s, but even now many continue doing it) interpret the transformation as the confrontation of antagonistic systems, the Bad and the Good Society, totalitarianism' and 'democracy'. This normative approach is politically understandable, but makes the manifest descriptions and interpretations of continuous processes and structures hard to interpret or even invisible.

2. International research cooperation functions as a strong thematic filter for systematic interpretations of that reality. Almost every international project in the region in the 1990- 2000s used questions developed by the 'transitology' of that time, especially its American versions. So, the transition societies both in Central and Eastern Europe and in the post-Soviet states were described in close comparison. Again, two different approaches can be observed in this context. The first is

interested in the typology, or at least in the morphology of transforming societies and can be termed the Arboretum approach (Kaase, Sparschuh, Wenninger (eds.), 2002). The second one is the Assembly Line model, which believes in the existence of only one socio-political technological line of Westernization. Descriptions of the given societies can be constructed according to the speed and character of their divergence from ideal types of the Western model. In these years, almost no work is available that compares the transitional societies with real Western societies or societal processes.

Since the late 1990s, the dominant trend has been just the opposite. Researchers in the region were invited to take part in large European programs of social science cooperation. But in practically every case, both the coordinators and the basic questions formulated as starting points in the projects were presented by West European research centers. These projects are usually not interested in the dynamics of transformation in the post- Soviet countries, but only in the 'Eastern' equivalents of problems formulated by the coordinators in their Western European social and research environments. The 'post- Soviet' researcher is interested in joint activities and therefore tries to do his best, identifying local analogues of the 'central' problems of the projects offered. Investigations of transition are consequently marginalized in these projects. The work emerging here may be interesting or even original, but usually only weakly related to local intellectual traditions and cultural environments, and cross-national comparative accents or efforts will normally be absent here.

3. The structure of the post-Soviet social order is usually determined by specific institutional roles and informal ties and mentalities. In these countries, very often, the institutional approaches are focused on events around institutional transfer, and rarely show high-level analytical skills in analyzing the local institutional mix. The most interesting local work is in the other area: describing informality, hidden mentalities, the political culture, and networks of trust or distrust. The world of

informality is more interesting than that of institution building for the local research community. The research process thus simply mirrors the processes in the 'real' social settings.

4. There are significant differences in the structures of social theories, as well. Current theories on the international markets nowadays are non-philosophical, and usually their moral or normative elements are marginal. The dominant style of theories developed in post-Soviet countries is just the opposite: even now it is very philosophical, and its normative elements are still very central. Concepts tied to new social players (feminism, theories of social movements, the risk society, and problems of social justice) are still insignificant. Research focuses on the presentation of general value systems. In the region, the projects perceived as leading are the qualitative or distribution-oriented ones, rather than those focused on behaviorist, game theory, or discursive languages. The region's middle-range theories for special analytical purposes are still underdeveloped, so macroanalytical approaches are used to explain in areas, where they remain too general, and therefore inefficient. The theoretical mix is usually supported by methodological eclecticism.

5. It is possible to expect that the substantial part of researchers in social sciences in post-Soviet countries will continue efforts, aimed at integration of their studies with mainstream Western theories. It is even possible to expect that this tendency will be dominant in the region, notably in countries with pro-Western, and, especially, pro-American political regimes, like Georgia or the Ukraine. There is nothing wrong if they are included into international networks and receive access to the recent advances in the various disciplines. The problem is that the research agenda is determined predominantly by the interests of foreign partners, who are usually grant holders for international projects. At

the same time, it is possible to expect some strengthening of positions of 'traditionalists' in social sciences, especially in Russia, bearing in mind the sharpening conflict in the political sphere between this country and the 'Western' world. Supporters of the "Russian' way of development could rely on ideological and financial help from the country's authorities. This could lead to the emergence of interesting discourse and academic debates, which is already evident in some disciplines within the Russian scientific community. However, in most research areas, co-operation and mutual exchange is possible, and it could produce valuable results of significance for all parties, but only if the intention to seriously take into account the partner's (opponent's) position becomes a rule in relations between research groups and schools.

# References

Amosov, A. (2014). On the economic mechanism of the new industrial development. *Ekonomist, 2,* 3–12.

Archangelsky, Yu. (2014). Neo-industrialization: some polemical considerations. *Ekonomist, 5,* 3–5.

Avtonomov V. (1998). *Model of man in economics.* Moscow: Moscow School of Economics.

Balatsky, E. & Sergeeva, V. (2014). Scientific and practical effectiveness of

Russian universities. *Voprosy Economiki , 2,* 133–143.

Balatsky, E. & Yekimova, H. (2013). *Academic performance of economic schools in Russia. – Capital of the Country.*

Fortov, V. (2002). Domestic science in the transition period. *Otechestvennie Zapiski, 7,* 43–53.

Geyets, V. (2012). Society, state and economy: the unity and contradiction [Scientific report]. Moscow: Institute of Economics, Russian Academy of Sciences.

Glazyev, S. (1998). *Genocide.* Moscow: Terra.

Gokhberg, L. et al. (2014). *Indicators of Science.* Moscow: HSE.

Gritsenko, A. (ed.) (2008). *Institutional dynamics of architectonic and economic*

*transformations.* Kharkiv: Fort

Gubanov, S. (2014). Neo-industrialization of Russia and poverty sabotage of her criticism. *Economist, 4,* 3–32.

# Chapter 10: The Impact of Internationalization

Kaase, M., Sparschuh, V. & Wenninger, A., (eds.) (2002). *Three social science disciplines in Central and Eastern Europe: handbook on economics, political science and sociology (1989–2001)*. Bonn/Berlin: GESIS/ Social Science Information Centre (IZ):

Kantorovich, L. (1960). *Optimal Utilization of Economic Resources*. Moscow: Publishing House of the USSR Academy of Sciences.

Khromov, A. (1996). *What Science We Have Lost*. Moscow: TSISN.

Kirdina, S. (2013). Methodological individualism and methodological institutionalism. *Problems of Economics 10*, 66–89.

Kleiner, G. (2014). Rhythms of evolutionary economics. *Problems of Economics, 4*, 123–136.

Kolodiy, A. (2006). Ukrainian Regionalism as a Situation of Cultural and Political Polarization. *Agora, 4*, 69–91.

Kuzninov, Ya., Radaev, V., Yakovlev, A. & Yasin, E. (2005). *Institutions: From Borrowing to Fostering. Experience of Russian Refors and the Possibility of Cultivation of Institututional Change*. Moscow: HSE (in Russian)

Majewski, V. & Malkov, S. (2014). Prospects of macroeconomic theory of reproduction. *Problems of Economics, 4*, 137–155.

Malkov, E. (2014). The theory of general equilibrium in the Soviet economic science: bibliometric analisys. *Problems of Economics, 3*, 106–125.

Mirskaya, E. & Rabkin, Y. (2004). Russian academic scientists in the first post-Soviet decade: empirical study. *Science and Public Policy, 31(1)*, 2–14.

Oleinik, A. (2011). *Power and the Market: The System of Socio-Economic Domination in the Russia of "Zero" Years*. Moscow: ROSSNEP

Shor, N. (1998). *Nondifferentiable optimization and polynomial problems*. Boston; Dordrecht. London: Kluwer Academic Publishers

Shulga, N. (2015). *Academy of Sciences the need for audit – financial, managerial and recruitment*. Ukrainska Pravda – http://life.pravda.com.ua/person/2015/04/9/192354

Sukharev, O. (2013). Status of economics in modern Russia and objectives of economic knowledge. *Ekonomicheskoe Obozreni, 1*, 54–66.

Tambovtsev, V., (ed.) (2009). *Property Rights, Privatization, and Nationalization in Russia*. Moscow: Fond 'Lberalnaya Missia' and Novoe Literaturnoe Obozrenie.

Voronin, Yu. & Labzunov, P. (2014). The need for management of the economy. *Economist, 5*, 36–4.

Woodrodrow Wilson Center (ed.) (1999). *The Humanities and Social Sciences in the Former Soviet Union: An Assessment of Need*. Washington, D.C.: Kenan Institute

Zayonchkovskaya, J.A. (2004). Labour emigration of Russian scientists. *Problems of Forecasting, 4*, 98–108.

# Chapter 11:
# Poverty and Social Sciences: Pauperology as Apology for Modernity

Kumaran Rajagopal

## Introduction

The emergence of Poverty Studies in development organizations (or NGOs as they are known here in India) and their increasing prominence in this part of the world has resulted in heightened interest in processes of marginalisation and social exclusion and consequently a host of research studies and projects is being undertaken outside the academic institutional contexts. Claiming that they are more pro-poor and grounds-ups, these research endeavours aspire to distinguish themselves from the conventional social science research by variously portraying themselves as counter-hegemonic, counter-epistemological, alternative etc. The alternative stature they arrogate to their research concerns is predicated upon the centrality they accord to poverty and marginalization. Hence all poverty-specific research that is principally conducted under the banner of Poverty Studies by these NGOs now aspires to understand marginalization and exclusion. Although such research enterprises aspire to claim a place in the fold of social sciences, there is a crucial difference in their treatment of their respective objects of study, poverty—both in approach and in emphasis. The difference between them is decisive, as some mutually challenging and reciprocally critical foundational notions guide them. Choosing one over the other is not just a matter of research focus but also expressive of the values and worldview we stand by. In this paper I will try to demonstrate how an understanding of the difference between them can help us learn a few lessons on alternative conceptualization and theorization of poverty. Before doing this, a discussion on the commission and omissions of the mainstream social sciences in relation to the issue of poverty is warranted.

The biggest problem with studies about poverty is that there is poverty of studies about issues of poverty in sociology. But in reality "Poverty was never a problem but destitution was" writes Ashis Nandy (2002). The pre-modern societies or even the pre-modern minded in modern societies, did not regard poverty as a problem. It exists sometimes as a voluntary renunciation of worldly pleasures or as the outcome of *karma*, or as a punishment for too much boasting or ill-will for others. It never meant starving or abandonment. The person in poverty had clothes, food and shelter, perhaps lesser in quality or quantity than what was normal for the wider society. But he had them. Starvation death and famine are modern inventions, as Amartya Sen would have us convinced. It is worth quoting Nandy further on this:

> Poverty is not destitution. When some intellectuals and activists talk of poverty being degrading or reject any critique of development as romanticization of poverty, they actually have in mind destitution, not poverty, but are too clever by half to admit that. By collating or collapsing these two terms, apologists of development have redefined all low-consuming, environment-friendly lifestyles as poor and, thus, degrading and unfit for survival in the contemporary world... Destitution, or at least large-scale destitution, is a more recent phenomenon. It has been increasing among many traditionally poor communities over the last hundred years, partly as a direct result of urbanization and development. The most glaring instances of destitution are found not in traditional, isolated tribal communities, but among the poor communities that are uprooted and fragmented and move into cities as individuals or nuclear families. It is also found among landless agricultural laborers who for some reason lose their jobs in a situation where agriculture is industrialized or becomes nonprofitable. They are the ones who find themselves unable to cope with the demands of an impersonal market or the culture of a modern political economy. Indeed, when we talk of poverty, we usually have that other kind of created poverty in mind, but are too defensive to admit that. We suspect that our world-views, ideologies and lifestyles are in league with the creation of this new kind of modern poverty. (Nandy, 2002)

Poverty as an integral part of social existence, but not as the opposite of wealth or richness has got transmorphed into a stain or shame, only thanks to the sleight of hand of modernity and the disciplines that it spawned.

It all happened in 1949 January 10, when Harry Truman declared nearly two billion people and the most nations of southern hemisphere as underdeveloped or poor. Before this the peoples of Asia, Africa and Latin America did not always see themselves in terms of "poverty." This is relatively recent; it goes back only as far as the early post-World War II period, when the apparatuses of knowledge production and intervention (the World Bank, the United Nations, bilateral development agencies, planning offices in the Third World, etc.) were established and when a whole new political economy of truth—different from that of the colonial or pre-war period—was set into place. None would have predicted that this qualification would become part of the self-image of the people in these nations. It unleashed such a sudden sense of shame and self-disparagement in the psyches of these nations and the people in them, that removing this became the avowed mission of every nation, elites, international agencies and governments.

They have more or less successfully transferred this self-definition onto their non-cash earning, non-monetized asset possessing people who never thought that they were ever poor. In this, the entire army of international development experts, agencies and national elites and bureaucrats joined hands to declare first the nations as poor then the vast sections of the people in them. Thus poverty became shame—national and personal shame at that. Now, poverty as shame tends to generate self-images in the countries and people in them that treat poverty as problematic to be immediately dealt with and instantly banished. "Normal" middle class citizens, particularly those belonging to the liberal-democratic tradition, are uncomfortable with these paradoxes. They usually push them under the carpet through various psychological subterfuges. Who wants to live in moral discomfort when easy escapes are available in the form of popular ideologies of development?" For them poverty assumes a life of its own as a ghost that must be exorcised. It is not caused by those who wish to banish it. It is something that exists before. As Maia Green explains, "Poverty is ascribed agency to impact on the lives of people who 'fall into' it. Poverty is not described as a consequence of social relations, but represented as an evolving entity that must be 'attacked'. Size matters. The growth in poverty, its sheer scale, prompts a response. Poverty in these development writings is represented as inherently problematic, not only for the poor themselves, whose suffering is graphically documented, but for the wider society which is threatened by it" (Global Poverty Research Group, 2014).

But what was getting defined as poverty was lack of money or lack of absorption of certain amount of calories. This has sidestepped that which produced real shame, namely, destitution and kept itself busy with something that can be managed technocratically and bureaucratically, because it has been de-contextualized, universalized and quantified. It was contented that this disembodied disease called poverty can be eradicated and managed only with modern institutional apparatuses. It is important to be sensitive to the resonances of disease metaphor. Just as disease management and control became the means to define diseases and normalize modern institutions and the attitudes consistent with them, poverty management institutionalizes modernity and modern knowledge through privileging of an array of institutions and an army of experts. If the spread and ferocity of disease say like cholera were attributed to the 'potentially threatening' behavior of the poor who steeped as they are in traditions, poverty too was traced to the non-internalization or non-intrusion of modern outlook and attitudes in the poor. Hence the study of poverty becomes the study of poor. With poverty as a subject the poor, who by definition lack the resources and entitlements to reframe the terms of this engagement, become objects of study.

It is one thing to internalize the ethos of modern labour and all other concomitant value frameworks associated with it, and it is another thing to accept the intruding power of the experts. They derive their intrusion rights in the form of grand narratives such as "Industrialization", "family planning", the "Green Revolution", "macroeconomic policy", "integrated rural development" and the like. These become the conduits for radically reorganizing the lives of the wider society in the image of modern societies who have supposedly banished the disease of poverty. They repeat the same basic 'truth', namely, that permitting their interventions is tantamount to paving the way for the heralding of those conditions that characterize rich societies: industrialization, agricultural modernization, and urbanization. In this process poverty itself is regarded as the vestige of pre-modern societies and truly modern persons cannot and need not be poor.

## Poverty as not-modern

The logic of modernity by aligning with the discourses on poverty tends to produce a definition of poverty as something that is non-modern. 'Modern Man' may not be the richest, but he is definitely not poor, even in the economic sense. If someone is poor, it is because of his personal inadequacy to absorb the virtues of modernity and its ethos[1] (Goode and Maskovsky, 2001:3). As Max Weber would argue, poverty under conditions of capitalism, with protestant ethics having modernized itself, would only mean that if someone is starving for want of money, he or she has not acquired the capitalist spirit, which is very much a product of modernity. Bauman affirms this association in a different way, by explaining the perennial concern of the modern societies and state about poor and poverty as an attempt at converting the lazy poor into productive labourers, who would learn to work in the factories by absorbing modern work ethics. He further adds strength to the thesis that the *poor person is non-modern*, by tracing the sudden elision of poor from the discourses of development in the developed world to an assessment normalized in these societies' that poor are not important anymore as they have not internalized the virtues of consumption and also do not possess resources to participate in consumerist culture. The post-modern societies do not need the poor any more. The indispensability of the poor is an abandoned idea. Now societies can do without poor. But that is a story for the west. *The east still needs the poor!* Not only that, it is only in the name of the poor that it can even continue its modernizing and self-serving missions. Historically informed perspectives on poverty reveal not only the social construction of the category within specific historical and institutional settings, and the key role of powerful institutions in globalising the poverty agenda, but also the fact that the constitution of the kind of poverty that development practitioners aspire to reduce is itself a product of the socio-economic relations of modernity.

At another level being poor is equated with being non-modern, is in the way poor were disciplined in hard labour. This equation is as old as industrialization itself. Poor are poor because they have not internalized the virtues of industrialism, an unmistakable modern product. They were the basis of discourses about poverty and social responsibility for the destitute in England until the mid-twentieth century, hence the intentionally punitive welfare regimes in workhouses where the destitute could go to seek food and shel-

---

[1]   It has been stated differently by Goode and Maskovsky, who treat "Poverty as a political, economical, and ideological effect of capitalist processes and state activity. Poverty as a function of power, as an essential and utterly predictable effect of the ideological and political-economic processes of late capitalism."

ter in return for hard labour in conditions that were explicitly designed to replicate the prison. Related attitudes live on in popular perceptions of poverty even within poor communities (Woodhouse 2003) and within the international development community. The latter's Food for Work programme and other food-aid in place of direct cash as relief is predicated on the assumption that the poor should learn to earn his/her food through hard labour, thereby learning the virtues of modern industrial society.

All these lead to the dichotomous and dualistic construction of the poor as reified category and further imputation of same solidity to a society of the poor, as if there is such a reality existing, and the simultaneous construction of non-poor universe consisting of the experts who study poverty and the poor[2] (*Yapa,1998*). The world of non-poor appropriates the right to criticize and alter the lives and universe of the poor. As has been forcefully argued by Yapa, "Dualistic thinking pervades the entire notion of a poverty sector which is viewed as a distinct, measurable, bounded entity, that part of the economy where the poor reside—the locus of the poverty problem; those who are not poor reside in the realm of the non-problem. The poverty sector has little capital and no resources. Presumably that is why it is poor. Capital, technology and resources must be infused from outside. The sector of the non-poor is the seat of intellect, resources and solutions—the knowing subject reflecting on the problems of the needy object, an idea well captured in the term 'poor as target group" (*Yapa, 1998: 99*) Crucially, the criticism against the poor tends to get further leveled against the society of the poor, there by exonerating the wider society from the crime of creating poverty in the first place. With this, not only the incommensurability of worlds of the poor and the world of the non-poor become firmly established but also the right of the world of the non-poor to intervene into and *construct knowledge* about the world of the poor. The victors now have no ear for the losers. The

---

[2] The poverty sector is viewed as a distinct entity with stable internal characteristics whose study will reveal the causes of poverty (Yapa 1996a). The point of such a study is to devise operational methods that will help 'solve' the problem. This is what I mean by reification of poverty: the lack of basic needs by large numbers of people has been transformed into a quantifiable poverty problem existing in a distinct and coherent sector with stable inner characteristics, the study of which will reveal the causes of poverty and thus help us to find solutions.

emphasis on poverty as the problem and the locus of analysis diverts attention from the social relations, local, national and international, which produce poverty as an attribute of people.

But the experts and their disciplines would not problematise the role of the world-outside-poor, both at the national and international levels, as the reasons for spewing poverty in the lives of the poor. But either would ignore or reify poverty as if it resides in the world of poor caused by endogenous factors specific to the society of the poor. This has led to a paradoxical situation of complete neglect of or excessive obsession with poverty. While the act of ignoring has been adopted by social sciences such as sociology and social anthropology, the act of attributing poverty to endogenous factors has been the stance of development and poverty studies. Within the realm of social science practices, once poverty has been conceived as caused by factors immanent in the society of the poor, in the name of 'Culture of Poverty' debate for example, poor are left on their own and focus gets shifted onto a wider social system whose abnormality is poverty. Hence poverty occupies least space in the consciousness of the social scientists, even while it assumes enormous importance in the minds of the state and NGO sectors, aided as they were by Poverty Studies, for they seek to legitimize modernization processes and thereby their own centrality in heralding them in post-independent India. At another level, what has been the omission of social sciences has become the reason for development studies' engagement with poverty and the poor as social categories, thereby creating a rationale for the imposition of modernity.

# The Poverty-Focus or the Lack of It in Social sciences

In what follows, let us try to grapple with the question of why poverty was not the proclaimed object of study for mainstream social science disciplines such as anthropology, sociology and political science and the politics of knowledge production around issues of poverty.

That sociology had a lack of concern for poverty and the poor has been well argued. G. K. Lieten (2002) laments, "Although the focus on poverty of international development institutions has spawned an army of anti-poverty specialists and a burgeoning literature on its constitution and definition, this has not been reflected across the social sciences, with the exception of the satellite disciplines to development. To this Boothe agrees, "Social anthropology has produced remarkably little about the problem of 'poverty'. (Booth, D., Leach, M. & Tierney, 1999)

The same has been echoed by S.C Dube (1994) in the Indian context, when he says, "In the mid-sixties there was a revival of interest in the study of poverty. The subject had attracted serious social science attention earlier also but its pursuit was neither intense nor sensitive. It had remained peripheral to the concerns of mainstream social science" (Dube, 1994:177). In another context P.C Joshi has this to say: "If one considers the quality of Indian social science in terms of its sensitiveness to the existence of the poor, one finds social science much more deficient than even literary writing...Indian social science, however, has failed to mirror the life of the poor in India in any significant and meaningful way, even though naked poverty is fast emerging as the most conspicuous fact of Indian life as a sequel to the much faster dislocation of the old economic and social order than the creation of a new order" (Joshi, 1979: 355).

Even when exceptionally poverty has been engaged with by social scientists, P.C. Joshi mourns that they as "Poverty experts travel round the world for seminars on poverty and unemployment without ever coming into direct contact with the poor themselves. Social science, with few exceptions, thus, provides a rich man's view of poverty and not the poor man's view." (ibid, 355 &356). He further adds, "Indian society has invested a vast amount of money, time and man-power in several dozen village studies by sociologists and social anthropologists. But the identity of the poor is lost, or the identification of the poor is completely obscured, by the failure of the social anthropologists to explore the fundamental division into haves and have-nots and by their tendency to give exaggerated importance to the less fundamental forms of social stratification like caste which mystify this division between the haves and have-nots "(ibid, 356).

"Social anthropologists have by and large ignored the role of caste as an ideological force obscuring the identity and crystallization of the poor. The absence of any contribution by social anthropologists to poverty studies has not only impoverished social anthropology; the absence of a direct interaction with the people which was central to the classical anthropological perspective has also impoverished the very conception of anti-poverty planning and mobilization" (Joshi,1979).

I would like to argue below that there are two kinds of reasons one may attribute to the reasons for exclusion of poverty in the social sciences: One, those concerning the inherent politics and methodological rigidities of social sciences and the other, the politics intrinsic to conceptualizing poverty itself.

## Historical Legacies

The first kind of reasons flows from the historical and methodological legacies of social sciences. Historically social sciences were born in times when the western hegemony was establishing itself through colonialism very stridently. As the products of modernity these disciplines mostly sided with the colonial empires and furthered their agendas. Though there were dissenting voices within the social science fold, the dominant voices were supportive of the colonizing forces as they saw the latter as the harbingers of modernity. Though the criminal intentions of the colonizing forces were taken note of by the most conscientious among the social scientists, they were pardoned for they were treated as necessary costs to be paid for promoting and disseminating modernity. In this sense the social scientists were willingly missing the trees of criminal acts of colonialism for the wood of modernizing intentions of the imperial forces.

Thus the social sciences were more focused at the processes that contributed to the dissemination and effects of modernity. As a result poverty was treated as the reality specific only to the non-modern societies, and poverty was regarded as the manifestation of the deadweight of traditions. Hence social science research was obsessively fixated with modernity and the factors that promote it. In India context too, if caste, race, agrarian economy, rural power structure etc were studied by social sciences, it was not so much for the impoverishment they caused but for the challenges they posed for the spread of modernity[3] Poverty and other social ills were thought to melt into thin air with the arrival of modernity. The untrammeled optimism for modernity and the redemptions it will bring upon the societies mired in traditions had persuaded the social scientists to give scant attention to poverty. If any, poverty was regarded as a problem coming in the way of modernity marching successfully. Thus, by strengthening modernity, poverty was thought to disappear.

## Methodological Rigidities

Secondly, on the methodological front too there was least encouragement for grappling with poverty, let alone conceptualizing it. Much of social science disciplines particularly sociology, political sciences, and anthropology, were steeped in the functionalist and systemic paradigm due to which they were intensely concerned about the normal state of affairs in society and about the processes and means for maintaining it. (See, 1987) Poverty and all its manifestations were regarded as abnormal and therefore dysfunctional to society. While social scientists were alarmed at the higher incidences of abnormality in society they still treated them as the excreta that would be washed away by the oncoming waves of normalcy achieved by the engulfment of the entire society by modernity. The social scientists' persuasive recommendations for social engineering were aimed at working on the reinstatement of normalcy. It was believed that normalcy defined in modernist spirit will establish the equilibrium and will banish abnormality in its wake. This resulted in the whole focus centering on social engineering and the effects of it on the wider society.

Poverty thus was consigned to the status of the crust on the surface of society that will have to be eliminated forthwith through social engineering efforts. Social sciences, as they were growing in the shadow of the supremacy of scientific rigour in natural sciences, had assigned the task of studying poverty to less theoretical disciplines like social work and development studies. However the latter were 20th century phenomena and very much the product of the social engineering orientation of the social sciences. While So-

---

[3] Like Durkeim's lamentation about Anomie, Marx's notion of Alienation and Weber's Iron Cage.

cial Work has come as an answer to the concern of the mainstream society to integrate many 'marginal' (read deviant) groups into mainstream modernity, Development Studies aspired to objectify poverty so that doing so would help development professionals and the agencies to which they belong to have a "problem" that can be "managed". (Pathy, 1981) The results: social work located the problem of marginalization and impoverishment in the groups that were marginalized, rather than in the forces that marginalized them in the first place. Development studies, on the other hand, solidified the multifaceted experience of impoverishment into a managerial issue for the development sector. Impoverished persons too were understood in the same sense. Poor are persons who failed to integrate themselves into the redeeming processes of modernity, for reasons mostly personal—personal incapacity, inability and inadequacy. Many of the development studies disciplines in various incarnations too took this up uncritically and went about understanding, assessing and measuring poverty without ever problematising it as a relational product. Poverty was understood by Development studies only with a biomedical perspective, which treated poverty as a disease that has crept into society like a germ into the human body. It was in the manner of going to war that poverty was approached

## The Concern with Processes

It does not however mean that the social sciences were not concerned with poverty. The social sciences too studied poverty in the sense of grappling with the experiences and various ways of coping with it. This was happening, even while the social sciences grew out of their modernity fixations, crossed on to post-modern territories and became critical of social engineering as such.

The post-colonial period saw social sciences becoming characterised by their reflexivity about their own practices and the politics they had normalized. This brought to light how social sciences were engaged as pamphleteers for modernity and in the process invented the backwardness of non-modern societies. This brought the curtain down on even the peripheral possibility of studying poverty per se, as it itself was the invention of a modern mind to suit and privilege the colonizing modern mind. And also as ever, with the primary concern centering on understanding social, political and cultural processes, social sciences virtually ceased to engage with creating an object called poverty that could be measured and grasped tangibly. If anything, they only became critical of such objectification of poverty. Their interest in processes led them to study how social actors dealt with and became part of social processes. Simultaneously another camp within the social sciences was engaged in studying the institutions and structures that sustain and maintain the social processes. Accordingly, in the social sciences the understanding of poverty begins from the processes and leads to people who are impacted by these processes. This is the inverse of what transpires in development studies in which such understanding proceeds from and ends with the poor and what happens to them.

Curiously, despite the dearth of exclusive attention paid to poverty *per se*, much of the alternative conceptions of poverty have come from the social sciences. Particularly the contribution of anthropology in highlighting alternative conceptions of poverty is immense. It has to be remembered, however, that anthropology was the handmaiden of colonial forces throughout the period when imperial forces were riding roughshod over many third world societies. However in their concern with understanding the cultures of many third world societies, they brought to limelight many new ways and perspectives of experiences of poverty. More significantly their contribution towards the cross-cultural understanding of poverty and the differential experiences of poverty in different cultural settings is very valuable.

Therefore, various categories of people identified to be among the poorest population such as disabled, widows, beggars etc were not studied in the same way as development disciplines studied them. For the latter it was a 'given' that they are poor because their life circumstances fit into models already developed to identify poor persons. But in the case of the social sciences what is more important are the social processes that operate in relation to them. In that sense these groups of population are as significant for study as the groups development studies would have qualified as nonpoor. Moreover for the social sciences, the development studies' cardinal division of the population into poor and non-poor is immaterial as they are interested in the interaction among social actors in the generic sense of the term.

## Development as Elimination of Poverty

The absence of poverty discourses in the social sciences can also be explained in terms of how they conceptualize development. Development in the social sciences is understood in mostly positive terms in that it was treated in terms of several presences that affirmed development. For example development was measured in terms of what have to be established rather than in terms of what have to be eliminated. A society was regarded as developed if it had acquired scientific spirit, rational attitude and economic prosperity. It was believed that the establishment of these traits would drive away all other problems and social ills. With this understanding, social sciences had taken upon themselves the task of informing various social forces as to how these presences can be brought in. Such conception of development compelled them to study those processes that maintain or facilitate or act as impediments to these traits. Most of the social sciences' energies were spent on the functional aspects and other equilibrium-maintaining processes. Sadly those absences and dysfunctional elements were treated with contempt and were thought to disappear in the face of modernizing forces. Moreover the western bias was also the reason which, as suggested by Krishnan Namboodiri has meant "that Indian sociologists have tended to confine attention to research issues raised by their Western colleagues, that national concerns such as mass poverty and other social problems have been ignored..."( Namboodiri,1980).

However the heightened attention given to poverty in International development studies had a lot to do again with their conception of development. In their conception, development was understood in terms of the elimination of negative presences. Development is such a state in society when poverty and other such 'social ills' are eliminated. In the development studies' perspective poverty and other such phenomenon were given the kind of place that disease occupied in biomedical disciplines. Therefore maintenance of normalcy calls for singling out the disease and bringing it under the microscope for analysis, measurement and management. Poverty was a disease and it was studied in the same spirit in which diseases were studied in medical sciences. For these disciplines development is the 'normal' state that every society has to strive for. However, now there is an easy way out to achieve development (easy way out only conceptually but not in reality where poverty elimination proves to be an elusive task)—eliminate poverty and there comes development! The easy equivalence of development with the absence of poverty triggered off unfettered interest in poverty, its kinds and types.

This explains why social development knowledge is all about poverty. Yet the generation of such knowledge has an instrumental purpose. The politics of such equivalence between development and elimination of poverty will be elaborated later. However it suffices here to say that the arrival of international development studies has a lot to do with sudden concern with poverty in the last three decades. It all began with the World Bank becoming actively engaged in poverty eradication after few decades of wishful thinking that economic growth leads to the elimination of social ills like poverty. The linkage of this knowledge to management-of-poverty-anxiety is quite evident in the way many development organisations and state agencies use them for control and evolving interventions strategies. The proliferation of knowledge about poverty soon reached its crescendo with the institutionalisation of Development Studies across the globe, promoted and sponsored by international finance organisations, among other big forces. What was missing in Development studies discipline was the kind of reflexivity that became so crucial for the social sciences. Hence the politics of studying poverty never came to light until social scientists probed into it. The next section will deal with it.

## The Politics of Understanding Poverty

Poverty became an issue of grave importance only in the last three decades. Ever since human and social development was no longer assumed to be an automatic concomitant of economic development and as something that had to be actively pursued and established, social development has become a big techno-managerial concern of development agencies, both that of the state and non-state. This shift has bred a different understanding of poverty and who the poor are. This shift has also legitimized the arrival and continued presence of an army of development institutions, organisations and professionals that have assumed the mandate of facilitating, achieving and consolidating development in the societies and groups deemed underdeveloped by them. They have all come together to create a particular reality called poverty in a fashion that validates their interventions in the society and the lives of the impoverished members in it. The way, in which international development organisations, particularly World Bank, have suddenly brought poverty at the centre of the development discourse, hides certain self-serving intentions of these institutions, rather than just the noble concerns for the poor. At once, poverty was very extensively and vigorously studied by Development/Poverty Studies. Many poverty studies soon ensued. In the long run, both the noble and not-so-noble intentions of poverty studies have conspired and worked overtime to establish a distinct ontological reality of being poor and poverty. It is as if they have carved out a new species of human—the one who is in poverty. Presently let us examine a series of assumptions that have acquired axiomatic proportions in Development research and have gone great length to invest species-specific qualities in the poor, as it were.

## Convenient Assumptions—Insinuating the inevitability of Development Interventions

One such convenient assumption is that persons in poverty cannot cope with poverty without the support of the development sector, be it the state or NGOs. These Development actors justify their interventions into the lives of the persons in poverty without taking into account those people's abilities of self-help and coping. Development studies and even practices conveniently gloss over the truth that the poor have always coped with poverty and survived it in history. If anything, it is only with the arrival of many of those very forces that seek to remove poverty in the lives of the poor, that poverty has become an unmanageable challenge in the lives of the poor to a large extent. That is why in much of the anthropological research undertaken in Africa we find that the essential component of the actions that the poor undertake to deal with poverty involves moving beyond the perimeters of the circles within which both the state and development organisations operate and influence. Even in Indian contexts a sensitive researcher may discover the desire of those being poor to evaluate their capabilities to deal with poverty outside the support, parameters and definitions provided by the development actors of both the state and non-state variety. In other words, modern forces, including the development actors such as the state and development organisations of all varieties, have incapacitated the poor not only by what they omitted to do, but also by what they committed to do.

This is true even in those individuals, categories of populations and communities that have decided to selectively relate to the state and development organisations. In their poverty-confronting efforts of the poor, there are many situations that do not have any scope for the involvement of either state or development organisations. It may thus be said that, in many aspects of the lives of those being the poorest, the development actors may not have any relevance at all, or at best only a marginal presence. It should awaken the development personnel from their delusions that poverty cannot be eradicated without their active support, involvement and presence. As a matter of fact, in specific situations, the poor are well served by the development sector when they do not serve them at all. This is because these development actors bring in their train a whole lot of value systems, moral frameworks and cultural scales (in this context, they are that of modern or other dominant paradigms such as Brahminical Hindutva) that not only define them as poor or the poorest before commencing their poverty elimination work, but also by a stroke of definition and conceptual jugglery push them to the peripheries by locating the centres in some other places other than the ones that are the native to the people they choose to work with.

It is exactly for these reasons that development is conceived of by some sensitive minds, not as the product of the expansion and influence of the development sector, but by banishing their influence from the respective territories. Gandhian vision was one such alternative conception of development that visualized the return of self-worth and self-sufficiency in the people the moment they abandon the civilizational attributes of modern western societies.

# Convenient Assumption—
# The Singular Social Identity of the Poor

Another crucial self-serving assumption that poverty studies have valorized in the discourses of poverty is the singular social identity for the poor. Indeed the cursory perusal of many poverty studies points to the way they have variously confirmed, very unfairly, that for the persons they have studied, being poor is the only social identity. By fixing and freezing the impoverished people in the identity of poor, through its deployment of externally evolved indices, poverty research has served its personal interest well, even while obviating other social identities which people move into and out from. It is exactly because of this congealment of individual identities in their beings as poor, poverty studies have largely lost sight of the processual aspects of both poverty and being poor.

Ethnographic research of various varieties in anthropology confirms the fact that being poor is one among the many social identities people possess. And it is not that on all occasions they call themselves poor, even when the external variables evolved by development professional would label them so almost oppressively. Many such policy formulations also aim at trapping them in their poor status across all times and space. In contrast, in many of the life stories we have collected as part of the LPP project, one is often struck by the interest and concern of the persons interviewed, to deal with many other things in life, other than just poverty. This was, notwithstanding our story collectors obsessively relapsing into asking poverty-specific questions. Those persons interviewed were aspiring to represent themselves as being equally, if not more, concerned about other challenges in life, than about poverty alone.

## The Plea for Different Ontological Conception of Human Person

The arguments should not be construed to mean that development research should not be aimed at studying poverty at all. Far from it, such efforts should take into account the processes that trap as well as free people from fixed social locations. This will also help us to move towards those sections of population which do not have the luxury of even such fluidity, and gets fixed in such poor status forever even by their own definitions. Nevertheless we have to be very cautious in positing such idea of person with singular identity, for the sociological wisdom warns us that social actors can never be trapped into a singular identity consistently as they always move from one social region to another, while assuming varying identities as they move through. Thus our understanding of the poor and poverty can benefit from the qualification we have mentioned above. This would boil down to mean that the poorest person would be one who continues to treat oneself as being poor despite moving across different social regions or, even worse, would not be able to move into different regions at all, other than the one that locates that person as poor in the given moment.

Therefore, firstly, our commitment to treat people as an end in themselves and not as a means for enhancing economic productivity should be based on our vision to see 'being poor' as one of the many ways of being persons by the people we work with. Such commitment behooves us to move beyond the much-vaunted conceptualization of poverty as multidimensional experience and phenomenon. We should proceed to the multidimensional nature of poverty, from the decisive premise that being a person in society is a multidimensional experience, within which being poor is an experience that certain individuals undergo recurringly. Our focus is on these individuals who by their own definitions move into and occupy the identity of poor more often than others and more permanently than others.

Secondly such commitment should also be informed by the learning that the multidimensional aspects of poverty are socially embedded in relationships and processes. Therefore locating poverty experiences and poverty processes in the terrain of social relationship is supremely essential. Therefore a proper analysis of the social relationship and social processes assumes importance. Sadly most of the participatory approaches have failed to capture the relational and processual aspects of being poor, for even the longest of the Participatory Rural Appraisal (PRA) or Participatory Poverty Assessment (PPA) exercises, is short when measured by ethnographic research standards. The latter guide us to focus on social processes and patterns of social relations that constitute an individual experience and sense of identity.

## Poor are not in Groups

In the same breadth one has to critically reflect on the practice of poverty studies to categorize people into groups that are labeled as poor. For example, the classic understanding of disabled, homeless, widows, beggars, street children and others as groups of poor population is, in true sociological sense, problematic and even questionable. For one thing, they do not share the essential characteristic of groups or communities, as, apart from that which we attribute to them, they do not necessarily have common experiences specific to being disabled, street children, homeless etc. If, anything many of the attributes are applicable to all these groups. Such groupings tend also to gloss over their socially embedded experiences of being poor, as well as their singular strategies to deal with that identity of being poor. For example in the case of the disabled and elderly, that person's experience of poverty is not so much to do with being elderly and disabled but rather to do with whether or not s/he has family members or other forms of social support to turn to. Thus, there is a great deal of variability as to how the persons being poor use social relationships and make meanings out of social processes. This may be common between ones classified as poor with that of other ones from another category, and not necessarily common with another person like him/her.

We are not arguing that these classifications are not important, but they must be treated as such, and not attributed an uncritical commonality, thereby flattening the multiplicity of experiences of being the same type of poor, as arising out of differing relational contexts occupied by them. The danger is that by reifying these classifications, a whole array of development efforts and policy-making is made that eventually end up causing more distress than they seek to eliminate. It is instructive to remember that much more than poverty, it is the solutions to get out of poverty that have proved problematic to people.

## Conclusion

Poverty research is inevitably tied to the aspirations of policy-making as they are concerned about propelling actions. But the last few decades of policy making and the actions resulting out of it, duly assisted by action research of the development studies, have compelled many of the sensitive ones among us to conclude that a lot of bad actions is much worse than no action at all. It was because action research and the consequent actions were guided by much of self-serving notion and assumptions elaborated above in this essay. Poverty and the discourses around it become a major legitimizing force for the modernist paradigm and privileges knowledge-making practices championed in western intellectual power centres. It achieves this by creating a sense of inadequacy and low self-esteem in the psyches of the impoverished geographies world over through a skillful conceptualization of poverty. Poverty Studies by calling a whole array of social sciences into service has become a central agent in this mission.

## References

Booth, D., Leach, M. & Tierney, A. (1999). 'Experiencing Poverty in Africa: Perspectives from Anthropology.' Background paper No.1b for the World Bank Poverty Status report 1999.

Dube, S. C. (1994). Understanding Poverty. *Tradition and Development*, New Delhi.

Goode, J. & Maskosky, J. (2001). *The New Poverty Studies: The Ethnography of Power, Politics and Impoverished People in the United States.* New York: New York University Press.

Joshi, P.C. (1979). Perspectives on Poverty and Social Change: The Emergence of the Poor as a Class. *Economic and Political Weekly*, 14(7/8), Annual Number: Class and Caste in India pp. 355–357, 359, 361, 363, 365, 366.

Lieten, G. K. (2002). Faltering Development and the Post- Modernist Discourse. *Social Scientist, Vol. 30(7).*

Maia Green: Representing Poverty And Attacking Representations: Some Anthropological Perspectives On Poverty In Development: GPRG-WPS-009, accessed at http://www.gprg.org/. p.12.

Namboodiri, N. K. (1980). On Sociology in India: Yesterday, Today, and Tomorrow. *Social Forces, 59( 1), 288.*

Nandy, A. (2002). The Beautiful, Expanding Future of Poverty: Popular Economics as a Psychological Defense. *International Studies Review, International Relations and the New Inequality, Vol.4 (2),* 115.

Pathy, J. (1981). Imperialism, Anthropology and the Third World. *Economic and Political Weekly, 16(14),* 623–627.

See, M. N. S. (1987). Development of Sociology in India: An Overview. *Economic and Political Weekly, 22(4),* 135–138.

Woodhouse, P. (2003). Local identities of poverty: poverty narratives in decentralised government and the role of poverty research in Uganda. Working Paper, IDPM, University of Manchester.

Yapa, L. (1998). The Poverty Discourse and the Poor in Sir Lanka' Transactions of the Institute of British Geographers. *New series, 23(1),* 95–115.

# Chapter 12:
# Academic Working Culture: Shifting from National Competitions towards Transnational Collaborations

## Kazumi Okamoto

## Introduction

Today, discussions on the internationalization/globalization of academic work have become almost routine in the social sciences discourses. These discourses particularly focus on their different working conditions, on inequalities in publication opportunities, especially in 'prestigious' academic journals, on the issue of power and science, and on numerous other topics relating to skewed balances under various conditions framing academic work. Although the number of such studies and discussions is abundant, a substantial diversity in these discussions cannot easily be found. That is to say, the existing discussions on the above topics almost always argue about how so-called scientific 'centres', the 'North/West' and 'dominant' academic circles in North America and Western Europe are privileged in academic work making them widely visible around the world, and how the rest have been suffering from all sorts of disadvantageous academic working conditions compared to their dominant counterparts.

Underlying such discussions is an excessive emphasis on the idea that international scientific activities are about competitions among academics, mainly seen as competition among nationally constructed entities, the national science communities. While one might raise the question if academics really engage themselves in international activities as contributing to such a competition among nationals, this view is exactly shared by the nation states' views on science that consider international scientific activities as a mean for nations' competitiveness. Simultaneously, the competitive nature of the discussions among academics about their great interests in discussing such things as rankings or the number of citations that are frequently used to benchmark academic productivity, prominence, and quality of work, ever measured along national units, can be well interpreted as coinciding with the nation state view on international science.

A number of scholars express concerns that the method exploits science citation indices such as the Social Science Citation Index to benchmark academic work in social sciences. These scholars argue that this is rather inappropriate due to some biases which are often included in available citation index databases and that it seems problematic to keep this method in order to discuss topics on quality of academic work. However, employing the same or any amended methodology and discussing the skewed balance in academic work, would lead us substantially to the same conclusion that certain academic circles, which are North America and Western Europe, are privileged and dominating in global social sciences.

Whatever the methods measuring such skewed balances might be, it would not change the main topic of such discourses: Not surprisingly, within discourses, focusing on international science activities as a competition among national entities, such a discourse knows winners and losers, and those who are not included in these privileged circles, inevitably complain about 'unfair' working conditions to achieve the same status as the privileged—as long as international science activities are mainly seen as a global competition, in which unprivileged ones would also like to show their academic presence to the world, just as their national governments would like them to be. Consequently, as it has already been shown, scholars' interests in such discussions tend to be various types of analysis that focus on 'winner-loser' relationships in academic work (Okamoto, 2013). Thus, whatever the ways of measuring the strength of national sciences might be, the relationship between science and competition tends to indicate more national political interests and implications in academic work and activities, than discussing the scientific substance of academic work and its scientific quality.

This article attempts to exhibit a new approach towards constructing a new direction of discussions on international academic work. Advocating this new approach is necessary in order to overcome the repetitive nature of current discussions on this matter, which are often national comparative studies that tend to end up with repetitions of mere descriptions of one country/region in which international academic activities are implemented, ever pointing out the differences and particularities of the national science units. This is not to deny such differences and particularities; however, it is rather problematic to put so much emphasis on differences and particularities in each country and/or global region, especially in order to further deploy discussions in relation to international academic activities, since such differences inevitably result in simply creating more distance between academics, and in an extreme case end up in a kind of unnecessary hostility between academic communities, in which people might work well under different academic circumstances, but should possibly not discuss them as if internationally working academics were fighting the competitive battles nation states may see in international scientific activities.

In order to achieve the purpose of this article, suggesting shifting the discourses about international scientific activities from this competitive view of nation states towards the more scientific interests of academics, this article addresses the following topics:

Firstly, it reviews the current mainstream discussions on structures of globalized academic work in social sciences. Secondly, it explores the meanings of international collaboration underlying these discourses. Thirdly, it analyses what intercultural studies about international collaborations contribute to these nationally driven discourses. Fourthly, I will try to sketch an alternative approach established via a cultural study of academic work, conceptualized by and based on Adrian Holliday's concept of "small cultures" (Holliday, 1999). Simultaneously, the overall framework of such cultural studies of science, which is called "academic culture", will also be introduced, and the necessity and validity to use this framework to better understand and analyse scientific relationships between academic culture and academic work in international collaborations will be discussed.

# Structures of Globalized Academic Work in Social Sciences

Although it is very difficult to grasp all the discussions that exist in each disciplinary field of social sciences regarding academic work that crosses national borders, the World Social Science Report published in 2010, can be a useful source to draw an overview of the current principle status and issues discussed in international social science discourses about international academic activities[1]. This report is heavily committed to describing how skewed the work in social science across the world is. In other words, as the title of this report already shows[2], how academic work in social sciences is divided across the world between those who have more privileged working conditions for carrying out conventional academic work such as publishing in academic journals, participating in international conferences, and other activities. Just looking through some chapter headlines[3] of the report, it becomes obvious what the main debate in this report is about: Without reading each article closely, one can conclude from the topics of the headlines that the world of social sciences is divided into a two-fold distinction: According to the debates in this book, gathering many names of the most prestigious scholars from around the world, the world of social sciences is divided into one group of scholars and/or academe that, according to this image about the world's social sciences, leads the whole social science world, not only theoretically but also institutionally; the other part of this dichotomist world view are those who feel un-noticed, left behind, and even dependent on their powerful counterparts in the North American and European global regions.

Some similar "either or" contrastive terms are frequently indicated, by such terms as North versus South, centre and periphery, dependent, power, and hegemony, in order to depict the current situation in social sciences, presenting the world of social sciences as a skewed balance of human resource, funding, publication, and other items framing academic practices that are seen as characterizing the globalized academic work. Whichever term and topic is used, the central message advocated by these terms is this twofold divided world, pointing out a small and less powerful academe, particularly in developing countries, arguing that they are not able

---

[1] However, quite some number of authors in this report seems sociologists and bibliometricians. Therefore, in a strict sense, the discussions do not necessarily represent all social scientific disciplinary fields.
[2] The title is "Knowledge Divides" (UNESCO, 2010).
[3] For instance, chapter three is titled as "unequal capacities, chapter four as "uneven internationalization" and chapter five as "homogenizing or pluralizing social sciences?".

to join international academic practices, such as publishing in prestigious academic journals, making presentations in international conferences, and participating in academic collaborative activities, mainly due to the lack of financial and human resources, a lack of English language abilities necessary to join the mainstream social science academe and, on the other side of this dichotomic division, a lack of theoretical and conceptual understanding by their Euro-American colleagues, considered to be representing a hegemonic power in the divided social science world. It is the image, of a science world in which a winner of competing national units of sciences oppresses the smaller participants in this social science world, the world of social sciences presented a battle between the losers and winners of politically constructed science units[4].

It is certainly relevant to discuss such disparities in globalized academic work in the social sciences. On the one hand, however, it also seems to be a great drawback to endlessly continue this type of discussion. On the other hand, ever repeating this opposition, someone must be the winner and the loser in this view of the social science world. This contrastive discussion, however relevant it may be if one discusses within the ideas of a science world consisting of such national science units, this debate will ever be confined to depict and emphasize the different working conditions among social science academics around the world. Drawing attention to the fact that there is disparity in academic work seems meaningful as a starting point to discuss the globalized academic work in social sciences; however, blaming academic people and/or academe for the so-called dominating academic communities in social sciences would only leave the need to think about how to create international knowledge, by insisting on stressing the antagonisms expressed by those who do not dominate in the world of social sciences. Kuhn criticizes this discourse, discussing the social science world as "a battlefield of national science communities" (2013:40) and questions:

> Are they seriously thinking an internationally acting academic is a kind of intellectual soldier gathered and organised in national science entity fighting a battle between national science organisations from different countries? (ibid.: 43)

---

[4] For more detailed discussion about this, see "Hegemonic Science: Critique Strands, Counterstrategies, and Their Paradigmatic Premises" (Kuhn, 2013).

Presenting international scientific activities as a "battlefield" is a metaphor of the current status of the globalized knowledge generation practices, and really brings one to the point of discovering the competitive nature of the discourses among social sciences about academic activities as a whole and, in particular, about international academic activities.[5] If it is only these discourses about the social sciences or if it is really the nature of international social science work to internationally compete among national entities, may be another question. However, it is the image of international activities consisting of national science communities, nation state views on the international social science world indeed have, that is considered as the nature of international science activities, then thinking and discussing the current status of globalized social sciences, it is no surprise that the above-mentioned discourses are only able to have this contrastive view such as North versus South, centre/periphery, and dominating/dominated while discussing the issue of international academic activities and never arriving at a discussion of how to craft international academic activities across these different working conditions. It is, to my mind, the most problematic point in these discussions, that such comparisons, or complaints, can merely focus on the fact that social sciences are different and that they do have different working conditions from our powerful counterparts, but that any competitive science world will face such differences and has to find ways to work through such differences. If, however, the main point of these discourses is to shift the position between winners and losers on this battlefield, then these debates will only repeat these debates about unequal working conditions. It is quite obvious, if you look at what is happening in the global economy, that globalization implies more severe worldwide competitions among participants. There is no harmonious competition, no equal competition in which everyone is the winner at the same time, due to the fundamental nature of competition (Okamoto, 2012). At this very point, such discussions are really stagnant, and can only be repetitive, since any other interests would not be required to participate in such discussions than being a winner on this battlefield.

---

[5] Ranking system for Higher Education Institutions worldwide also indicates this competitive nature in academic activities.

The advocates of these discussions might insist that there are so many difficulties in working internationally, that there are different working conditions, and that there are fixed frameworks for academic work, such as publication practices under which certain groups of academic people have more advantages than the others. It is though necessary for future academic collaborations to know where people with different academic backgrounds and experiences could meet and how they could work together, since, as long as the social science world is a competitive science world there will be no equal working conditions. Albeit, most of their claims about their working conditions/circumstances may be the reality; a strong wish that they would also like to be recognized and dominant in the globalized academic arena can be seen behind the terms such as 'inequality', 'dependent', 'periphery', and others. It is not to say that people should not be ambitious in their work[6], but to question the validity of the argument that they are not recognized and therefore are not prestigious because of disadvantageous working conditions and the current structure of globalized academic work, because such an advocacy is very contradictive: It opposes the current system and conditions where this unequal work takes place, but at the same time, the same argument advocates being included in the very competitive system that the same critique fiercely impeaches. (Okamoto, 2013).

The same applies to the nature of the current discussions on international collaborations as the above-mentioned competitions about individual prestige. What makes this debate about international scientific activities so confusing and so difficult to focus thinking on, when this is so affected by political issues, is the fact that in such international activities more than in non-international activities very political implications become involved, such as that country A is better than B and C in the region, since science nowadays has indeed been made a means to enhance the competitiveness of a nation state[7]. It is certainly necessary to closely observe

---

[6]  Becher and Trowler (2001) point out that majority of academicians are motivated to acquire individual prestige in their academic fields.

[7]  In the case of Japan, the Ministry of Education, Culture, Sports, Science and Technology (MEXT) has just launched a new funding project, namely "Top Global University Project" in autumn 2014. This is "a funding project that aims to enhance the international compatibility and competitiveness of higher education in Japan. It provides prioritized support for the world-class and

the current status of the globalized academic work in social science; nevertheless, we should also realize the great discrepancy between collaboration which means working together with others to create something and competition which means, as discussed, deciding the winners and the losers, the political views that national politics have on international science activities and the view academics have on this. Identifying such political views on international sciences with the political views national politics have on this, is the view that limits the current discourses about international activities on the above issues of the different conditions for the competition of national science units. I doubt that it is competing with other nationals about the conditions of academic work that should motivate academics to join international activities. And I also doubt that discourses which consider international academic collaboration partnerships as being reciprocal obstacles for each other is what in reality builds the basis for international collaboration among academics in social sciences.

In the next section, I will discuss what international academic collaboration involves in the fields of social sciences, what it means for social scientists, that is, how globalized academic collaboration is understood among social science scholars.

## What Does 'Collaboration' Mean in Social Sciences?

The term "collaboration" in fact may give us an impression that this relationship is smooth and harmonious, sharing the same objectives and ways to achieve them. However, while the assumption of academics encountering each other in international joint scientific activities as representatives of national scientific interests is the rather problematic image in the above mentioned discourses, it is also not necessarily the case what the notion of collaborations implies.

Unfortunately, only very few studies on international collaborations, such as cross-national research projects in social sciences,

---

innovative universities that lead the internationalization of Japanese universities." (MEXT, 2014 Retrieved on 5 December 2014 from the MEXT website: http://www.mext.go.jp/b_menu/houdou/26/09/__icsFiles/afieldfile/2014/10/07/1352218_02.pdf) exist; instead, co-authoring articles seems to be considered a synonym for academic collaborations (e.g. Franceschet & Costantini, 2010; Shin & Cummings, 2010; Sonnenwald, 2007; Glänzel & Shubert, 2005; Katz & Martin, 1997). Consequently, the extent and/or impact of collaborations tend to be reduced to being measured by a database, focusing on citation indices, an appropriate measurement criterion, measuring the impact of this kind of collaborations, given the interest of this measurement is to measure the visibility of authors in co-authored publications. Thus, again, the implication of measuring the visibility of authors in co-authored articles has the competitive orientation, because it measures the impact co-authoring has on the rankings of the individual participants quantitatively. Although a number of scholars, not only in the social sciences but also in natural sciences, argue that measuring scholars' quality of work and/or internationality by such a database of science citation indices is inappropriate (e.g. Bedeian, Van Fleet, & Hyman, 2009; Lariviere, Gingras, & Archambault 2006; Hicks, 2005; Klein & Chiang, 2004; van Leeuwen et al. 2001; Seglen, 1997) because of various bias in those databases, this approach, though it be biased or not, to evaluate the work of scientists, is not only very common but seems to be the only approach widely used in discussing the quality and productivity of scholars in the international contexts. The consequence of the usage of this approach to measure collaborations is again ranking scholars (or again by countries) by the number of citations, and, thus, it repeats and reinforces seeing collaborations as mere competitions among scholars about their status and omits any other motivation and interest of academics.

Scientific outcomes and caring about status are surely significant aspects of academic work; nevertheless, in respect to academic collaborations, co-authoring is not the only form of collaborative work, but a work that allows one to trace their impact on rankings to reduce thinking about collaborations as an aspect of competiveness, that is also again often measured along national entities. What all these considerations blind out from the reflections, is what happens, not as the outcomes of such collaborations, but what happens inside the collaborative production of joint articles. It can be assumed that there should be many more phases in collaborative work, until they achieve the form of co-authored publications, and even collaborations without ending in any publication such as journal articles and books are also possible. In any case, what all these reflections omit is the core aspects of collaborations, the work that needs to be done to arrive at the outcomes of collaborations. In this sense, it seems too reckless to consider that co-authoring is the exclusive and representative form of academic collaborations and even more to consider the results as saying much about what happens in the collaboration process. Then, the question needs to be raised: How do we define international academic collaborations, if measuring it via their outputs in terms of publications and measuring in relation to how it contributes to the competitions among the collaborators rather omits looking at the core aspects of joint international academic activities?

In order to deploy a new discussion path on international academic collaboration, to understand what happens in the process of creating joint academic "products", it seem to be necessary to go beyond reflecting on all the competitive aspects of conventional understanding on international collaboration, reducing such discussions to either the "unequal" conditions of academic work or to their outcomes, reproducing such "inequalities", leaving the whole process of collaborations in the darkness and, thus, creating a view as if the joint production of knowledge was nothing but a battle about prestige. If this were the case, as the current discussions on the issue of academic working conditions and structure of knowledge dissemination seem to say, social science scholars, who are involved in international scientific activities, are basically engaged in competing and comparing what they contribute to a nationally measured academic prominence and this seems to be an odd image of what academics do. If this were the case, the nature of international academic activities would be indistinguishable from any Olympic games.

Indeed, such discussions, obviously falsely identifying the *conditions* and the amount of publications of international academic work with the *nature* of international academic activities, always discussed and measured in national units, incline to focus on the perspectives national policies have, which in fact do exclusively put great importance on the competitiveness of people/organizations in a country, and who, on the other hand, just as in the above discourses, do not care about what happens inside international academic activities either. As a result, all these very political discourses, both those about the working conditions and those about the quantitative impact on nationally measured rankings, seem more like political debates than thinking about the academic and scientific qualitative aspects of international science activities. One might raise the question: if academics working internationally in social sciences are not much more interested in, when joining international research collaborations, that they do this due to their intellectual curiosity, to know and understand what other scholars in the same field in other global regions think about a social science topic, how they carry out research activities and what they find in their research about these topics (Kuhn & Okamoto, 2008).

Assuming that it is this interest that motivates international academic activities, and that it is this interest in the creation of joint knowledge, I attempt to suggest a discussion on international science collaboration in a new direction, one may coin "academic culture", which is an attempt to explore what happens inside academic work in the social sciences in the process of creating knowledge and to thus see international collaboration in a different light, in a light that focusses on truly academic interests in knowledge, their interest in creating and exchanging theories, rather than the political interest in competitive national science communities.

Shifting the discourses about international academic activities towards the joint creation of knowledge confronts academics with the fact that the whole endeavour of internationalising knowledge production in the social sciences starts from social science practices in which international academic activities were and still are an exception in social science practice which tends to be confined to national activities, both with regard to the topics they reflect on as well as with regard to the discourses. In this sense, the above discourses conceptualising international academic activities as a kind of battle among national social science communities is a continuation of this national orientation of international academic activities. Therefore, shifting the discourses about international activities in the first place rather than reinforcing the borders between academics via discussing them as competing nationals, leaves a need to think about how to support joint activities among academics, who are used to working in the nationally confined contexts.

As the few studies that have been carried out about international academic activities show, international academic activities are in all respects of academic work most challenging, due to lacking knowledge as to how academics interpret academic activities in different national contexts. (See for example, Kuhn and Weidemann, 2005). In fact, even if it were true that academics join international activities as competing national representatives, competing about prestige and rankings, even then, once they collaborate, they are confronted with the challenges academics face in the joint creation of knowledge, may it be in joint research or in joint publications.

Providing academics with knowledge about how they work and with which ideas of academic work they enter international academic activities, is therefore a contribution towards shifting the discourses about international academic activities towards collaborations as opposed to all those ideas discussing international activities as the competition of nationals.

## Different National Cultures?: Irrelevance of National Cultural Traits in Analyses on Academic Work

The very few studies providing such knowledge are mostly carried out as an application of the concept of "culture" to the academia.

As soon as the term "culture" comes into play, culture is mainly discussed as "national culture". Intercultural studies are a very common approach analysing behaviour and phenomena occurring between people, mainly in the world of international business, coming from different global regions.

Using the term "culture" to discuss people's behaviour, is neither easy nor straightforward, since the term "culture" is almost always interpreted as implying differences between 'we' and 'others/foreigners', and consequently, thinking through the concept of culture is easily caught up in the categorization of 'we' and 'others' as if 'we' and 'others' were always mainly different when people have different ethnicity/nationality. Also, academic discussions, especially in the context of discussing international academic activities, take, somehow, for granted that when using the term 'culture', it means large cultures, as Holliday (1999) notes. Culture, even more when used in international contexts, naturally seems to be conceptualized based on geographical regions/countries. This is not to deny that there could be such regional/national cultural traits in people's behaviour and mind; however, there is certainly a risk to over-generalize when the concept of large cultures is the only one that is available as a conceptual framework to study diverse people's behaviour.

Intercultural studies are widely adopted to the study of other social settings such as international corporations (e.g. Hofstede, 1984), local communities where many immigrants live, etc. Therefore, it is widely assumed that employing this intercultural approach to studying interactions in *any* groups of people who come from different countries, according to the existing studies, is an appropriate way to also study international academic activities.

Thus, it seems very conventional to employ this approach to culture, that originates from studying international business relations, when studying the international educational/academic settings. Particularly, studies on international students, which often means Asian/non-Western origin students, in Western (often English-speaking) higher education institutes, employ this intercultural study approach to the world of academia, mostly focusing on explaining why international students tend to experience difficulties and challenges in their degree courses or how to better handle these students from an administrative and/or the educational staff's perspectives.

However, a study on Japanese scholars of social sciences and humanities in international academic activities, focusing on disagreement discourse, some years ago (Okamoto, 2010), proved that applying this approach to the world of academia starts from false assumptions. My hypothesis was that Japanese scholars would have difficulties when encountering disagreements in scientific discourses, articulated by their foreign counterparts in international academic collaborations. Because Japanese cultural characteristics are often defined as "collectivism", "uncertainty avoidance" (Hofstede, 1984) and "high-context culture" (Hall, 1976), the assumption was that Japanese scholars would have difficulties with handling scientific disagreements in academic discourses. The definitions of the above cultural theories about Japanese people saying that it is a particular image about Japanese people that their style of discourse is so implicit that they would not express their feelings to others directly, that Japanese people respect harmony in groups or in the society as a whole, rather than having individual opinions and/or interests. Furthermore, such studies say that Japanese people might be generally understood as people that would not reveal what they really think when they witness that other people have diverse opinions contrary to their own, due to these national cultural traits.

However, very much in opposition to my study hypothesis, assuming that Japanese scholars must have difficulties in very direct controversial scientific debates, it turned out that Japanese scholars, who participated in my study, confirmed that the opposite to my hypothesis was the case in their international academic practices. This research outcome allows us to question the reliance of intercultural theories, which most roughly classify people's behaviour around the world with national stereotypes, and to apply these stereotypes to analyse activities of academics.

In the following section, I introduce a non-essentialist approach to analyse culture, the concept of "small cultures" deployed by Adrian Holliday to "academic culture" as the new framework to develop discussions on international academic collaborations in social sciences towards gaining some insights about how academics work, focusing on aspects of them which are relevant to international academic activities.

## Holliday's 'Small Cultures': A Non-Essentialist Framework to Analyse Academic Culture

Among other linguists who have teaching experiences with the English language in non-English speaking countries (e.g. Guest, 2002; Stapleton, 2002; Littlewood, 1999), Adrian Holliday is one of the scholars who felt uncomfortable about the essentialist approach to investigating students' learning attitudes, arguing that using stereotypical national cultural traits only generates "reductive statements" (Holliday, 2000: 40) usually known already before any research activities start. This means, since the national cultural traits are already defined and fixed, any research findings would only re-confirm that their research samples/participants *do* have the same cultural traits, confirmation for which such studies are constructed. Holliday therefore critiques that frequented cultural traits such as 'individualism versus collectivism' or 'masculinity versus femininity', which allude that one culture is right and the other is wrong, "supports various spheres of political interest" (1999: 243). To avoid bringing such political interest into academic research and repeating such stereotypes about people studied, Holliday took another non–essentialist approach to bridge people's behaviour and culture. For Holliday (2000), culture can only be "discovered" by a non-essentialist approach, because it "can help us to unlock *any* form of social behaviour by helping us to see how it operates as culture per se." (Emphasis in original). His intention is not to define culture as "X rather than Y, but to clarify what we mean when we use the word in different ways for different purposes." (1999: 238)

Hence, what Holliday claims is not that a non-essentialist approach that is later introduced as "small cultures", is correct or the only approach to analysing people's behaviour, but he introduces an alternative way to approach understanding people's behaviour in a way that is more explorative than looking at pre-defined ethnic/national cultural traits of people.

From the aforementioned conceptual standpoint, Holliday distinguishes two forms of culture: He distinguishes large cultures and small cultures. This distinction is not exclusively done only by Holiday; however, the meaning of small cultures advocated by him is different from other concepts of non-essentialist approaches. In his view, large cultures mean cultures that are classified by a geographical region/country such as the Asian or Japanese culture, which is the foundation of the essentialist approach, as the ones mentioned above. On the other hand, small cultures see people differently: though small cultures might be just seen as distinctive from large cultures as a matter of size, and therefore, might see them as sub-cultures, and simultaneously, sub-cultures are considered as a deviant form of large culture. However, as Holiday argues, then sub-culture is "essentially a large culture concept" (ibid.: 238-9). That is to say, sub-culture is only small in terms of the size of the units it analyses compared to large culture, but it conceptually belongs to a way of thinking in the large culture concept. Holliday calls this structure and the relationship between large and sub-cultures a "Russian doll or onion-skin" to visualize what he wants to distinguish between his concept of small culture and sub-culture.

> The idea of small cultures (...) is non-essentialist in that it does not relate to the essence of ethnic, national, or international entities. Instead it relates to any cohesive social grouping with no necessary subordination to large cultures. (ibid.: 240)

Thus, the distinction between his concept of small culture and subculture has nothing to do with size, but with a concepts of culture in which both large and sub culture are categorized under ethnic or national constructs. In the table below, the two paradigms of small and large cultures are briefly explained and characterized. It seems quite obvious that his emphasis on small cultures is based on a strong disagreement to observe 'culture' as something pre-defined, fixed, and an over-simplified stereotypical categorization by mere ethnicity/nationality. Therefore, Holliday's concept of "small cultures" can be considered as a new concept of culture that would attempt not to bind people's behaviour to ethnic/national constructs, but to understand their very behaviour by looking at them as a unit of cohesive social groups.

|  | Small cultures | Large cultures |
| --- | --- | --- |
| Character | **Non-essentialist, non-culturist** Relating to cohesive behaviour in activities within any social grouping | **Essentialist, culturist** 'culture' as essential features of ethnic national or international group |
| Relations | No necessary subordination to or containment within large cultures, therefore no onion-skin | Small (sub)cultures are contained within and subordinate to large cultures through onion-skin relationship |
| Research orientation | **Interpretive, process** Interpreting, emergent behaviour within any social grouping Heuristic model to aid the process of researching the cohesive process of any social grouping | **Prescriptive, normative** Beginning with the idea that specific ethnic, national and international groups have different 'cultures' and then searching for the details (e.g. what is polite in Japanese culture) |

(Source: Holliday, 1999: 241)

In the following sections it will be discussed how to exploit the concept of small cultures towards generating the concept of "*academic* culture" and how this concept of "academic culture", based on the small culture approach, can be used to reflect on academic work in social sciences with regard to its contribution to the debates on international academic activities.

## Constructing the Study of Academic Culture

As a first pilot study investigating how academics carry out their work, the concept of academic culture is constructed in order to investigate and analyse aspects of academic work that could be related to and therefore influence academic activities in international collaborations. Even though most social science scholar's work is committed to teaching and supervising students, academic work related to teaching is not reflected in this pilot study about academic work, since any aspects of teaching do not play any important role in international academic activities.

Rather than presenting any findings, I present in the following section only how this study about academic culture is constructed.

It should be mentioned that fundamental aspects of academic work are certainly shared by academics around the world, that is to say, there is no nationally confined or nationally specific academic work, though they might very well interpret the same essentials of academic work in diverse ways. Looking at the diversity of the same essential elements of academic work, is what has been much ignored when studying what academics are actually doing in their working life. Due to the focus on national peculiarities of the above mentioned discourses, including essentialist cultural studies, such discourses, captured by overstressing national identities tend to overlook what the diversities in practicing essentially the same elements of academic work really are. It is therefore important to look at elements academic work shares around the world, which seems normal, usual, and well known, in order to find out in which ways these "universal" activities are carried out with diverse purposes and in very diverse ways, which create all the obstacles when academics work internationally.

Investigating academic culture, this study distinguishes three levels of factors shaping academic culture related to international academic activities[8], which are the macro level, the micro level and the level of social relations shaping academic work.

---

[8] The three levels and individual factors are identified and set up, according to a variety of literature reflecting on the structure of the Higher Education (HE) system, the roles of HE institutes, and other studies on HE in general. Strictly speaking, all these studies are too broadly discussing mainly science policy issues to identify and define academic work at a more individual and practical level. However, since there is very little literature which has similar orienta-

## 1. Macro level of academic work

The macro level can be circumscribed largely by the social, political and institutional environment, in which academic work is carried out. In order to investigate such background aspects crafting the work of academics, the following four factors are studied:

- *National science policy*

    Under the notion of science policies, funding systems/programmes and nationally prioritized research topics/fields are considered as directly influencing the ways in which academic work—mainly research activities—are structured. Additionally, it is assumed that national science policies have, to some extent, also certain impacts on the funding programmes/topics of private funding agencies. In this sense, academic work is largely framed by national science policy, and is influenced by research stakeholders' interests in academic knowledge. It is apparent that there are always research trends among social sciences, "fashions" for research topics/themes, derived from societal/national demands for academic research; however, it is assumed that such trends are also largely defined and decided by national science policies.

- *Institutional infrastructure: Roles of Higher Education in a society*

    For many, universities are the place for their academic work. However, universities have diverse roles in different countries[9], which are not necessarily related to academic knowledge generation. Even though universities are considered to be places where various forms and processes of knowledge generation take place, in the context of discussing what the factors shaping academic work are, it might not be the main and/or the only role university plays in the overall social reality. Such broader social missions of universities and how they influence academic work are easily overlooked, since universities are considered as institutions sharing universally shared concepts, roles, and systems across the world, the most important of which is the idea of their independence. It might be true to a certain extent that universities share the idea of independence, nevertheless, how they interpret their independence and their relations to the so-

---

tions to this study, no clear definition of academic work in this context could be found in the existing literature. Hence, the components structuring academic work, the levels and factors shaping academic work, had to be newly constructed for this pilot study.

[9] In the case of Japan, universities are expected to contribute to education and research, and to contribute to issues relevant for local communities/societies.

cieties needs to be reflected on as a substantial factor shaping the work of academics, just as the ways that universities can be influenced by national science policies, by demands for knowledge from society, and other social, political and economic elements, setting the social environment in which universities and thus academics work. This social working environment could impact their academic working life, since the working environment could also be an important element that defines what work they are expected to do in universities.

- *Mission of academics in society*

    Connected to the above roles of universities, the mission of academics in society is another factor structuring the study exploring how academics work. That is, it looks at how academics are seen/understood in society, what the public expects academics to contribute to society. Such issues are raised to unfold how academics are perceived by the public and how this perception impacts their way of working. It might seem less relevant, at a first glance, to investigate such aspects, but, considering that academic work and scholars do not exist only in academic environments such as universities and other academic societies/institutions, their work is certainly connected to the public world, the expectations the non-academic society has on what academics contribute to society's agenda. Investigating the position and perception of academic people in the public society would help to clarify the relationship between the academics, who are people who generate academic knowledge, and the society for which this knowledge is produced. Reflecting on the relation between society and the academia could also reveal some relevant aspects of some essentials of the society with regard to the role academic knowledge plays in society[10] in and for which they generate academic knowledge.

- *Academic knowledge in society*

    Connected to the previous aspect (academics in society), the role of academic knowledge plays in and for society is examined. Assuming that academics are part of society and that it is their particular mission to provide knowledge for society that is knowledge for education, for solving political problems and for the economy, under this notion, what type of knowledge society

---

[10]   Such a question is raised because societal demands have influence on academic work, as previously pointed out. Although the societal demands do not directly come to scholars, what the society requires can often be top priorities as today's research agenda (e.g. poverty, aging population, unemployment, etc.). Under such circumstances, it is not unimportant to understand what the public society thinks about academics as people generating knowledge.

expects to gain from their academia is investigated, thus shaping the creation and distribution of knowledge, as major aspects of academic work.

2. Micro level of academic work

Contrary to the macro level, at the micro level constructing how to study the particular nature of academic culture, the more practical and internal aspects of academic work will be explored. The factors on this level of scholars' practical daily work will again focus only on the activities and aspects of academic knowledge generation and distribution, rather than on teaching, due to the orientation of this study towards factors shaping academic work that have an impact on international academic activities.

As relevant factors at the micro level, the following five factors are considered as factors shaping academic work:

- *Academic discourse practices*
- *Publication practices*
- *Managing academic activities*
- *Knowledge acquisition practices*
- *Disciplinary practices*

By investigating these academic practices, a closer look at scholars' academic working life will be possible. Such reflections include inquiries such as: What the topics of knowledge are, how they reflect on such topics, how they communicate with their colleagues about knowledge, what they discuss with their colleagues, where, how and why they acquire academic knowledge, what, where, and why they publish their academic work, as well as other aspects of their daily working life.

3. Social relations in academic work

In this section, the factors below contributing to academic culture are explored:

- *Hierarchy/ Status*
- *Gender*
- *Nationality/Ethnicity*

These factors are often considered as components of nationally constructed cultural characteristics. Including such factors in this study implies no intention of replacing the concept of small cultures and to fall back into an essentialist concepts of culture. However, such factors of national cultures are shown to be a possible element while investigating academic culture, scrutinizing if and how academic culture includes elements of national culture. This also encompasses whether or not such broader social relations that also occur beyond the academic environment influence the ways academics interpret these aspects of their work. Further, even if it turns out that such social relation factors influence academics, this would not directly relate to any influence of national cultural traits, because the same observation could be true in other countries regarding such factors[11]. Additionally it has to be stressed, there could be many more other social relation factors at this level of investigating academic culture; however, this study limits this type of factor to those which presumingly could be related to the practices of knowledge generation and distribution, and according to the focus of this research, to international academic activities.

Thus, investigation on academic culture is constructed with the four elements shaping academic culture as described above. However, there are many other possibilities to construct academic culture dependent on the research question of studies. Nevertheless, in any case the construct of the aforementioned academic culture is strictly focused on academic work, particularly on academic knowledge generation and distribution as the core elements not only of individual academic work but also of international, collaborative academic work. In the next section, therefore, I will discuss some aspects of the interrelationship between academic culture and international collaboration in the social sciences.

---

[11] At this moment, we cannot know whether or not it is the case, since this article is based on the study on academic culture focusing on the Japanese SSH scholars as a case. Therefore, the impact of such national cultural elements would be clearer, if the similar studies were implemented to investigate social sciences in other countries. This pilot research project does not yet aim at making a grand generalization on academic culture worldwide, but so far just attempts to suggest other approach to discussion on globalized academic work as such.

# How Studies on Academic Culture Can Be Exploited for Discussion on International Collaborations

Theorizing about academic culture is an attempt to better understand international academic collaboration. Captured through the discourses about the working conditions between national science communities as the conditions to distribute theories, there are hardly any attempts to establish discourses trying to go beyond the political views of nationally confined discourses which can only be used for comparative, country-specific studies. As discussed earlier whatever the conditions under which knowledge is created and distributed are, international collaborations must allow knowledge to be created jointly, providing knowledge beyond the nationally confined theories, satisfying the intellectual curiosity of academics by internationally working together with others.

The concept of academic culture, based on the concept of small cultures advocated by Holliday, would be more helpful to observe and analyse academic work, which is carried out within a country, since, after all, such everyday work is the foundation of all work, whether it is carried out nationally or internationally. In my current research project, I focus my study on Japanese social science scholars. Studying how Japanese scholars interpret the essentials of academic work shows no intention to study any "Japanese" academic culture, but sets up a methodology for a study of academic culture that aims at being widely applicable to academic work in any other countries based on sharing the same essential elements of academic work. Studying the case of social sciences in Japan is only a case for the first attempt to test how the concept of academic culture works. Needless to say, the factors constituting the above sketched model to study academic culture in Japan can be constructed in a diverse way from any one setting compared to this study that is directed towards studying elements that are related to international academic activities. Nevertheless it should be stressed, studying academic culture is not studying any specific confined country's cases and any differences between such confined entities, as essentialist studies emphasize, rather, it is studying academic culture focusing on how factors shaping the same essentials of academic work across countries influence academic work in global settings.

Having a better understanding of how academic work interprets the shared essentials of academic work through studying academic culture in this direction would lead us to better analyses on academic work carried out in international settings, showing us the ways in which academic work is carried out in different national settings and thus enables us to explain and analyse academic activities that could have an impact on international collaborations between academics coming from diverse interpretations of what they share as the essentials of academic work.

Academic culture does not provide any fixed definitions on academic work, instead, it provides a broad framework in which diverse activities and phenomena could be observed to analyse academic work. Since each scholar carries academic culture, this framework could be used to explain and analyse joint academic activities when they meet their counterparts, be they foreign or of the same nationality. Hence, academic culture could provide a different analytical framework to discuss international academic activities beyond the national cultural framework and beyond the competitive nature of all the discourses so far dominating the debates on international social sciences.

## Acknowledgement

This article is based on my ongoing doctoral thesis project "Investigating Elements in Academic Work for International Knowledge Production in Social Sciences and Humanities: The Case of Japan" (the title is provisional). The project was awarded ta research fund by the Konosuke Matsushita Memorial Foundation for the period of October 2012-September 2013.

## References

Becher, T., & Trowler, P. R. (2001). *Academic Tribes and Territories: Intellectual enquiry and the culture of disciplines* (2nd ed.). Buckingham, U.K: SRHE and Open University Press.

Bedeian, A. G., Van Fleet, D. D., & Hyman, H. H. (2009). Scientific Achievement and Editorial Board Membership. *Organizational Reseach Methods, 12*(2), 211–238.

Franceschet, M., & Costantine, A. (2010). The effect of scholar collaboration on impact and quality of academic papers. *Journal of Infometrics, 4*(4), 540–553.

Glänzel, W., & Schubert, A. (2005). Analysing Scientific Networks Through Co-Authorship. In H. F. Moed, W. Glänzel, & U. Schmoch (Eds.), *Handbook of Quantitative Science and Technology Research* (pp. 257–276). Springer.

Guest, M. (2002). A critical 'checkbook' for culture teaching and learning. *ELT journal, 56*(2), 154–161.

Hall, E. T. (1976). *Beyond Culture*. Anchor Books.

Hicks, D. (2005). The Four Literature of Social Science. In H. F. Moed, W. Glänzel, & U. Schmoch (Eds.), *Handbook of Quantitative Science and Technology Research* (pp. 473–496). Springer.

Hofstede, G. (1984). *Culture's consequences: International differences in work-related values*. Newbury Park: Sage.

Holliday, A. (1999). Small Cultures. *Applied Linguistics, 20*(2), 237–264.

Holliday, A. (2000). Culture as constraint or resource: essentialist versus non-essentialist view. *Iatefl Language and Cultural Studies SIG Newsletter*(18), pp. 38–40.

Katz, J. S., & Martin, B. R. (1997). What is research collaboration? *Research Policy, 26*(1), 1–18.

Klein, D. B., & Chiang, E. (2004). The Social Science Citation Index: A Black Box—with an Ideological Bias. *Econ Journal Watch, 1*(1), 134–165.

Kuhn, M. (2013). "Hegemonic Science": Critique Strands, Counterstrategies, and Their Paradigmatic Premises. In M. Kuhn, & S. Yazawa (Eds.), *Theories about and Strategies against Hegemonic Social Sciences* (pp. 31–54). Tokyo: Center for Glocal Studies.

Kuhn, M., & Okamoto, K. (2008). Through international collaborations towards a multipolar SSH 'world order'. Research project report.

Kuhn, M., & Weidemann, D. (2005). Reinterpreting Transnationality—European Transnational Socio-economic Research in Practice. In M. Kuhn, & S. O. Remoe (Eds.), *Building the European Research Area: Socio-Economic Research in Practice*. New York: Peter Lang.

Lariviere, V., Gingras, Y., & Archambault, E. (2006). Canadian collaboration networks: A comparative analysis of the natural sciences, social sciences and the humanities. *Scientometrics, 68*(3), 519–533.

Littlewood, W. (1999). Defining and Developing Autonomy in East Asian Contexts. *Applied Linguistics, 20*(1), 71–94.

MEXT (Ministry of Education, C. S. (2014). *Top Global University Project*. Retrieved December 5, 2014, from MEXT (Ministry of Education, Culture, Sports, Science and Technology, Japan): http://www.mext.go.jp/b_menu/houdou/26/09/__icsFiles/afieldfile/2014/10/07/1352218_02.pdf

Okamoto, K. (2010a). Challenges for Japanese Social and Human Scientists in International Collaborations (Unpublished Masters Degree Thesis submitted to the University of London).

Okamoto, K. (2010b). Internationalization of Japanese Social Sciences: Importing and Exporting Social Science Knowledge. In M. Kuhn, & D. Weidemann (Eds.), *Interntaionalization of the Social Sciences* (pp. 45–65). Bielefeld: transcript.

Okamoto, K. (2012). Presentation: What is Hegemonic Science?: Power in Scientific Activities in Social Sciences in International Context. *Presentation document: World SSH Net Thinshop in Tokyo.*

Okamoto, K. (2013). What is Hegemonic Science?: Power in Scientific Activities in Social Sciences in International Contexts. In M. Kuhn, S. Yazawa, & K. Okamoto (Eds.), *Theories about and Strategies against Hegemonic Social Sciences* (pp. 55–73). Tokyo: Center for Glocal Studies.

Seglen, P. O. (1997). Why the impact factor of journals should not be used for evaluating research. *BMJ, 314*, 498–502.

Shin, J., & Cummings, W. K. (2010). Multilevel of analysis of academic publishing across disciplines: research preference, collaboration, and time on research. *Scientometrics, 85*(2), 581–594.

Sonnenwald, D. H. (2007). Scientific collaboration. *Annual review of information science and technology, 41*(1), 643–681.

Stapleton, P. (2002). Critical thinking in Japanese L2 writing: rethinking tired constructs. *ELT Journal, 56*(3), 250–257.

UNESCO. (2010). *World Social Science Report.* Paris: UNESCO. Retrieved April 10, 2014, from http://unesdoc.unesco.org/images/0018/001883/188333e.pdf

van Leeuwen, T. N., Moed, H. F., Tussen, R. J., Visser, M. S., & van Raan, A. F. (2001). Language biases in the coverage of the Science Citation Index and its consequences for international comparisons of national research performance. *Scientometrics, 51*, 335–346.

# Biographical Notes

**Carmen Bueno** is a social anthropologist. She is Professor at Universidad Iberoamericana in Mexico City, specialized in globalization studies from de local and in the evolution of the discipline in Mexico and its relation to hegemonic knowledge. Actively involved in the Mexican Association of Anthropologist and past president of the network of educational programs of Anthropology in Mexico (RED MIFA), past president of the Commission on Policy and Practice of the IUAES.
Email: carmenbuenocastellanos@yahoo.com.mx

**Reiner Grundmann** is Professor of Science and Technology Studies at the University of Nottingham. His current research looks at the public discourse on climate change, comparing various countries. He is also interested in the relation between knowledge and decision making, focusing on the role of expertise in knowledge societies.
Email: reiner.grundmann@nottingham.ac.uk

**Huri Islamoglu** is Professor of Economic History, Bogazici University, Istanbul , Visiting Professor of History, University of California, Berkeley; and currently senior Fellow at the Institute for Advanced Study ,Nantes, France. Publications include: (with Peter Perdue) *Shared Histories of Modernity in China,* India and the Ottoman empire (2009), *Constituting Modernity: Private Property in the East and West* (2004), *Ottoman Empire and the World Economy* (1987); *State and Peasant in the Ottoman Empire* (1994)
Email: huricihan@gmail.com

**Michael Kuhn** is President of the World Social Sciences and Humanities Network ad director of Knowwhy Global Research. His background is philosophy, political science and international economics. His current interests focus on theories of social sciences.
Email: michaelkuhn@knowwhy.net; mkuhn@worldsshnet.org

**Mauricio Nieto** is professor of history of science at the University of los Andes, Bogotá, Colombia. His main research interest is the relation between science and empire in the context of European exploration of the New World from the 16th to the 19th centuries.
E-mail: mnieto@uniandes.edu.co

**Kazumi Okamoto** is the Secretary General of the World Social Sciences and Humanities Network, Germany. She is currently pursuing her PhD study at Karlsruhe Institute of Technology, Germany on 'academic culture' in the Japanese social and human sciences. Her research interests are internationalization of social sciences and humanities (SSH), working cultures in SSH in the context of international collaborations, and internationalization of Higher Education.
Email: okamoto@worldsshnet.org

**Sujata Patel** is a sociologist at the University of Hyderabad. An historical sensibility and a combination of four perspectives-Marxism, feminism, spatial studies and post structuralism/post colonialism influences her work which covers diverse areas such as modernity and social theory, history of sociology/social sciences, city-formation, social movements, gender construction, reservation, quota politics and caste and class formations in India. She is also an active interlocutor of teaching and learning practices, and has written on the challenges that organise its reconstitution within classrooms, University structures. She is the author of more than sixty papers and is the Series Editor of *Sage Studies in International Sociology (including Current Sociology Monographs* (2010-1014), *Oxford India Studies in Contemporary Society* (Oxford, India). She is also the editor of *The ISA Handbook of Diverse Sociological Traditions*, Sage London (2010). She has been associated in various capacities with the International Sociological Association and has been its first Vice President for National Associations (2002–2006).
Email: patel.sujata09@gmail.com

# Biographical Notes 277

**Kumaran Rajagopal** is assistant professor at the Department of Sociology, Gandhigram Rural Institute – Deemed University, Gandhigram, Tamil Nadu India. His disciplinary background is sociology, his interests are alternative science practices and theories.
Email: rkumara@gmail.com

**Kwang-Yeong Shin** is professor of the Department of Sociology at Chung-Ang University in Seoul, Korea. His research areas are class analysis and inequality, comparative social welfare regime, and philosophy of social sciences. Recent publications include "The Dilemmas of Korea's New Democracy in an Age of Neoliberal Globalization"(Third World Quarterly. 33(2)) and "Economic Crisis, Neoliberal Reforms, the Rise of Precarious Work in South Korea"(American Behavioral Scientist, December 2, 2012 online)
Email: kyshin@cau.ac.kr

**Pal Tamas** is Professor of Scoiology in Corvinus University in Budapest, Hungary, and in Moscow Lomonosov University in Moscow, Russia. He has diversifiesd research interests, including studies of elites in Central European and post- Soviet states, mass media, science systems, political sciences and journalism in Europe.

**Hebe Vessuri** is a social anthropologist, Emeritus researcher at the Center of Science Studies, Venezuelan Institute of Scientific Research (IVIC), Caracas, and a Collaborating Scholar at the Center for Environmental Geography (CIGA), National Autonomous University of Mexico (UNAM). Dr. Vessuri's general interests are on the sociology and contemporary history of science in Latin America, science policy, and sociology of technology. She is also interested in the challenges and dilemmas of expertise and democracy in developing country contexts.
Email: hvessuri@ivic.ve

**Doris Weidemann** is a cultural psychologist and professor of intercultural training with focus on the Greater China area at the University of Applied Sciences of Zwickau, Germany. Her research interests include intercultural science collaboration, indigenous psychologies, and methods of intercultural training. M. Kuhn and D. Weidemann. (eds.), (2010), Internationalization of the Social Sciences, Bielefeld: transcript
Email: Doris.Weidemann@fh-zwickau.de

**Igor Yegorov** is Professor of Economics and Department Head in the Institute for Economy and Forecasting of the National Academy of Sciences of Ukrainein Kiev. His research is focused on innovation theory and science studies with special attention to transformation processes in these areas in the post- Soviet states
Email: igor_yegorov1@ukr.net

***ibidem*-Verlag**
Melchiorstr. 15
D-70439 Stuttgart
info@ibidem-verlag.de
www.ibidem-verlag.de
www.ibidem.eu
www.edition-noema.de
www.autorenbetreuung.de